365 Days
In The Presence Of God

Daily Devotions
From The Sermons of Dr. Frank Ray

Edited by Linda Perry

BETHESDA BOOKS

Bethesda Ministries, Inc.
Cincinnati, Ohio
www.ApostolicBooks.org

365 DAYS IN THE PRESENCE OF GOD
Daily Devotions From The Sermons of Dr. Frank Ray

Copyright © 2004 Frank E. Ray, Sr., Ph.D.

Scripture quotations are taken from The Holy Bible, King James Version, or are the author's paraphrase of that version.

Published by Bethesda Ministries, Inc., Cincinnati, Ohio
Design by William L. Pettiford III

10 9 8 7 6 5 4 3 2 1

ISBN 1-59744-006-X

Printed in the United States of America

This book is dedicated to my beloved wife,
Deborah Joye Nolan Ray,
who is an inspiration to me.
She is my prayer warrior and my best friend
that I love dearly.

Announcement

Dr. Ray's second book, entitled,
"Making It Through The Weak Days"
is a healing reminder of God's promises,
His grace, and His love. For as Christians we know.
"In this world you will have troubles.
But take heart! I have overcome the world."
– John 16:33

Contents

Preface

It is so important for each of us to have time in our day to spend in God's Presence. We receive new purpose as we come before our heavenly Father and experience Him personally in our lives. Our entire existence centers on a personal relationship with our Lord and Savior, Jesus Christ, and an understanding of the plan of salvation and the sacrifice He made for you and me.

My purpose in bringing to you a devotional is to encourage you as you walk on this planet, our temporary home. Each day brings new dilemmas for us to deal with. Each day requires a fresh dose of God's word along with God's wisdom. We need Him to give us discernment and discretion in our daily walk. As we dwell in His word, we receive the answers we need for every situation we may face.

It is my hope that this devotional will point you toward our Lord and help you to find daily renewal as you spend time with Him and understanding His word. The Lord has been my friend, my guide, my provider, my burden-bearer, and my Savior for many years. I continually thank Him and praise Him for all He's done for me. May God bless you always and be your closest friend!

Dr. Frank E. Ray, Sr.

Introduction

How difficult it seems to be for many of us to confine our plans just for today just to be concerned about the evils of the day. It seems perfectly normal to look ahead and to plan for tomorrow.

It seems totally irresponsible not to look ahead and do your best to care for your temporal needs not only for today, but for the rainy days that lie ahead.

Acts 17:28
For in Him we live, and move, and have our being.

Proverbs 27:1
Man at best lives but a day at a time for tomorrow may never come.

James 4:14
Yesterday is in the tomb, Tomorrow is in the womb,
Yesterday is a canceled check, Tomorrow is a promissory note,
Yesterday is history, Tomorrow is a mystery,
Today is a gift.

Foreword

This book provides the needed support and sustenance for days of weakness in the life of the believer. Dr. Ray has drawn deep from the well of human experiences and has allowed God's word to give us instruction on how to make it through our weak days. This book is a reflection of the genius and creativity of Black preaching and providing us strength and comfort in difficult times. Dr. Ray is not a novice when it comes to trouble, and has shared with us in a straight forward, practical, and biblical manner how to overcome our struggles.

Dr. R. A. William, Jr.

January

Don't Miss Out

Revelation 1:7

Behold, he cometh with clouds; and every eye shall see him; and they also which pierced him: and all the kindreds of the earth shall wail because of him. Even so, Amen.

I know that many of us are sitting here comfortably satisfied in our dilemma or situation. We don't have a worry or a care in the world. But when I read this passage, and I looked at it every day last week at least two or three times a day, my heart would get so tender to the point that it almost started bleeding. So many of us are so eager trying to get; trying to accumulate; trying to be who's who, and what's what, that we're overlooking the fact that "he's coming." Whenever I see this, I have mixed emotions because I know that when he comes, some will not be ready. And it could hit close to home. It doesn't bother us very much when they pick up people across the street or down the road. But when death comes to our house and invades the privacy of our own families, it's different.

The text says, "Behold He cometh." The book of Revelation is written using many pronouns instead of the nouns. The Lord seems to say, "You ought to know by now who it is that's coming." Revelation 1:4-18 speaks very specifically concerning Jesus and who He is. At that point, He is saying, "I shouldn't have to mention my name on every occasion."

He says every child of God that's born again knows him. And so the text says that He wants to spend some time telling us what's getting ready to happen. Behold, he cometh. There will be some that won't want to meet him–the ones that don't know him and haven't departed from their sins. They will run to the rocks and beg the rocks to fall on them. Can you imagine a person running from death and being unable to even kill himself? It will be an awesome day when the Lord returns again.

Don't Get Complacent

Genesis 6:12
And God looked upon the earth, and, behold, it was corrupt; for all flesh had corrupted his way upon the earth

Noah preached one sermon a hundred and twenty years and nobody paid him any attention. The tragedy of the millions of people that were on planet earth is that only eight of them were saved. I wonder how many in the church are really saved. I didn't say how many have religion, but how many in my church are really saved? There's a difference in standing on his promises and sitting on the premises. And just going to church doesn't anymore make you a Christian than hanging around in a garage will make you a Rolls Royce. You must be born again.

And Noah preached and the people paid him no attention. As a matter of fact, they laughed at him. They criticized him. Noah was mocked year after year by people who didn't have a relationship with God. They didn't listen to him, but continued in their day to day living. They had become complacent. Not until the rain started coming did they run for safety. But I hear Noah saying after he reached the ark, "I'm sorry. The key to the door is not in my hand. God has the key."

Remember during the days of Sodom when Lot went to the town. Lot pitched his tent in Sodom. Lot found a wife in Sodom. He raised Sodomite children. He gained his wealth in Sodom. According to the book of Peter, he had a sodomite spirit. He had somewhat of a worldly nature. However, because he was saved, God would not destroy the city until He got Lot out of it. I wonder what town is being spared today because of some Christians, because of some saved person that God planted in a certain place that has been criticized yet whose name has been hung on the wings of the morning. But God saves the community because of saved saints in the area.

Don't Give Up

Matthew 25:6
And at midnight there was a cry made, Behold, the bridegroom cometh; go ye out to meet him.

I remember the story of the ten virgins. Five were wise and five were foolish. And they thought they had the time of the wedding feast at hand. Somebody said that the invitation said the wedding would be at six-thirty. But when six-thirty came there was no wedding. The bridegroom didn't come at seven. He didn't come at eight. He wasn't there at nine. He was not there at ten. He didn't show up at eleven. He wasn't there. And when you wait for such a long time, sometimes you think the wedding is over. But at midnight, there was a cry and the people that were ready went in. Only the ones that were ready went in.

However, there were other virgins that were waiting–without oil. They trimmed their lamps, but there was no oil. They cleaned their wicks, but there was no oil. And the reason they couldn't get in was because their lamps had gone out. Do you remember the time you used to shout and get happy and you don't do it anymore. Nothing is exciting to you about church any more. Is your spirit is dead and dampened? Do you need a fresh supply of oil in your Christian walk?

I don't know how you feel about it, but when I look at the text, one part of me wants to get happy. I have peace within when I know He's coming because I have already made provisions. If I were you and I hadn't made the right provisions and hadn't gotten it together with the Lord, I would walk starting today and say, 'just a closer walk with thee, grant it Jesus if you please.' Let me walk a daily walk close to thee because one of these days the hour will come and the time is up. There won't be time to seek God at that moment. We must keep our lamps filled and our lights shining. Jesus is coming! Make sure there is some oil in your lamp because He will show up.

Be Prepared

Acts 1:11
Which also said, Ye men of Galilee, why stand ye gazing up into heaven?
This same Jesus, which is taken up from you into heaven, shall so come in like
manner as ye have seen him go into heaven.

Several years ago our National Convention was held in New York City and our headquarters was the hotel right in front of Madison Square Garden. Forty thousand delegates came to New York for the convention and when I arrived, there were people sitting all out in front of the hotel and in the lobby, trying to get reservations When I walked in, I stepped around the people that were in the lobby and those standing in line. I walked up and gave them my name and they gave me my room key in spite of the other people. I had reservations ahead of time. I didn't know how crowded it would be, but I didn't want to take any chances.

And I tell you that I don't know how it's going to be when the Lord returns, but you will do well if you take a few moments to make a reservation because sooner or later you'll have to check out of here. The sooner the preparations are made, the better your life will be.

If God didn't do anything else for me on planet earth, I could praise him from now on because he brought me farther than I ever dreamed of going. I've traveled all over the country. I've seen everything I want to see. I don't know anything else I want to see. I don't know another building I want to see. I don't know another state or country I would rather go to than Heaven. There are no famous people that I'm looking forward to seeing. If I don't accomplish anything else, God has been good to me. And many of you can say the same thing. I may not live in a big mansion, but within the little dwelling I have, I have peace on the inside. When you think about what God has done for you and the ways He has brought you and kept you and delivered you. I tell you, it's enough to be thankful for.

Don't Get Discouraged

Romans 8:23

And not only they, but ourselves also, which have the firstfruits of the Spirit, even we ourselves groan within ourselves, waiting for the adoption, to wit, the redemption of our body.

You remember how you used to be young and had a lot of vigor. You used to move fast, run up hills, climb steps, jump and hang and swim and play. But now you walk to your car and you're out of breath. There was a time you didn't need eyeglasses for anything; now you have to have eyeglasses to find your eyeglasses. There used to be a time, you'd get up anytime of day or night. Now you want to sleep as long as you can. Time has a way of changing things. Just looking at us will tell us that we didn't come here to stay. Hair starts changing colors on our head or it will fall out, and teeth start leaving one by one. The heart starts skipping in its beat. When you get my age and older, you will discover that you've got more friends over there than you have here.

The text says he's coming and I like that because when he comes, he'll do some stuff for us. As a matter of fact, when Jesus got up himself, he had a new body. Luke 24:39 tells us Jesus could eat and be seen and heard by others. So we won't be only spirit when we get up; we are going to have a body. We will not only be recognized by those gone on, but we will also know them. Once we get rid of this body, we'll be able to praise Him endlessly. And when we bow down before the King and start praising Him, when we rise up we'll think of something else that He did for us. We'll bow down again. And when we rise up, we'll think of something else that the Lord did for us. We'll bow down again, and that will go on and on because if you're honest with yourself now, with our fevered minds, when you start thinking about what God has already done for you. You can't help but to shout and praise him everyday.

Every Eye Shall See Him

Revelation 1:7

Behold, he cometh with clouds; and every eye shall see him; and they also which pierced him: and all the kindreds of the earth shall wail because of him. Even so, Amen.

Not only good eyes will see Him, but bad eyes will see Him. People that were born blind will be able to see Him. Some of the people that live in countries where they never had a chance to preach the gospel or hear the gospel preached will be able to see Him. Two or three people in the Bible already saw him.

Do you remember Isaiah? He said, In the year that King Uzziah died, I saw also the Lord. He was high and lifted up. His train filled the temple. Seraphims stood with six wings, with two wings, they veiled their face, with two wings they veiled their feet, and with two wings, they did fly. And when Isaiah saw the Lord, he was so shaken up that he started confessing, Woe is me, I'm a man of unclean lips."

There were others that saw him. Stephen saw him. The first deacon, after he was stoned, looked up toward heaven. The Bible says that he saw the glory of God and Jesus standing on the right hand of God. What a great look that must have been to be able to look up and see the Son of God. Also the apostle Paul saw Him. He was caught up into the third heaven and when he went up he saw something he couldn't tell anybody. And then he said he finally got a chance to see the Lord.

But there's another. The writer of the book of Revelation saw him and described his face as the sun shining in all its brilliance. John said that when he saw him, he fell at his feet as though he was a dead man. And I like that because whenever we come into "his presence" we can't walk around with our heads in the air as though we think we're something that we are not. Every eye shall see Him and it will be a powerful moment.

17

Get Ready For A New Body

1 Corinthians 15:4
There are also celestial bodies, and bodies terrestrial: but the glory of the celestial is one, and the glory of the terrestrial is another.

What kind of shape will I be in when the Lord returns? There is one glory of the sun, another glory of the moon, and another glory of the stars. For one star differs from another in glory. So also is the resurrection of the dead. It is sown in corruption. This means that when I die, I might have only one leg; I might have only one arm; I might have only one eye. But it is raised incorruptible. It won't deteriorate. It is sown in dishonor; I might have a crooked limb; I might have one eye looking one way, the other looking the other way. It will be raised in glory. It is sown in weakness, but it is raised in power It is sown a natural body; it is raised a spiritual body. There is a natural body; and there is a spiritual body. The former things will be passed away. 1 Corinthians 13:12 says, "for now we see through a glass darkly, but then face to face: now I know in part; but then shall I know even as I am already known." Life is a little blurry now. Some things I can't understand but one of these days, I'll be able to understand it all.

Now you can live a week without food, you can live days without water, but you can live only minutes without hope. God gives us what you call a renewed hope. Romans 8: 24 and 25, says we are saved by hope. But hope that is seen is not hope. But what a man seeth why doth he yet hope for it. It says but if we hope for that we have not seen, then do we with patience wait for it. This patience comes from the word meaning under. It means carrying a load under you and moving with your load. You see when you know you've got something you're looking forward to, sometimes it helps you live a little longer, patiently serving our Lord and bringing others to Him.

The Blessing Of Giving

Malachi 3:6–12

Bring ye all the tithes into the storehouse, that there may be meat in mine house, and prove me now herewith, saith the Lord of hosts, if I will not open you the windows of heaven, and pour you out a blessing, that there shall not be room enough to receive it.

I was introduced to this passage by my pastor when I was 20 years of age. A light came on and I have never been the same This passage literally changed my life to the point that I am scared to death not just by me even thinking of not fulfilling this passage, but I'm frightened for you. I see so many blessings that God has in store for you.

Maybe you're trying to use other means to make it and survive. It's bad when saints resort to things of the world to try to make ends meet such as scheming and conniving, sitting in front of a slot machine, resorting to begging and gambling, cheating and lying. God says you are a royal priesthood. You are a chosen generation. You are a peculiar people. Hear me when I tell you saints of God that when you abide by his word and make sure that you are in his will, then God will bless your life.

I have discovered in life that there are some things you will need that money can not buy. There are some things in life that you may want to accomplish that you won't be able to use your connections to get. Only God can open certain doors. Only God can do certain things for us. Now this is not a reflection on my part, but it will be if I fail to warn you. The Bible states, "I am the Lord." This is not a scheme that preachers have cooked up and schemed up to try to talk you out of something that you think is yours This is the Lord speaking. And when the Lord says something, it is settled whether you believe it or not; it is still true. He says "I am the Lord, I change not." God needs us to know that He doesn't change. Bring the tithes into the storehouse.

Life's Windows

Malachi 3:10

And prove me now herewith, saith the Lord of hosts, if I will not open you the windows of heaven, and pour you out a blessing, that there shall not be room enough to receive it.

Have you ever noticed how God provided for you when you were out of work? Not only did He sustain, but He kept you with your dignity. You didn't have to walk with a hung down head. You see that alone ought to tell you that you're not surviving because of your job, because jobs come and go. Possibly you have been married and perhaps your spouse died or moved away and you kept on surviving. Have you had your health and then all of a sudden it was gone and God kept putting food on your table. You're not surviving just because of your health. God is the one that makes ends meet.

Whatever your needs are, God has a window for that need. If you need a friend, he will open up a friend window; friends are worth more than money. That's why if you have one good friend, you should cherish that friendship. Most people don't have a lot of friends in a lifetime; they have associates. Associates will get in your business and tell it all over town and laugh while you're falling down. A friend will love you in spite of problems. There's a difference between an associate and a true friend.

If you need help, God has a help window. If you need health, He has a health window. If you need finances, He has a financial window. If you need a mind to be regulated, He has a mind-regulating window. He says, "I'll open the windows of heaven and I'll pour you out blessings that you don't have room enough to receive." You see God is not concerned with how much you have, he just wants you to be in his will. He just wants you to put him first and give him the first part of the money that He has allowed you to make.

Take Your Spiritual Temperature

Malachi 3:7
Even from the days of your fathers ye are gone away from mine ordinances, and have not kept them. Return unto me, and I will return unto you, saith the Lord of hosts. But ye said, Wherein shall we return?

We have strayed from God. We must recognize our failure. I don't care how much you shout and how holy you look, your tithing is the thermometer that measures your commitment. Now you can know the Bible from Genesis to Revelation, from cover to cover, but when you fail to tithe you're saying something about your spiritual status. Even if you're flat broke, when God blesses you with something you will make sure God gets his when you are in his will. But when you're out of his will you find every reason not to give. In verse seven He says, "Return unto me what is my part and I will return unto you." This means that when I fail to tithe God turns away from me. Can you handle God turning His back on you?

There's a big difference between existing and living. A lot of folk are just existing. When you ask a person how they are doing, the one that is just existing will say, "Come here, let me show you what I'm driving. Come let me show you where I stay. Come look at my rags." But when you're living, you don't have to show a person your possessions because the possessions come and go. When you're living you don't have to focus on being happy because you have joy. And you heard me say happiness is based on what's happening. But joy is never based upon your surroundings. It's based up on the person that's living in you. And when the person in you is happy then you're happy. You may be in rags and tags, but you have joy on the inside of you.

And life is too short to be miserable and on top of being miserable knowing that you are not pleasing God. Have you looked at your spiritual thermometer lately?

Don't Rob God

Malachi 3:8

Will a man rob God? Yet ye have robbed me. But ye say, Wherein have we robbed thee? In tithes and offerings.

I was on my way to church one Sunday morning and three young boys were riding in an open jeep. Two young ladies were riding right behind them. They stopped at the red light right in front of First Baptist Church. One of the fellows pulled downed his pants and bent over and patted it at the young ladies behind them. That's low morals. But can I let you in on a little secret. You're just like those fellows when God gives you a job and health and strength and protection down dangerous highways and lets you work on the job all week and gives you a paycheck and then lets you make it home. Then on Sunday instead of paying God, you act like God doesn't exist. It's like bending over in front of God, patting yourself and saying, "Take it." It is only by His protecting you everyday that you do the things you do.

Will a man rob God? Have you ever heard of a child holding up the parents? Can you imagine how you would feel if your 16 year old boy walked straight up to you and put a gun in your nose and said, "Momma, give me every dime you've got." Not only would you be mad, you would be hurt because you raised that child from birth. You took care of that baby. You remember all the times he was sick and you sat with him. You remember times that you gave up stuff for yourself for him to survive. And now for him to show how he appreciates you, he robs you. Now there's a difference between robbing and stealing. A thief is a coward. The thief catches you with your back turned. A thief waits until you leave the house and then slips in the window and rushes out before you get there. That's a thief. But a robber has nerve. He stands and looks at you right in the face. Notice the text didn't say, "Will a man steal." We have the audacity to rob him and then tell him, "Bless me."

Will a man – a little puny finite man rob and infinite God?

Permanent Resurrection

Revelation 1:5
And from Jesus Christ, who is the faithful witness, and the first begotten of the dead, and the prince of the kings of the earth.

When I read the text, I was baffled for a moment because I remembered there were others that got up while Jesus was alive. You remember that Jesus raised Jairus' daughter from the dead. Jesus also brought back the son that lived in a city called Nain. And you do remember Lazarus died, and the Lord brought him back.

The text says that Jesus was the first begotten of the dead. These other people had gotten up, but yet the Bible says that Jesus was the first. Here is the answer; you see even though Jairus' daughter was raised from the dead, she died again. Even though Lazarus was brought back, Lazarus had to die again. The widow's son had to die again. They experienced two deaths. But Jesus, after he died, didn't die anymore. He was the first.

And then he died, and they buried him and put him in Joseph's new tomb that he had lent to Jesus. Whatever you lend to the Lord, he will give it back to you, but it will always be better. And by just letting Jesus use his grave evidently, the spirit had said, it will be given back to you again. When Jesus got up that morning, he wrecked the grave. I mean he robbed the grave of its victory and took the stain out of death.

The Greek text says that he was the first in rank, the first in line. In other words, he showed us how it was going to be later for us. He was the first begotten of the dead and He was the Prince of the king of the earth. Jesus got up with rank. He didn't lose anything because he died. And when you die in the Lord, you don't lose anything. As a matter of fact, you gain. As Paul said, "For me to live is Christ, but for me to die is gain." We will live again!

Not Because Of

Revelation 1:5
...Unto him that loved us, and washed us from our sins in his own blood.

I'm shocked when I read the text because I didn't have much to bring to the table. I didn't have much to give him, for him to love me. Most people love "because of." Whenever somebody tells you they love you, keep listening; they will tell you why. It is always a "because of." I love you because you look good. I love you because you treat me nice. I love you because of how you talk. I love you because of how you act. We even send cards now and write on it, just because. And of course love now is based upon "because of." And if there is no "because of" it's not much love.

Jesus' love is different from that. He doesn't love us "because of." We had nothing to give Him. I mean he would have been better off if he had left us where we were. I had nothing to present to Him. I was a wretch undone; I was filthy. Neither was I fit to live nor was I ready to die. And the text says he didn't wait until I got right to love me. Romans 5:8 says, "...while we were yet sinners, Christ died for us." It meant he loved me in my mess. He loved me at my worst stage. He loved me because he knew he could take nothing and make something. Whenever God looks at us, he sees a diamond in the rough.

There was a man who had been very prosperous and successful with all the finery that any man would ever want in life including clothes, cash, cars, commodities and comforts. However, he had a son that was severely asthmatic. The boy spent many nights in bed and in the hospital because of the asthma. But his father loved him and spent many nights by his side. Not "because of" his strength, abilities, or charming personality, he loved him because he was his son. This is God's love toward us.

The Divine Washing Machine

Revelation 1:5
...Unto him that loved us, and washed us from our sins in his own blood.

He washed us. I like that because some scholars and theologians say that the word should not be translated 'washed' but 'loosed'. Loosed implies that we were in chains. But by saying washed, it meant we were in stain. Now a lot people can be in chains and get loose and still act like they're in chains. Have you ever wondered how elephants are trained? The trainer takes an elephant while he is young and still a small creature. He gets a rope or chain and ties around his leg and puts a stake in the ground. The elephant stands there pulling on the stake, just pulling trying to get a loose. But because he's weak, he can't pull it up from the ground. But after he gets of age, the stake and chain are taken away and just a little rope is wrapped around his leg and just thrown around the stake. If the elephant wanted to, he could break away any time he got ready. But mentally, he thinks he's still chained. And so he just stands there, wobbling from one side to the other wondering, hoping he can get a loose. When he's really all ready loosed. And that's what happens sometimes when people have been in chains. You are a loosed, but you think you're still in chains. And so when you think you're in chains, you'll act like you're in chains, because the scar moves from the outside to the inside. It's a mental scar.

Being washed means the stain has been taken away. Nobody can de-stain us like the Lord. He gave His blood in place of my sins–His blood. My sins—out; his blood—in. The blood of Jesus is so powerful that it can get the stain out. As a matter of fact, the Lord used what you might call a divine washing machine. He takes that washing machine and once he places you in the divine washing machine, when you come out you're whiter than snow. You are washed and free of stains and chains.

From A Wretch To A King

Revelation 1:6

And hath made us kings and priests unto God and his Father; to him be glory and dominion forever and ever.

And hath made us kings. Here I am, a wretch undone, and yet the Lord takes a sinner like me, and makes a king. That means royalty and authority. We don't have to yield to any and everything; we have authority. I need to explain what I'm saying. Matthew 28:18, "And all power is given unto me." The Greek word for power is exousia, which means authority. Then Matthew 16:18 says, "Upon this rock I'll build my church." The Greek word for church is ekklesia. And then Acts 1:8 says, "But ye shall receive power." This Greek word power is the word dunamis. The word dynamics and the word dynamite are derived from dunamis. The Lord gets his exousia, which is his authority and places it behind his ekklesia, which is His church. Then He gets his dunamis, which is his dynamite and puts it in the church, and tells the church to seize the opportunity placed before the church.

Whatever dynamite comes in contact with, it is always rearranged. Dynamite is like the working of the Holy Spirit; it moves you above certain things. What he said; what she said; what they said; what I don't know but it looks like to me. When that dynamite gets on the inside, it takes that which was unorganized and organizes it. It gives you power and authority and arranges your life.

You see when you are a king; you shouldn't get upset with your subjects. A king doesn't pace the floor wondering where he's going to get his next meal. A king doesn't get upset just because somebody has been lying on him. When you're king, everybody talks about you and picks at you. It's almost like being in the field playing football and getting upset because you've been tackled. When you're in the field expect to be tackled. He has made us kings. Let the King rearrange your life.

Instant Access to God

Revelation 1:6
And hath made us kings and priests unto God.

He made us priests. What was the role of the priest? If I had a problem, then I would go and tell the priest and the priest would take my problem to the mercy seat in the temple. He would sprinkle blood on the mercy seat on my behalf because I couldn't go any farther than the outer court. I wasn't holy enough to go into the holy place. In between the inner court and me was a veil. And behind the veil was the mercy seat. And I would tell the priest what my needs were. The priest would go sprinkle blood on the mercy seat. He would have to kill a dove or a pigeon or a lamb and use his blood. If you were rich, you had a lamb; if you were poor, you used a turtledove. And they sprinkled blood and then the priest would stand and tell God what I told him. And then I'd have to stand out there and wait on the priest to get an answer from the Lord.

But at Calvary, the veil was split from the top to bottom. Now you can tell by the way the veil was split that man didn't split it because he would have begun at the bottom and started tearing upward toward the top. But this veil was split from the top to the bottom. I don't have to wait on a priest to talk for me. He might have an upset stomach that day or be unavailable for a number of reasons. I can go (and I don't have to go crawling to the mercy seat, saying, "Lord I don't want to disturb you; Lord I don't want to upset you.") boldly to the throne of God. Why? Because He made us priests. We do not need to carry any blood from animals. Hebrews 9:13-14 For if the blood of bulls and of goats, and the ashes of an heifer sprinkling the unclean, sanctifieth to the purifying of the flesh: How much more shall the blood of Christ, who through the eternal Spirit offered himself without spot to God, purge your conscience from dead works to serve the living God?

I didn't make myself a priest. Jesus did the work!

A Closer Look

Revelation 1:7
Behold, he cometh with clouds; and every eye shall see him, and they also which pierced him...

E very eye shall see him. Jesus will wake up some people that are already dead. He will visit every cemetery, funeral home, and hospital because every eye will see Him. Those who did not accept Him and the ones that pierced Him will have to look at Him also. Can you imagine his enemies standing, looking at the Lord with eyes like flames of fire and feet like polished brass, his voice sounding like many trumpets? Jesus isn't going to just slip in quietly.

I long to see Him. When no else would look at me, he saw me. When no one else would pay me any attention, the Lord did. He didn't look at who I was; he looked at what he could make out of me. When everybody else said, you're nothing, you're nobody, Jesus said, "I can take that person, and I can do something with him.

The next reason I want to see Him is because I get tired sometimes of talking to somebody and haven't got a face to go along with it. Every now and then, somebody tries to paint a picture of Jesus. They paint Him looking like a sissy without any scars in His hands and long hair on His back. A man who has been living in the desert and in the wilderness would not have that type of appearance. I don't think we've got the right picture. If you go in a white church, he looks white; in a black church, he looks black; in a Chinese church, he looks Chinese, etc. But one of these days, I'll be able to look at Him face to face. Do you want to see him? The man that died for me, the man that set us free. Hallelujah! Oh, I want to see Him.

Every eye will be focused on him on that day. People will not be watching their favorite football hero or movie star or looking at the stock market report, but every eye will be on the Lord Jesus. We will personally see him.

Honoring The Son

Revelation 1:18

I am he that liveth, and was dead; and, behold, I am alive for evermore, Amen; and have the keys of hell and of death.

I know that many of you are in a terrible dilemma. Your heart is heavy; there are problems steaming all around you and in your life. And you have said to yourself, "If it were not for bad luck, I wouldn't have any at all." You've tried to make ends meet and the harder you try, the worse things become. Your doctor and your psychologist haven't been the answer. You haven't found it in magazines, in the bottom of a liquor bottle, or at the other end of a stick of marijuana. But I stopped on my way to heaven to tell you that He that honors the son, God will honor. Take time out of your busy schedule; stop complaining; stop worrying; stop giving up your right for the fellowman's wrong and prancing the floor every night and focus on the Son. When you focus on the Son, he seems to have a way of drying the tears and easing your fears. He makes your burdens lighter and your pathway brighter. When you decide to honor the Son, He will supply all your needs.

A winner never quits and a quitter never wins. Satan may approach you many times and tell you to give up, throw in the towel. But you need to know that the devil doesn't have a Heaven for you. However, he will certainly try to keep you out if he can. And sometimes on this journey and pilgrimage, the road may not be as sweet as it should and ought to be, but stay in the race; don't give up the ship; don't throw in the towel. The race is not given to the swift or the battle to the strong, but to him that endures to the end. When John penned the book of Revelation, he was in his nineties. At the age of twenty-five, he left his parents and occupation to follow Jesus. At ninety, he's still walking with the Lord and yielding his life to the Son, honoring Him. Honor the Lord to the very last moment!

I Am Whatever

Revelation 1:8
I am Alpha and Omega, the beginning and the ending, saith the Lord, which is, and which was, and which is to come, the Almighty.

I am. Whatever your need is, Jesus says I am that. For instance if you're sick, you'll hear him say I am a doctor. If you're in a storm, you'll hear him say I am shelter. If you don't know you way, he'll tell you I am the way. If you're dead, he says I am the resurrection and the life. If you're in the dark, I am the light of the world. If you're lost, I am the good shepherd. Whatever my needs are, he said I am that. He said I am Alpha and Omega—He is omniscient. In other words, he is an all knowing God. Isn't it amazing how Jesus knew so much, yet he spent so little time in school? His education and mind did not come from man. More books have been written about Jesus than any other one person I know of. Libraries are built for the sole purpose of studying about Jesus.

Jesus is all knowing. I like that because I'm serving a God that's not ignorant. He cannot be deceived. You can deceive me, but not him. He knows me from the inside out and from the outside in. He knows my name; my number; my need, and my nationality. He is an all knowing God. You can't dispute him; because nobody has the knowledge that God possesses.

Notice the way Jesus handled the devil when he went up on the mountain and was transfigured and when he was tempted in the wilderness by the devil. I wondered why Jesus didn't just dialogue with the devil and confuse his mind. But Jesus dealt with the devil the way we have to deal with him when he tempts us. Jesus was my example. By him saying, I am Alpha and Omega, He is saying I cannot be deceived, disputed, or discredited because anything you bring up, I can handle; I have all knowledge.

I AM encompasses everything we can ever imagine.

Shake Your World

Revelation 1:9
John, who also am your brother, and companion in tribulation, and in the kingdom and patience of Jesus Christ, was in the isle that is called Patmos, for the word of God, and for the testimony of Jesus Christ.

John begins by telling the reader something about who he is and his circumstance. He identifies himself as a witness for Jesus, a brother and companion in tribulation and in the kingdom and patience of Jesus Christ. John was in exile because of the gospel. When was the last time you got in trouble because of the gospel? When was the last time you got in trouble on the job just because of the word of God? When was the last time you got in trouble at your house with the word of God. Most of us, if we are around folk that we don't think want us to be in the word, will back off. We don't want to disturb anybody. God called us to disturb folk. God called us to shake other folks' worlds when they don't want to learn the word of God; you are to be a living epistle in the midst of them. Let your light so shine before men that they might see your good works and glorify your Father who is in Heaven.

Your spiritual life ought to be first of all private, then public, and then purposeful. It doesn't mean that you need to leave your job because nobody there is saved. Light shines better in dark places. Let your light shine while on your job. Sooner or later somebody will recognize that you have been with the Lord and spent time in His presence.

Be thankful for the things you're going through because God is preparing you for something better. You haven't always had the ability to accomplish what you can accomplish now. God has done many things in you. We ought to look back and thank God for every negative situation in our life. Our spiritual muscles must get in shape so we can leap over difficult situations. We will be able to look back and see the growth God brought in our lives during those times He allowed our world to be shaken.

31

Turn Your Traps Into A Trapeze

Matthew 5:11–12

Blessed are ye, when men shall revile you, and persecute you, and shall say all manner of evil against you falsely, for my sake. Rejoice, and be exceeding glad: for great is your reward in heaven: for so persecuted they the prophets which were before you.

Don't get upset when you've been criticized. Instead, go and throw a party and be exceedingly glad because great is your reward. There was a time that folk used to rejoice because they thought they were worthy to be persecuted for calling on Jesus' name. Persecution has fringe benefits. You will benefit from calling on and lifting and carrying his name. If you've got the gospel, Jesus has a way of keeping you from being lonely at night. The gospel has a way of drying tears from your eyes and healing sick bodies. The gospel has a way of keeping you from focusing on your enemies and focus on the one that can bring you through these situations. Whatever you are going through, remember somebody else is going through the same stuff. Let the gospel take your trap and turn it into a trapeze.

I call it the God-spell, because whenever you digest the gospel it will put a spell on you. You will be loving your enemies and treating your neighbors right, going when you don't feel like going, singing when ain't nothing to sing about, laughing when ain't nothing funny. Crying when ain't nobody bothering, running when ain't nobody behind you. There is joy. No wonder Paul said he was not ashamed of the gospel. Every one of us ought to be a witness for the Lord; there is something He has done for each of us.

The gospel has different effects on different folk. The gospel might make Annie pout, but Mattie shout. The gospel will make Sally mad, but Mattie glad. So don't think it will work on you exactly the same as it works on me, but if you take a good dose of gospel, it changes your life.

Praise Under Pressure

Acts 16:25
And at midnight Paul and Silas prayed, and sang praises unto God: and the prisoners heard them.

Paul and Silas were out doing missionary work when they met a little girl who was notorious for fortune telling. When the little girl got saved, the community fell out with Paul and Silas. The proceeds were no longer coming in because the girl stopped her fortune telling business. We see even today there are lots of people in the world who do not want certain people to get saved. Income sources would be cut off. A lot of corrupt business practices would stop So it is no wonder how much difficulty is thrown at the person who is trying to win folk for the Lord. The devil will throw fiery darts at you to try to dampen your spirit; he will try to get you to sit down and shut up. But I am convinced that if you honor the Lord, in spite of what the devil doesn't want, Jesus will be with you always.

So Paul and Silas were arrested. Their backs were beaten; they were put in jail with shackles on their hands and on their feet. A rack was put around their necks. They were thrown in an inner jail and stripped of their clothing. And the devil thought he had them. But they didn't sit down and give up. At midnight Paul and Silas started praying and singing praises unto God. We can worship under pressure. When trouble comes, pray your way through and while you're praying, go on and praise. Don't wait until God answers your prayer. Praise him while you are praying. Pray and praise, praise and then pray. But the story doesn't end here. God used an earthquake to set Paul and Silas free and then more people got saved. The prison guard and all his household believed on the Lord Jesus. Paul and Silas were not defeated. I like to take my lesson from Paul and Silas and praise at all times. Something takes place every day of my life to make me want to praise him.

Interrupted Plans

Acts 9:3

And as he journeyed, he came near Damascus: and suddenly there shined round about him a light from heaven:

Some of you have had your plans interrupted by God. Even though you thought you had everything in order and in place. You had laid out your plans and made decisions what to do next. And lo and behold, the Lord interrupted. He does have a right to detour our lives, since he is the controller of our lives. I've seen people that set out to take vacations and the Lord said, "I don't want you to take it yet." So he interrupts your vacation. Other people set out to make good careers and they set out to do one thing, but God says, "I don't want you to do that." So he interrupts the plans. He alters your schedule and sends you in another direction. He can interrupt anytime he gets ready because many times we don't know who we are or where we're going. We don't know what we're going to do.

The Apostle Paul had an interruption of his plans. He had heard that there was a church in Damascus calling on the name of the Lord. Saul, who became Paul, had plans to slaughter the disciples of Christ. He went to the high priest and received letters of permission to go to the synagogues in Damascus and find those who were the disciples of Jesus so he could arrest them and bring them to Jerusalem. When he and a group of like-minded men were on the Damascus road, there shone a light from heaven brighter than the noonday sun. Acts 9:4, And he fell to the earth, and heard a voice saying unto him, Saul, Saul, why persecutest thou me? Paul was shaken and began to tremble when he realized Jesus was truly the Lord. Jesus interrupted Saul's plans and even blinded him until a disciple prayed for him. Saul became Paul and changed the direction of his life. God interrupts the plans of man.

In The Midst

Revelation 1:12–13

And I turned to see the voice that spake with me. And being turned, I saw seven golden candlesticks; And in the midst of the seven candlesticks one like unto the Son of man...

John said when he turned to look that he saw several golden candlesticks. Now these candlesticks (Revelation 1:20) are symbolic of the churches of the living God. Golden candlesticks were also used in the temple and in the tabernacle before sacrifices were offered. It was a standard format for a table to be prepared. Candlesticks were placed on the table. Each candlestick had seven prongs on it and each prong had seven cups. There were always at least twelve loaves of bread on the table to represent the twelve tribes of Israel. These seven-pronged candlesticks were all filled with oil that was symbolic of the Holy Ghost. Each candle having a cup had a wick in the cup. And that wick actually represents us. It seems to say that before you can see the fire, the wick must be connected with the oil. In other words, before there will be a shining, there first must be a burning. And you see too many people who want to shine without the burning. You need to get the burning and then shining will show up.

In the midst of the seven candlesticks was Jesus; notice he was not somewhere afar looking down. He was in the midst. And remember the candlesticks represent the church, which means that Jesus does come to church. He spends his time in the midst. Now have you ever asked yourself, when Jesus comes to church, what does he do? Does he sit back, cross his legs and nod his head ever now and then. I think not. When Jesus comes to church, he comes to examine the saints. On every pew somebody is hurting, needs help, is depressed, sitting with a hung down head. But they leave with their head up and a song in their heart. It's amazing how Jesus supplies the needs of so many during a single worship celebration. Jesus is in the midst of his church.

In The Middle Of The Fire

Matthew 18:20
For where two or three are gathered together in my name, there am I in the midst of them.

Jesus says he is there in the midst for many reasons. Not only does he show up in the midst to heal and deliver but he also appears in the midst to correct. Occasionally, a church fighter will show up at church. Critics will make their appearance. People with negative attitudes and negative dispositions will arrive. And the Lord knows how to handle that each and every one. Sometimes your enemy is sitting right next to you and can't bother you because the Lord is in the midst. When your enemy tries to come up against you he stumbles and falls. That's why you don't have to walk around with a 357 magnum. No, you don't have to have your switchblade; just leave it to the Lord. Your enemies can come behind that switchblade or magnum, but they can't overpower the Lord. He has all power. And a God that's got all power, I want him on my side. And definitely I want Him to know I am on his side.

Shadrach, Meshach and Abednego, three Hebrew boys, got in trouble because they would not bow in worship to a golden image of an earthly king or worship his gods. They were willing to make a stand and even die for their faith if necessary. These young men were bound and thrown into a fiery furnace that was so hot that even the mighty men who threw them in died from the heat. When the king looked in the furnace, he saw not three but four persons all walking and rejoicing free from their bonds. The princes, governors, captains, and the king's counselors saw these men, upon whose bodies the fire had no power, nor was their hair singed. The Lord arrived on the scene and corrected the situation. It's amazing how when the Lord shows up he makes little numbers, big numbers. You see God plus any number is a majority

All Power

1 John 4:17

...that we may have boldness in the day of judgment: because as he is, so are we in this world.

The Lord gives us five calls in life. The first call is the call of birth. You had nothing to do with that. The second call is the call from darkness to the marvelous light. You do have something to do with that call. That's when you accept Christ or reject him as your personal Savior. The third call is the call to death. You really don't have anything to do with that because sooner or later, we're all going to die. But then there's a fourth call, and that's the call to resurrection. Whether you've been bad or good, you're going to have to get up. Last is the fifth call, the call to judgment. Let me tell you how that's going to work.

The second call will determine the fifth call. 1 John 2:1 "My little children, these things write I unto you, that ye sin not. And if any man sin, we have an advocate with the Father, Jesus Christ the righteous:" You see, your attorney and your judge are the same person. Jesus is your Savior right now but on judgment day, He will be the judge. You may say Lord, "I was aiming to come and I just didn't. Didn't nobody tell me." The Lord will remind you when you were fifteen years old and your classmate told you about Jesus Christ and you laughed in his face. Or when you were thirty years old and had your appendix taken out, do you remember when the Chaplain came to your room, and said "son, do you believe that Jesus died for you?" And you told him you didn't want to talk.

When you walk up to the bench, Jesus will be sitting there as well. However, if you have accepted Him as your Savior, the judge is going to see you coming and say, "Case dismissed." The case has been handled out of court. I've got a good attorney. My attorney knows the judge. He died one Friday and got up Sunday with Al-l-l-l-l-l power.

Supernatural Strength

Revelation 2:8–11
Unto the angel of the church in Smyrna write; These things saith the first and the last which was dead and is alive;

Smyrna was a city infiltrated with Jews. Some believed in the Lord Jesus Christ while others were merely pretending practitioners of the faith. They tried to carry on the cover of loving God, but Jesus said that they were of the synagogue of Satan. He sends a message to the church at Smyrna telling them He knows of their works and tribulations and poverty and the blasphemy of them which say they are Jews and are not.

You see the strength of the church is not based upon the size of the membership. It is not based upon scholarly preachers in the pulpit or business-minded men on the deacon board or educators in the pews. Neither is it based upon finances or wealth. The church's strength is based upon the person that founded the church. It is in Jesus that we live and we move and have our being. The foundation of the church and my faith must be built on nothing less that Jesus Christ and his righteousness.

Jesus gives us a concept of his strength when he says, "I am the first and the last," indicating that whatever trying situation you find yourself in, he is there first. Jesus doesn't wait until we get into trouble and then show up. He's there before we get to the trouble. When Shadrach, Meschah, and Abednego were thrown into the fiery furnace, the Lord had already arranged to be there to protect them ahead of time. He made a way for Noah and his family before the flood took place. All you that labor and are heavy laden, Jesus has already arranged for rest. Not only is Jesus the first, He is also the last. He won't abandon us while we're still on the ship. Other friends counsel, visit, talk with us for a while, but if we keep on worrying them, they may abandon us. But we're serving a God that will not leave us. He is the first one to show up at your house the last one to leave.

Stand Firm Under Pressure

Revelation 2:9
I know thy works, and tribulation...

I **know thy works.** Jesus knows my name; he knows my number; he knows of my necessities; he knows where I'm going before I leave home; he knows my thoughts before I think them because he is an all knowing God. He says I know thy works – and then he adds and tribulations. Now the word tribulation here comes from the word meaning pressure. Isn't that exciting to know that the Lord knows the pressure you're under? And the good part about it is not only does he know, but he is also able to do something about it.

The people of the church in Smyrna were experiencing crisis in their lives. Many of the Jews there believed in worshiping Caesar. Once each year every person in Smyrna would have to stand before a court of law and say that Caesar was his Lord. But the saints couldn't say Caesar is our Lord. And since they refused to say that Caesar is our Lord, they got in trouble within the city. If they were merchants, it got all over town that they wouldn't worship Caesar. And so folk stopped buying products from them. If they worked on a public job and everybody else was bowing to Caesar then they would get demoted. A person could lose their job if the boss became upset when he didn't bow to Caesar. Students would get picked on at school by the professors and everybody else because they didn't bow to the god of Caesar.

So Jesus says I know what you're going through and I know your pressure. He let them know what was ahead, prison and hard times, because of their unwavering stand. But He also told them to be faithful unto death and He would give them a crown of life. These people had tapped into the real life and were not willing to deny Jesus and lose their eternal reward. He says, "I know your tribulation."

Poor But Very Rich

Revelation 2:9
I know thy ... poverty, (but thou art rich).

I also know how poor you are. Because of your stand for me, you've had your chariots taken away; you've lost good jobs, your wife and children walked away. He says I know your poverty. There are some people that believe what Ike use to say concerning the prosperity gospel–that if you do what the Lord says, you'll get rich. Now you can prosper following the Lord, but you don't have to prosper financially. Some of the closest folk I've seen to the Lord didn't have a quarter. It doesn't mean because you doing everything right for God, that you're going to have a pocket full of money. Nor does it mean if you have a pocket full of money that you're doing what the Lord says. A whole lot of folk right close by, living real good have never bowed down to the Lord. They have great big houses and have never accepted Christ as Savior.

God is not disappointed in you if you are poor. He says I know your poverty, but thou art rich. How can I be poor and then be rich at the same time? James 2:5 Hearken, my beloved brethren, Hath not God chosen the poor of this world rich in faith, and heirs of the kingdom which he hath promised to them that love him? Now I may not have any money but if I have faith, I'm rich. Faith is the substance of things hoped for, the evidence of things not seen. Without faith it is impossible to please him. He that comes to God must believe that He is and that He rewards those that diligently seek him. So if I don't have faith God is not pleased. But if I do have faith my Father is pleased with me. I don't have to have any money because he knows what I have need of even before I ask him. The road may be rough, the going may get tough, the hills may be hard to climb, but I started a long time ago and there's no doubt in my mind, Oh I decided to make Jesus my choice.

Suffering Will Happen

Philippians 1:29
For unto you it is given in the behalf of Christ, not only to believe on him, but also to suffer for his sake.

I know we don't like to talk about it but saints if you are saved you are going to suffer. John 16:2 They shall put you out of the synagogue, the time cometh that whosoever killeth you will think that he is doing God's service. I mean that's suffering isn't it? There are those that tell you, you don't have to suffer. You even have folk out now saying that if you're saved, you'll never get sick. I don't know what you're going to do about Job. Job was a man that feared God and avoided the presence of evil. That boy got sick! Lazarus got so sick he died and he was Jesus' best friend. You don't get any closer to the Lord than that. Hezekiah got sick and turned his face to the wall and he was talking to the Lord all at the same time. In this earthly body, there will be sickness.

Philippians 1:29 says, "For unto you it is given in the behalf of Christ not only to believe on him but also to suffer for his sake." This type of suffering means to experience something painful. You see just because you believe, it doesn't mean that suffering is excluded. "Oh, I believe Jesus died for me; I believe his Father raised him from the dead; I ain't got nothing else to worry about." But you're still going to suffer. You didn't suffer before you got here; you're not going to suffer when you leave here. So if suffering is coming, it's got to come while we're here. Now a lot of suffering we bring on ourselves. If we're bogged down in debt, we can't blame that on the Lord unless we've been giving him our whole paycheck ever since we began working. Often when we're bogged down in debt, we've spent money we didn't have on things we didn't need, trying to impress folk we didn't like. It was not because we had been suffering for the Lord's sake.

The Mystery Of Suffering

Revelation 2:10
Fear none of those things which thou shalt suffer ... that ye may be tried.

Now why is there such a mystery about suffering? The Bible says that we're going to suffer. The mystery is not that we're suffering but the fact that God allowed it to happen. God says to fear none of these things which thou shall suffer. He says He is the first and the last with all power and knowledge and yet he's going to allow me to suffer. It is a mystery to know God loves me and still allows me to suffer. Is that a mystery to you? Because sometimes when you suffer, you'll find yourself asking, "Does God really care?" That's what the disciples asked you know when they were caught in the storm. They woke Jesus and said, "Master, do you care if we perish?" Now most of us know he can do something about it, do we not? But why is it that he will allow us to suffer.

The answer is in right there in Revelation 2:10. It says that you may be tried. The word tried means tested. Now any faith that cannot be tested cannot be trusted. Faith must be able to go through a test. You see anybody can love the Lord when the sun is shining or say, "I love you Lord," when horns are honking at your door. Anybody can say, "Lord I know you'll make a way," when you've already got your icebox full. Anybody can say, "The Lord is good to me," when you've got a good job to go to every morning. But testing time comes when you look in your icebox and nothing is in there. And you look in your pocket and ain't nothing in there; pick up your phone and there's no dial tone; turn on your light switch but the lights won't come on; and you look out and somebody's repossessing your car. It's then when testing time comes; it's then when you ought to be able to say, though you slay me, yet will I trust in you. Testing time is trusting time; testing time is trying time; testing time is delivering time. Suffering is a test.

February

The Secret Of Success

Revelation 2:10
...be thou faithful unto death, and I will give thee a crown of life.

It says to be faithful unto death. What does it mean to be faithful unto death? A man one day had some associates that walked up to him and said, "Sir, we're tired of you talking about this man named Jesus. If you don't stop talking about him we're going to banish you from this place. The man said, "You can't banish me from the Lord because He has promised to be with me always even to the end of the world. Well they went back to talk to their committee and returned because they wanted to stop this man from praising the Lord so much. They said, We'll take everything you own; you'll be broke." The man said, You can't break me because all of my treasures are laid up in heaven." The men said, Then we will just bury you. The man said, "I'm not worried about you burying me, because I'm stationed in Christ." So they realized the man had a conviction they couldn't change and they left him alone.

The root word of faithful comes from the word conviction. Now you won't be faithful until you first have a conviction. The three Hebrew boys had a conviction that prohibited them from bowing to the king's idols. They told the king, "If God delivers us from the fiery furnace, we'll be faithful. But if God doesn't deliver us, we'll still be faithful."

So whatever you're in, be faithful to the Lord. If you are singing in the choir and it's growing, be faithful. But if it's struggling along with only two or three members, continue to be faithful. If you are building a Sunday school class, be faithful whether you have five students or only one. When worship time comes, be faithful whether you are feeling jolly or whether you have pains all over your body. The faithfulness of the people determines the success of the church. Be faithful unto death and receive a crown of life.

Hold Fast The Name

Revelation 2:13
...and thou holdest fast my name, and hast not denied my faith...

In spite of where you are, hold fast to the name of Jesus. You see there are those now that cruise around too sophisticated to call the name of Jesus. Folk don't mind you going to civic meetings and singing, "How Great Thou Art." You know when people consider the stars, the moon, and the atmosphere they know how great Thou art. But when you verbalize, "In the name of Jesus," you upset some folk. They would rather you didn't call the name Jesus. I've been called to visit with family members who have somebody in their family that cannot accept the divinity of Jesus. When I begin to pray in Jesus' name, they head to the other room. Even if their family member dies, they'll stand outside the building during the funeral because they can't stand the name Jesus.

This is really the way it is with the devil. He can't stand the name Jesus. You see, when you start calling His name, you move to a higher plateau. A man, who was flying around in his airplane, looked back in the cockpit and saw a snake getting ready to strike him. He called headquarters and asked if he should try to land although he was quite a distance from the runway. Control said, "Oh no, don't come down. Point the plane upward." The snake began to lie still. Control said, "Keep on going upward," and the pilot went up a little higher. The snake began to lose its hold. Control said, Go on up," and the old snake just flipped over. Satan can't stand to go toward Jesus. Whenever you call the name Jesus, you're heading up! You're heading away from the devil and out of his striking distance. Jesus told the church at Pergamos they had done well to hold fast to His Name in all they did.

Balaam's Doctrine

Revelation 2:14

But I have a few things against thee, because thou hast them that hold the doctrine of Balaam, who taught Balak to cast a stumblingblock before the children of Israel, to eat things sacrificed unto idols, and to commit fornication.

Now what was the doctrine of Balaam? Balaam was a prophet that lived during the days of the children of Israel. The children of Israel had begun to multiply so much until Balak, king of Moab, became disturbed and felt threatened. Balak knew that Balaam was a prophet and whatever Balaam said, you could put your foot on it. So Balak sent his elders to pay Balaam to go down to the children of Israel and curse them so their population would dwindle. But the Lord told Balaam not to go. Balak then sent his princes with more money to offer. This time Balaam didn't wait on orders from the Lord. Numbers 22:21 "Balaam rose up in the morning, and saddled his ass, and went with the princes of Moab." But God dispatched an angel who stood in front of Balaam's donkey. The donkey feared the angel and tried to turn back. However, Balaam took out his whip and smote the donkey. Even after God used the donkey to speak to Balaam, he was still determined to go on.

Balaam prepared to curse the children of Israel, but every time he opened his mouth to curse Israel, he spoke blessings instead. Balaam told Balak he could not curse the children of Israel because God had blessed them. Yet, Balaam counseled Balak on how to corrupt Israel. That's the way the old devil is; if he can't curse you, he'll attempt to corrupt you. Corruption slipped into the church of Pergamos. They would take folk in who had not repented–just because they said, "Yes, I believe." They baptized them and allowed them to be members. The church became corrupted. That is the doctrine of Balaam, to compromise the people of God with sin. So God said he had against the church at Pergamos that the doctrine of Balaam was in it.

Change Of Mind

Revelation 2:16
Repent; or else I will come unto thee quickly, and will fight against them with the sword of my mouth.

R epentance really should be one of our daily practices. We don't need to just repent when we first meet the Lord because we go daily committing sin. The Bible says anything that is not of faith is sin. That means if you have doubts about something, you might be sinning right then and there. If you doubt the ability of God, you just might be committing sin. Talking about, "I don't know if the Lord..." Well it doesn't matter if you know whether or not, you know the Lord is able. He is an able God.

We know what repentance is, don't we? Repentance begins with a change of mind; first it's a change of mind about self. You stop depending on self because self will get you in trouble. Jesus says if any man comes after me let him first deny himself. Then it's a change of mind about sin. You see, you stop calling sin what you think it is and call it what it is. Have you ever noticed what we've done with sin now? We don't call it sin any more; we give it other names. We call adultery having an affair. Fornication is getting to know you better. We refer to homosexuality as doing your own thing. We don't even call it stealing any more; we call it embezzlement. But the Lord calls it sin. And if Jesus calls it sin, that's what we've got to call it. It doesn't matter how you dress it up, its still sin.

And, very importantly, we must have a change of mind about the Savior. We must know he means what he says when he says to repent or else I'll come to you quickly. Don't think you can hide because you're holding a position. The Lord will show you where your wrong spots are and give you a chance to get it right and repent of your sins. But, at some point, he will expect you to change in order to avoid a head-on collision. God is a quick God. Don't wait too long or you may have only enough time to beg mercy.

The White Stone

Revelation 2:17

To him that overcometh will I give to eat of the hidden manna, and will give him a white stone, and in the stone a new name written, which no man knoweth saving he that receiveth it.

To him that overcomes will I give to eat the hidden manna. You remember the manna that fell down during the days of Moses when Israel was hungry and there was nothing to eat. This manna represented Jesus Christ. First of all, the manna came from heaven; this represented the fact that Jesus came from Heaven. Secondly, the manna was white symbolizing the purity of Jesus. Thirdly, the manna was sweet typifying the sweet smelling Savior. Then fourthly the manna was round representing the immortality of Jesus Christ. Fifthly, the manna fell on the ground depicting the humanity of Jesus. Sixth, the manna was eaten representing the fact that Jesus is the bread of life. If you overcome, Jesus is waiting especially for you.

Then he says I will give him a white stone. Now that white stone may not mean much to you, but listen to what that stone really represents. In those days whenever a man committed a crime he had to go to court. A judge placed a black stone and a white stone in a container. If the judge took out the black stone, the man had been found guilty and received a death sentence. But if the judge brought out the white stone, it meant that man was acquitted. And just that alone is enough to make me buck and shout because you see I know without the shadow of a doubt if I'd been tried, a black stone would come out of my container. But thanks be to the God I serve, he put a white stone in that container on my behalf. One of these mornings when the wicked have ceased from troubling and the weary are at rest, when I bid farewell to every fear and I walk up to the gates, I'll have my white stone with a new name written inside.

Autopsy Of A Dead Church

Revelation 3:1
Thou hast a name that thou livest and art dead.

There was a pastor of a certain western church that called for the members to come to a Wednesday night prayer meeting, but no one showed up. He knew that there was a major problem in his church and so he went and rang the bell, indicating that someone had died. The neighborhood became disturbed because they had not heard the news of the passing of one of the neighbors. So they started inquiring who had died. No one knew. Finally, they rushed to the church to ask the pastor. After the church had filled to its seating capacity, he said, "I want to announce to you that this church has died."

The members decided to have an autopsy done to determine the cause of death. They cut the church open and looked on the inside to discover the church was suffering from low blood, heart trouble, and venereal disease. The low blood was causing blackouts when it came time to have Bible Class. Blackouts also interfered with mission work. The heart trouble made the members hard-hearted, with no feeling or compassion for anybody else. Don't you know God sends blessings to us so he can channel blessings through us? We may be all right at sixty, but God remembers us when we were sixteen and needed help. And the church had venereal disease resulting from sin. The gambling industry had many customers in the church. The dope dealers conducted business with the members and the prostitutes had many patrons from the congregation. These conditions were bringing about the demise of the church.

This church was living in the past. They used to have a good program; they used to pay tithes. I used to sing in the choir. I used to teach Sunday school. Always used to. God told the church to hold fast and repent and join with those that had not defiled their garments.

The Operation Of The Church

Revelation 3:1
And unto the angel of the church in Sardis write; These things saith he that hath the seven Spirits of God

Notice first that the Bible says the Lord spoke to the angel of the church in Sardis. Now remember that the angel of the church was the pastor of that particular church. If things go wrong, God holds that under-shepherd accountable. When a pastor has been in a church at least ten years, eighty or ninety percent of all the problems fall right at his feet. The pastor he should be spiritually strong enough to have the saints headed in the way that God has called him to lead them. If he's spiritual, then they will be spiritual. If he's carnal, the church will be carnal. If he's broad hearted, then they too will be broad hearted.

The number seven refers to being total and complete. When he said the seven spirits, he is talking about the total operation of the church – the total functioning of the work of the Holy Spirit. Isaiah 11:2 outlines the seven-fold ministry of the Holy Spirit: the Spirit of the Lord shall rest upon him; the spirit of wisdom and understanding, the spirit of counsel and might, the spirit of knowledge and of the fear of the LORD. (1) the Spirit of the Lord (2) the Spirit of Wisdom (3) the Spirit of Understanding (4) the Spirit of Counsel (5) the Spirit of Might (6) the Spirit of Knowledge (7) the Spirit of the Fear of the Lord. Isaiah is speaking about the seven-fold spiritual ministry of the church. A church cannot function as designed by the Designer if it is not functioning by the dictates of the Holy Spirit. We can not function and operate a church based upon our own knowledge, on our own ingenuity; on our own ability, or on our own thoughts; it must be based upon the finished work of Jesus Christ and the operation of the Holy Spirit. The pastor must lead by example and by yielding to the seven-fold master design.

A Faded Reputation

Revelation 3:1

I know thy works, that thou hast a name that thou livest, and art dead.

I know thy works. This church had a name for being a working, living church. This was the Who Church and the What's What Church. This was the church that everybody in the community talked about. If people were moving to Sardis, they would be told to move their letter to the First Church of Sardis. This was the church that was going on. Sardis was a great city at one time. It was a wealthy city, an aristocratic type of town, famous for its wool, used to make carpets. Also a wealth of gold ran down the stream in the valley of the area of Sardis. It was a well-fortified city built on a hill making it difficult for enemies to destroy. The church had an even greater name than the city. The church had a reputation. Oh what joy it must to have been for this church to have grown to the point that it had a reputation. One of the best choirs that could ever sing, a group of deacons that was second to none, Christian Education Board, Ushers were well uniformed; the Mission group were out on their job; it had a name. It had a department for the young folk; for the youth; for the young adult; for the married; for the single group. This church was together; it had whatever anybody was looking for in a church. It had a name that it lived, but Jesus said it was dead.

It had a reputation, but it was a deceiving church. It's dangerous to pretend to be something that you're not. We cannot be pretending practitioner of the faith. We have to walk our talk and live the life we sing about in our songs. We're deceiving ourselves when we shout on Sunday and raise hell on Monday, when we walk around in our saintly outfit, but have hell on the inside. That may be why we can't get some folk to follow us to church, because we brag about our holiness, but they see the hellishness.

Find The Burning Coals

Revelation 3:2
Be watchful, and strengthen the things which remain, that are ready to die: for I have not found thy works perfect before God.

God really knows how to stir us. Sometimes he'll allow things to happen in our lives to stir us. Sometimes He gives us some friends, but then he turns around and gives us some enemies. He gives us some sunshine, and then gives us a little rain, good days and then some bad days. And then He shakes it all up together and stirs our lives. He motivates us to get on the right track again. I have discovered, Saints, that if you've once been on fire, it doesn't take a lot to get you on fire again. When I was young at home at night, Daddy would put a big stick in the fireplace. And all of us would go to bed and go to sleep. When we woke up, we could see no fire; nothing but ashes; it seemed as though the big stick had burned out. But when Daddy would stir the ashes, live coals were still in there. He didn't need another match, he just put some kindling on top of the live coals and the fire started burning again. And that's really the way it is with saints that are truly saved. The fire is still there; you just need to be stirred a little bit.

Be watchful and strengthen the things that remain that are ready to die. He says you're at the point of death; it won't take much to push you over, but I want you to know you can still live. You must be spiritually alert. But he also says there must be spiritual broken-ness–repentance. Most people think that if they don't lie, don't steal, don't commit adultery, don't commit fornication, don't drink, and don't gamble that they are clear. But if you try to move in life without moving by faith, you're committing sin. The Bible says without faith it is impossible to please Him. For he that cometh to God must believe that He is and that He is a rewarder of them diligently seek Him. So he says to have brokenness and strengthen that which remains.

Recognize The Present

Revelation 3:3

Remember therefore how thou hast received and heard, and hold fast, and repent. If therefore thou shalt not watch, I will come on thee as a thief, and thou shalt not know what hour I will come upon thee.

If there ever was a time we needed to be right with God, it's now. We're living in a day of guided missiles and misguided men. In a day where folks know more about bombs and bullets than they know about the Bible. In a day where we practice more politics than we practice prayer. In a day of switching; from God to gold; from grace to grass; from soul sense to science. We've done some switching so if there ever was a time that we need to recognize where we are, it's now. God has put this in our hands; If my people, which are called by my name, shall humble themselves and pray and seek my face and turn from their wicked ways, then will I hear from heaven; forgive them of their sins and heal their land.

So God says to remember the past, recognize the present; and be ready for the future. Otherwise, He will come to you as a thief. Now notice when the Lord comes to get the saints, he's not coming as a thief; he's coming as a bridegroom. He's coming to get those of us that are ready to go. But when you're not ready, he says "I'll come as a thief in the night." And a person isn't comfortable knowing that a thief is coming because you don't know how a thief is going to react when you catch him even in your own house. You may have to shoot him or he'll shoot you. Or when you're nodding, that's when he'll show up. You're not ready for a thief at any time, but we'll be ready for the bridegroom if we are seeking our Savior. He says, "Look, you've got to recognize that the future is right before you. If you don't get it right, I'll come as a thief in the in the night."

Garments Undefiled

Revelation 3:4
*Thou hast a few names even in Sardis which have not defiled their garments;
and they shall walk with me in white: for they are worthy.*

In spite of the church being dead, there were a few that were still alive. And that's what I love about the God I serve. I've seen some real dead churches in my life. But if you hang around you'll find somebody in that congregation in spite of the church being dead, that is still on fire for the Lord and loves Jesus, a few names in Sardis, which have not defiled their garments. Can you imagine when Jesus walks in through the street of Jerusalem that he will have a faithful few that will walk with him in white?

One day there was a man that made it to the streets of Heaven and prepared to enter that Holy City, but said, "I have to find somebody that I can go in with." He first saw men dressed in white, about twelve in number, and asked the angels "Who are those folk?" The angels said, "These are the prophets of old." He said, "Well I can't go in with the prophets because I've never been a prophet." He saw another group about twelve in number and asked, "Who are these folk?" "These are the apostles—eye witnesses of Jesus Christ." He replied, "I can't go in with them because I was not an apostle." Another group came along and he asked, "Who are those folk?" "These were people that were murdered and did not live out their normal life." He said, "I can't go in with them because I was not murdered." And then he saw another huge number on their way to the gates, Rahab, that prostitute that hid the spies of Moses, and David, that brother that had committed adultery. He also saw Mary Magdalene, the woman from whom Jesus had cast several demons and the thief that confessed on the cross. "Who are those folk?" The angel said, "These are sinners that were saved by grace." And that man said, "That's my crowd; that's the crowd that I'll be able to go in with. Do not defile your garments. You've been washed.

Avoid The Blot

Revelation 3:5
He that overcometh, the same shall be clothed in white raiment; and I will not blot out his name out of the book of life, but I will confess his name before my Father, and before his angels.

I am an overcomer. I'm not going to let anything stop me from reaching the goal God has called me to reach. An overcomer shall be clothed in white raiment and will not have his name blotted out of the Book of Life. I'm glad that he's not going to blot out my name. Let me tell you how that works if you will. You see when you're born the first time, God will put your name in the Lamb's Book of Life. In other words the Lord doesn't want anybody to go to hell. However, if you don't accept Him as your Savior, he will blot out your name just as you are departing this life. Look at Exodus 32:32 where Moses says, "Yet now, if thou wilt forgive their sin–; and if not, blot me, I pray thee, out of thy book which thou hast written." Yet now if the Lord will forgive their sin– and then there's a blank there. That's the only time in the whole Bible you'll ever see a blank because Moses had never heard of anybody forgiving sin before. Verse 33 And the Lord said unto Moses, whosoever hath sinned against me, him would I blot out of my book.

In Luke 10:20 the disciples were excited because they had cast devils out of some troublesome people. Jesus told them not to brag about casting out any devils, but to rejoice that their names were written in the Book in Heaven. Revelation 20:15 And whosoever was not found written in the Book of Life was cast into the lake of fire. Revelation 21:27 speaks of the great city: "There shall in no wise enter into it anything that defileth, neither whatsoever worketh abomination or maketh a lie, but (only) they which are written in the Lamb's Book of Life." I may not be in Who's Who, but I'm glad I decided a long time ago to make Jesus my choice so when that day comes, he won't blot out my name.

He Has The Master Key

Revelation 3:7

And to the angel of the church in Philadelphia write; These things saith he that is holy, he that is true, he that hath the key of David...

This letter was sent to the Minister of the church so he could share the message with the parishioners. The first characteristic or attribute of Jesus is Holy. The word Holy comes from the idea meaning 'being the real thing.' Jesus is no phony. He's true, he is righteous, he is the Holy one. Everything about Jesus was Holy; his speech was Holy; his attitude was Holy; his thoughts were Holy. That's why he said in Philippians 2:5 Let this mind be in you which was also in Christ Jesus. If we are the children of God, then we too should be Holy. You can't really live a holy life unless you are a Holy person. So he is first of all holy.

Then the text states he is also true. Jesus doesn't major in error. As a matter of fact, He says before one tittle or one jot of his word shall fail, heaven and earth will pass away. Jesus cannot afford to tell one lie. I mean if Jesus would tell just one lie, the wheels would stop turning, horses would stop pawing in the valley, and roses would stop blossoming with just one lie. Not only is he true, he is the truth. John 1:9 says, "He is the true Light." John 14:6 "I am the way, the truth and the life." John 15:1 "I am the true vine." And so he is true.

He has the Key of David. He has the authority to open and to close. Revelation 1:18 I am he that liveth and was dead; and behold I am alive forevermore, Amen; and have the keys of hell and of death. You can't die without Jesus turning the key. Sometimes we think that what we do keeps us alive. No, it is the keeper of the keys. When things are falling all around you, He can hold that key open and you will remain alive. When he gets ready for you to go nothing you can do will keep you here because he has the key.

The Door Opener

Revelation 3:7–8

...he that hath the key of David, he that openeth, and no man shutteth; and shutteth, and no man openeth; I know thy works: behold, I have set before thee an open door, and no man can shut it...

Jesus has the accessibility, which means he can open and no man can close. And he can close and no man can open. It's amazing how many of us get upset because we think other people are standing in our way. I hear about all these ridiculous talk shows daily where people are criticizing one another, cutting each other down, talking about who's standing in their way. The only person that's standing in your way is you. You see, my blessings are tailored to fit me. They won't fit you. When the God I serve opens the door for your blessing, I can't get it. I don't care how strong a man is, he cannot close that door. Some of you may have had somebody try to stop you from getting a job. You really thought they were going to mess you up and maybe it seemed like they did. You didn't get the job you wanted. People weren't the ones in charge; the Lord stopped you because he had something better for you. The Lord has enough power and force to make a way when there is no way to be made. So Jesus has the key to accessibility; He can open a door.

The Lord set an open door of evangelism before the Church in Philadelphia that no man could shut. When it comes to winning souls, the Lord will open a door. He will send a sinner by just for you to witness to. The Lord will deposit you in some strange and unusual places so you can inform people about the man named Jesus. Be careful not to complain about how many crooks, outlaws and criminals are around you. The Lord knew you had the ability to win some of those people for Him, so He put you right in the middle. You don't need to be afraid. He will be with you and give you the words to say when He opens the door.

Let The Critics Live

Revelation 3:9
Behold, I will make them of the synagogue of Satan, which say they are Jews, and are not, but do lie; behold, I will make them to come and worship before thy feet, and to know that I have loved thee.

God is not only in control of the Christians, he's also in control of the critics. He will make them to come and worship before your feet. A lot of people get upset because they are criticized. Be aware of the fact that criticism is actually free advertisement. I've sold more than a few tapes from folk criticizing our church. Say did you hear what he's saying? Go get the tape. When they get it, they discover that I'm in the word and they change their minds about everything they had heard. A whole lot of folk tune in our television broadcast because of what somebody else said. Sometimes a woman becomes upset because some other woman got mad and criticized her. But what they do is just point you out to men. "She thinks she's something." And the man hadn't even paid her any attention before that moment. But then he goes looking for her. If people knew what they were really doing when they criticize you, they'd never say a word.

When a person criticizes you, he's thinking about you. He can't talk about you unless he's got you on his mind. You need to make sure you are right in what you're doing. Don't let them catch you doing wrong; make sure you're right in all you do and let people talk all they want. The Lord says He will make your enemies your footstool. Your enemies will help you reach some things you couldn't reach otherwise. They will give you a step up. Your enemies will help you accomplish some things. Now you don't do stuff just to make people talk, but when you are serving the Lord and you're right in what you doing, let them go on and talk. God will use the critics for his own purposes.

Don't Let Go!

Revelation 3:11

Behold, I come quickly: hold that fast which thou hast, that no man take thy crown.

ehold, I come quickly. Time is running out; we don't have very long to get it together. God tells the church to hold fast to what you have. There are those that are in and out of the church, faithful today yet they don't show up in a month or two. But know that a winner will never quits and a quitter will never win. If you have the love of Jesus, hold on to it. If you have the faith of the Master, he's saying "Don't let it go!" Hold fast to what you have that no man take your crown. Now the crown here doesn't mean your salvation because no man can steal your salvation. You say "Wait a minute preacher, I know some people that were saved and they're not saved any more." No, you know some people that were in the church, but you don't know anybody that was saved and then lost. They used to sing in the choir; that doesn't mean they're saved. They used to preach; that doesn't mean they're saved. You see if you're saved nothing or nobody can steal your salvation.

Any faith that fizzles before the finish had a flaw from the beginning. In other words, a person may look like a Christian, act like a Christian, sound like a Christian, but they aren't a Christian unless they have accepted Christ as their personal Savior. Every one of us have crowns that represent the works that we're doing while we are here. So what he's saying is not to let anybody make us mad enough to go home and sit down. Don't let nobody talk you out of serving the Lord; don't let anyone get you so upset that you hang up your robe or lay down your usher's badge or close your Bible. You've got to keep working until the day is done. I'm glad I represent His name—a name that soothes my sorrow, heals my wound, drives away my fear, and gives me joy in the midnight hour. Oh I love His name. Be faithful until death and receive a crown of life.

Movements And Motives

Psalm 139:2

Thou knowest my downsitting and mine uprising, thou understandest my thought afar off.

The Lord watches our movements. He is observing us. He doesn't just look at you when you are at church. Some of us think that when we leave church we're not only through with church until next Sunday but we are also through with God. We walk out and let our hair down; take our hat off; and go to cussing and get out bottles and all kinds of stuff. But you didn't leave God back here. He watches your every move. Can you imagine looking in your rear view mirror and seeing somebody following you? After you go in your house, you notice them looking in the window. You pick up your phone and it's bugged. You turn on your television and a picture of you comes on. They have a camera on you. Well can I let you in on a secret today–you're being watched. You're being trailed. The Lord is listening to everything you say, watching every move you make. Maybe you're not so good that you want him to watch you all the time.

Not only does he watch our movements, but he is also mindful of our motives. The Bible says he understands my thoughts. Motives added to movements don't always match up. Not everybody who shouts is happy. Everyone who grins at you doesn't love you; some times smiling faces tell lies. You may judge a person by movements although you don't know their real motives. And sometimes you embrace people with bad motives because they are good talkers and get in your heart. Later that person can stick a dagger in you because they were able to get close to you. Or you might turn someone away unknowingly that has a good motive. Sometimes we try to get people to change their ways thinking we could deal with them better. However, God made all of us unique with different tastes and ideas. God is acquainted with all my actions and motives.

You Can't Get Away

Psalm 139:7-9

Whither shall I go from thy spirit? Or whither shall I flee from thy presence? If I ascend up into heaven, thou art there: if I make my bed in hell, behold, thou art there.

Where can I flee from thy presence? David gives three directions people think of to try to get away from God. One way is through death. Some people think that when you die it's all over. That's why people commit suicide. No, it's not over when you take your life. When you take your life, you rush to stand before an angry God. At almost every funeral somebody will say, At least they ain't got to suffer no more." Well that depends on their relationship with God.

Another way is through distance – If I take the wings of the morning and dwell in the uttermost parts of the sea. No, if I start off in the east and I make my way over to the west, when I get there I will discover it was God's hand. Well, if it's trouble you're running from, it's going to be wherever you go. If you are tired of God, he's going to be wherever you end up. I have discovered something; you don't have to move for God to bless you. God can bless you in the spot you're in right now. So you cannot leave him with death or get away from him through distance.

Neither can you hide from him in the darkness for the darkness and the light are both alike to the Lord. Even if I make my bed in hell, he says he's there. Now you wouldn't think the Lord would be in hell. Somehow we put it out that hell is run by the devil. No such thing. The devil doesn't run hell; he isn't even there yet. Where is he? If there's a worship service, he's there. He prowls about like a roaring lion seeking someone to devour or trip up. So if you're running from the Lord and you've never accepted him as Savior, one day you'll still have to face him because if you go to hell, he'll be right there as a judge. And he will be so awesome when people see him they will run until death falls on them. Even though he's merciful, he's also just.

Resting, Not Fretting

Psalm 23:1
The Lord is my shepherd; I shall not want.

In Psalm 23:6 David says, "Surely goodness and mercy shall follow me all the days of my life and I shall dwell in the house of the Lord forever." But notice how he started off. The Lord is my shepherd and I shall not want. I won't have to want for food because You make me to lie down in green pastures. I won't have to want for forgiveness because You restore my soul. I won't have to want for protection when I die because yea, though I walk through the valley of the shadow of death I will fear no evil. How come? Because God is with me. I don't have to want for spiritual oil because my cup is running over. I don't have to want for a banquet because You prepare a table before me in the presence of my enemies. I won't have to want for comfort because I've got goodness on one side and I've got mercy on the other side. David said he might have to cry sometimes, but he goes on to say in Psalm 30:5 that weeping may endure for a night but joy comes in the morning.

Ever now and then I go God looking and I can't find him. Listen to what David says, "I waited patiently for the Lord; and he inclined unto me and heard my cry." If you wait on Him, won't he show up? Psalm 139:13, "For thou has possessed my reins; thou has covered me in my mother's womb." Before you were born, God was looking at you. When your mother almost had a miscarriage He held you. When you talked about getting rid of your baby, He changed your mind. God stamped a stamp of approval on that child. Psalm 37:1 "Fret not thyself because of evildoers." 'Fret not,' sounds like the words of a brave man to me. Neither envy the workers of iniquity for they shall soon be cut off. Delight yourself also in the Lord, and he will give you the desire of your heart. Trust in the Lord; Commit your way to the Lord. Rest in the Lord.

Dodge Danger

Genesis 3:2-3

And the woman said unto the serpent, We may eat of the fruit of the trees of the garden: But of the fruit of the tree which is in the midst of the garden, God hath said, Ye shall not eat of it, neither shall ye touch it, lest ye die.

Eve made several tragic mistakes. Number one, she allowed Satan to catch her alone. Satan loves to catch you alone. He cruises around to find you at your weakest point. The second problem she had was being in the wrong place at the wrong time. There were other trees that she could have been hanging around, but she was there in the midst of the garden gazing at the forbidden fruit. And the problem in the garden was not the apple on the tree; it was really the pair in the garden that created the major catastrophe. Eve made a third mistake and that was she did not utilize her Bible. I know there are those that say that there was no Bible during the days of Adam and Eve, but there was a Bible. What was their Bible? The word of God. Now they didn't have a Bible with sixty-six books, one thousand one hundred thirty nine chapters. No, Eve had only two verses but she misquoted both of them. She took the word freely out of verse two and the word surely out of verse three. Number four, she didn't consult her spouse. She could have said to Satan, "Every evening my husband comes home and we always sit down and have a fruit cocktail together." Or she could have said, "My husband is the head of this house and I recommend that you talk to him." The fifth mistake was in not telling the devil he needed to discuss the matter with God. Instead Eve tried to handle it herself. What the devil did then (and what the devil does now) is he planted a doubt in the mind of Eve. What started with a doubt ended in a denial. He did this by getting Eve to alter the word. Whenever the devil can get you to alter the word, you will lose the grip on your spiritual pilgrimage. Dodge the devil!

Desire Becomes Decision

Genesis 3:6

And when the woman saw that the tree was good for food, and that it was pleasant to the eyes, and a tree to be desired to make one wise, she took of the fruit thereof, and did eat, and gave also unto her husband with her: and he did eat.

There are four verbs here that we can hang our thoughts on to help us understand the text. Eve saw, she took, she did eat, and she gave. Saw—when the woman saw the first time she kept gazing…a look became a lust. Now sometimes the first look is a careless look but when you look again, it's not careless—it's a purposeful look. I cannot stop a bird from flying over my head but I can stop him from making a nest there on top of my head. You see I may not be able to stop a pretty woman from walking by me, but I don't have to keep gazing at her or have pictures of her hidden away. A look became a lust.

Then the woman saw that the tree was good food and that it was pleasant to the eye and a tree to be desired to make one wise so she took. You see that? A desire becomes a decision. You say well I got married and got caught up into this woman; she acted one way and then I found out that she's a nut. Your decision began with a desire, which swayed your decision. You say you're strung out on drugs because your brother persuaded you. No, it was your decision. A desire became a decision.

Then the woman did eat. A choice became a change. She chose to eat and her thinking was changed. She decided it was good. She wanted more and she wanted her husband to have some also. So she gave unto her husband. A sinner is a seducer. When a person is getting ready to do wrong, they feel better it they know others are doing wrong also. People are not satisfied in sinning alone; they will influence others into the same sin, bringing destruction in their lives. Withdraw from the temptation at the onset.

Fools And Fugitives

Genesis 3:7
And the eyes of them both were opened, and they knew that they were naked; and they sewed fig leaves together, and made themselves aprons.

In Genesis 2:25 the man and his wife were naked and they were not ashamed. But after they sinned, their conscience bothered them and they were ashamed. Sin brought about change. They sewed fig leaves together and made themselves aprons. Sin really makes a fool out of you because who with any sense would try to hide from God with fig leaves made into aprons barely covering up the front? And they are hiding from God not knowing which direction he may come from. The fig leaf aprons wouldn't help much if he arrived in the back. Sin makes a fool out of us in other ways. Some fathers will work hard all the week, spend every dime on some liquor and then go out and try to borrow enough money to feed his children. That's a fool.

Sin also brings about separation. It makes us fugitives, running and hiding from someone. Before they sinned, Adam and Eve enjoyed sweet communion everyday with God when He came walking in the garden in the cool of the day. Adam would be there waiting with Mrs. Eve. But as soon as they sinned, they ran from God; notice God did not run from them, they ran from God.

Sin brings about shame, separation, self-defense, sinners, and sorrow. First Adam and Eve experienced shame. Then they were separated from God's presence and their beautiful home. Adam began to defend himself and blame his sin on someone else. They had children, bringing forth more sinners. Women experience sorrow resulting from this sin through the pain of childbirth. Man could no longer eat the lovely fruits of the trees, but had to toil and eat from the ground, which was cursed with thistles and thorns. Man would have to sweat and toil for even this.

Persisting Problems

John 16:33

These things I have spoken unto you, that in me ye might have peace. In the world ye shall have tribulation: but be of good cheer; I have overcome the world.

Most of us are familiar with problems. You hear us saying if it's not one thing it's another. Problems seem to become attached to most of us in one way or the other. If it's not problems with the family then it's problems with the finances. If it's not problems with the finances, it's problems with our future. And if it's not a problem with our future, we have problems with our feelings. There are always some problems somewhere. I have discovered in life that the problems become smaller or larger depending on my attitude with the problem. It is amazing that some can have problems and walk straight through the difficulty. You never know they have one. They keep a smile on their faces. They never stop coming to church. They keep looking fat and fine.

There are others however, who give in to the problems. They resort to drinking, drugs, overeating, gambling, illicit sex and many other wrong pastimes to try to drown out the problems. Job 14:1 says a man's days are full of trouble. You cannot run from problems. You don't have to be a bad person to encounter problems. You don't have to be going in the wrong direction to have problems. Sometimes problems are heaven sent, for many of us would not have a personal relationship with the Lord if we had not experienced uncertainty. Problems often help us to have a closer walk with our heavenly Father. We stop taking life for granted. If you are honest with yourself today you will rightly say, "Because of problems I'm closer to the Lord." But a good attitude will diminish the problem and help solutions to be more obvious. It will be easier to focus on finding answers. Be of good cheer. Let your heart be happy. Your attitude can make all the difference.

Predictable Prayer

Acts 3:1
Now Peter and John went up together into the temple at the hour of prayer, being the ninth hour.

Peter and John were not just going just to be going; it was prayer time. They had a unique habit of showing up at church three times a day for prayer. They could have prayed in other places, but they thought it good to go to the temple to pray. Let me tell you it's a good habit to actually schedule your prayer. Many people pray haphazardly. They pray in crunches, or if it's convenient. But how many of us actually set out a specific time everyday for prayer where we say, "I'm not going to let anything interfere with me in this hour." The cell phone is turned off along with the TV, the VCR, and the radio, because I need to have some time to talk to my heavenly father.

If you ever get in the routine of praying you will look forward to the hour of prayer. When you learn how to sure enough pray, you will know you get strength from prayer. Some say, "I get great consolation when I pray. When I kneel in prayer knowing that the Lord will meet me there, I get strength on my journey." Can you imagine a personal God giving you twenty-four hours a day and you won't take one to tell him thank you? If you take life for granted, let me recommend several places you ought to visit. Start out at the mental hospital and go watch folk that look just like you, that used to live on your street, but their minds are disturbed and confused. Next, stop by any hospital in town and stroll down by the cancer ward, the diabetics ward, the burn ward, and the place where they fix up folk that have been shot and cut and realize you could be there instead. Stop complaining for a little while and tell him thank you that you can travel in freedom, that God brought us from no doors to a lot of doors, from the ghettos to the get mores. The reason you are here today is because God has kept you. So take some time each day to come before your Keeper.

A Forty Year Old Problem

Acts 3:2

And a certain man lame from his mother's womb was carried, whom they laid daily at the gate of the temple which is called Beautiful, to ask alms of them that entered into the temple;

There's a fellow in the text with a problem that was more than surface deep. Acts 4:22 says he was born a cripple. He was not crippled because of carelessness on his part. But he couldn't enlist in the armed forces or apply for a job. He couldn't play in sports or have a wife and family. His friends brought him to the temple every day of the year for forty years. He was in the right place, but still he had a problem. He knew if he was going to get help he had to come where he could find help. You will find more free-hearted people at the house of God than you will any other place. The man wasn't begging at the casino; he went to the temple because his hope for help was there. Now what the man wanted was a donation, but he needed deliverance. He wanted some money but he needed some mercy.

Peter, the impulsive talker and John, the quiet one, were on their way to the temple at the hour of prayer and saw the lame man. Peter said, "Look on us." We must not get upset because people look on us. We say to the world, "I'm the light of the world," and then we get mad because the world sees our light." This man was expecting to receive money from them, but Peter looked at him and gave him a great let down. Peter said, "Silver and gold have I none." Now the man wanted silver and gold, but that's not what he needed most. "...but such as I have give I thee: In the name of Jesus Christ of Nazareth rise up and walk." Peter had more than money; he had The Name. When Peter took the man's hand, the lame man stood up. The Bible says he began leaping and went on into the temple shouting and praising God. His problem was solved.

Needs And Deeds

Philippians 4:19
But my God shall supply all your need according to his riches in glory by Christ Jesus.

When the world looks at you they expect something special from you. The world expects you to have a different attitude than they have. The world gets upset, mad, and curses out folk. They don't expect you to do it. The world panics when things aren't going well. When gas goes up past $2 a gallon the world gets worried. Saints turn around and say, "But my God shall supply all my needs." We need to help folk learn how to live in contentment in Jesus and not just pacify them temporarily. When a person comes and says their lights are going to be cut off, the church can help with the bill one time. Instead of getting caught up in the material, the spiritual should be examined. We ought to sit down with the person and ask what happened. How did you get in this shape? They say, "I work; I just got behind." How did you get behind? Did you get behind by keeping up with the Jones' buying stuff you didn't need with money you didn't have, trying to impress people you don't like? You lost your job? Why? Did you have a bad attitude? Did you get up on the wrong side of the bed? Find out if there were wrong deeds and help them with the real problem.

Most of the time when people ask for help, they are folk that don't tithe. There is problem number one. You're cursed with a curse. When God curses you, how can the church bless you? When you deal with a person's physical needs you feed him for a day, but when you deal with his spiritual needs you feed him for a lifetime. You see when you get it right with God He will supply your every need. God can take nothing and make it work for you. When you're living in obedience, it takes longer for the gas tank to get down to E. Friends will invite you to dinner when the food is low. Someone who borrowed a little money from you twenty years ago will show up to pay. Needs are supplied!

An Excellent Spirit

Daniel 6:3
Then this Daniel was preferred above the presidents and princes, because an excellent spirit was in him; and the king thought to set him over the whole realm.

I am always threatened when I read about the life of Daniel. He's so straight; he is so upright. I'm at home with fellows like Abraham who lied about his wife and said she was his sister. Even that is pretty straightforward because he went down on record as telling a lie. If I could get out of here with nothing on my record but just a lie, I would be doing well. I can understand Moses who got mad, lost his temper, killed an Egyptian and buried him in the sand. I could understand how he would get upset with the complaining, rebellious people that he was leading. I can understand Samson getting his hair cut in the wrong barbershop. But Daniel's own enemies couldn't find a fault. You don't have to be my enemy to find fault in me. You could be my friend and find faults in me.

Daniel is old now. I watched him when he was just a teenager and refused meat at the King's table because of his beliefs. Daniel discovered then that when you stand for something, you won't fall for just anything. Now he's in his nineties and has lived through the reigns of several kings. The Bible gives us some holy helpful hints to tell us how Daniel made it to where he was.

The text says he had an excellent spirit. He was honest, good, humble and careful how he lived. So Daniel was put in charge of all the presidents and princes in the kingdom. Daniel was also faithful. Whatever you're in be faithful in that, your job, your family, your church, and most of all to God. Develop good habits of being on time, having a good attitude, and being happy for the success of others. Don't be arrogant, lazy, and self-centered. Daniel learned to be faithful to the Lord in good times and bad and became a powerful example for us all. Maintain an excellent spirit!

A Worthwhile Habit

Daniel 6:10

Now when Daniel knew that the writing was signed, he went into his house; and his windows being open in his chamber toward Jerusalem, he kneeled upon his knees three times a day, and prayed, and gave thanks before his God, as he did aforetime.

The princes and presidents of King Darius were jealous of Daniel's position and wanted to cause him trouble. They couldn't find anything negative on Daniel, but they discovered he had a very regular habit. Daniel had a habit of prayer. So these men had a law made that made it illegal to pray for thirty days. Can you imagine going thirty days without prayer? Here is a mother with a sick child and can't pray for the child for thirty days. But the text says, when Daniel knew that the writing was signed, he went to his house, opened the window in the direction of Jerusalem and knelt to pray three times a day just as he always did. Daniel had a place for prayer. We should have a special place for prayer. Not only did he have a place for prayer, but he also had a period for prayer, because the Bible says he prayed three times a day. He didn't change that habit even though the king had signed a decree stating that anyone caught calling on any God besides the King would be summoned to the lions den.

The king's men caught Daniel praying and hurried over to tell the king. However, Daniel had found favor with the king. Still the law could not be broken. I think the King got his best detectives and attorneys to see if any loopholes could be found. But the attorneys came back with their heads down and said, "There are no loopholes; he'll have to go to the lion's den." But Daniel also found favor with God. The lion's mouths were shut and he came out unhurt. The king sent for the men who had accused David along with their families and threw them in the lion's den because of the evil plan they devised. Daniel had a valuable habit!

March

Temptation Episode

Luke 4:1
And Jesus being full of the Holy Ghost returned from Jordan and was lead by the Spirit into the wilderness and being forty days tempted of the devil.

If Satan would attempt to tempt Jesus, then he will tempt anybody. If he will approach the Son of God, the Holy God, the one with all power, the one who knows everything and is everywhere at the same time, then he will certainly work on you and me. Jesus had just received his spiritual credentials. He had been baptized in the River Jordan, proclaimed the Son of God by a voice from heaven while the Holy Ghost in the form of a dove descended upon him. Jesus was lead by the Holy Ghost into the wilderness. So he was in the right place because the Holy Ghost had led him there. Then the devil showed up. Whenever the Lord rises to bless us, Satan rises to blast us.

Jesus, the Christ, was in the will of the Father and he was still tempted. I know many of you think because you're in the will of God you are safeguarded from temptation, but Satan cruises around to find people that are doing God's will. The devil doesn't bother you that much when you're doing nothing. But when you make up in your mind that you're going to make a difference, win somebody for the Lord, and live a life that's pleasing in his sight, it upsets the devil. And so he sets up traps to try to destroy you–to distract you. He tries to damage your testimony.

No person is exempt from temptation; you never reach a point in your life when you are no longer vulnerable to its appeal. And there is no place you can go where you can escape temptation. Adam was in the garden; Jesus was in the wilderness. You can be tempted in any environment. Temptation itself is not wrong; however, yielding to that temptation is wrong. The devil will attack; he will approach every last one of us sooner or later. Jesus was prepared for the attack.

Handling Temptation

Luke 4:4
And Jesus answered him, saying, It is written...

1 John 2:16 tells us "For all that is in the world, the lust of the flesh, and the lust of the eyes, and the pride of life, is not of the Father, but is of the world." The lust of the eye deals with getting; the lust of the flesh deals with doing; the pride of life deals with being. Doing, getting, and being are the three ways the devil tempts all of us. So he caught Jesus at what he thought was his weakest moment, when he was hungry. Jesus had fasted and prayed 40 days and 40 nights. Fasting backs you up from the physical table so you can be connected with the heavenly table. Satan said, If thou be the Son of God command that these stones be made bread." Jesus responded, Man shall not live by bread alone but by every word that proceeds out of the mouth of God." If Jesus needed bread he certainly wouldn't have gotten it from Satan. Anything you get from the devil is costly. Nor would Jesus alter what God had originally designed. If God made stones, he intended for stones to remain stones.

Now the devil is never satisfied at making one attempt. Then the devil took him up into a high mountain and showed unto him all the kingdoms of the world in a moment's time and offered them to Jesus if he would only bow. But Jesus told him there was only one person for Him to worship and that's the true and living God. So the devil brought him to Jerusalem and set him on a pinnacle of the temple saying, If thou be the Son of God cast yourself down." Let it get out all over town that you are a super Jesus. Jesus quoted the word, "Thou shall not tempt the Lord thy God." Jesus had disciplined himself through fasting and prayer and filled himself with the Word of God. Jesus handled temptation superbly.

Help In Handling Temptation

Luke 4:14
And Jesus returned in the power of the Spirit into Galilee…

1 You must be a Son of God in order to overcome temptation. You must be born again. Your flesh cannot overpower the devil. It is simple to become a son of God. Romans 10:9 says, "That if thou shall confess with thy mouth the Lord Jesus, and shall believe in thine heart that God has raised him from the dead thou shall be saved.

2) You must be submitted to God. God said, This is my beloved son in whom I am well pleased. Is God pleased with your life? God is keeping your record. Are you submitted to the cause of Christ? Do you keep working for him in spite of a broken heart or when you are lied on?

3) You must be spiritually filled. Jesus was full of the Holy Ghost, Luke 4:14, Jesus returned in the power of the spirit. Luke 4:18 The spirit of the Lord was upon him. Jesus didn't deal with temptation as a God. He dealt with Satan as a man filled with the Holy Ghost. You see when filled with the spirit you have an unusual power. The devil can't steal your spirit or pick the word out of your mind.

4) You must depend on the scripture. Jesus used the Word. You've got to study the Word, meditate on the Word and know the Word.

5) You must be satisfied. If you're satisfied with Jesus the devil cannot find an itch to scratch you. If I'm in a one-room shack and God gave it to me I ought to be happy. Find contentment in your present circumstances.

6) Remember to pray. No matter how you're troubled, learn how to pray. The devil really can't stand to see you on your knees, because a Christian is a powerful person down on their knees. Become a person of prayer.

Then when temptation hits, remember to look beyond temptation and see the guilt. Before you yield, look around and see the good things. Look up and see the grace. And look inward and see the goal.

Preserve Our Young Men

Exodus 1:22
And Pharaoh charged all his people, saying, Every son that is born ye shall cast into the river, and every daughter ye shall save alive.

Satan has launched an all-out attack to try to destroy our young men. Many of you ladies sometimes look at men with a critical eye because you are more learned than they are. You are now getting the better jobs. Sometimes you call the man lazy, ignorant, illiterate, not trying to make it. But what you don't know is that the world, in a sense, is promoting women and demoting men because they know a woman cannot stand very well by herself. Men have always been a problem for Satan and Satan's forces. If Satan can destroy the man, he knows he's got the family. And so he sets out to try to demote man to make him some kind of a bogeyman. Satan's plan is for the man to end up either in jail or in the grave or to find himself trying to figure out how he is – if he is an Adam or an Eve. As a result, our generation is suffering from the lack of strong men.

Satan tries to get young men while they are extremely young so he can program them. If he waits until you get saved, satisfied, and sanctioned in the body of Christ he has to deprogram you, which is much more difficult. So he is looking for young men he can put on his team that will be warriors for him. Have you noticed lately that most killing comes from young men? And most of the ones they are killing are other young men. There are no old dope pushers or dope addicts; they die young. But you say it's good money. Nothing that the devil has to offer you is good. If you look around you don't find any old bad folk. All of the bad folk die young. The devil doesn't give you nothing free; it always has a high price tag. So young people, live a life that is respectful to yourself and others. Let your deeds, conversation, and music be honorable to the Lord. If you are a parent, be a good example. Preserve your children!

Ungodly Snobbery

John 4:4
And he must needs go through Samaria.

Jesus had left Judaea on was on his way to Galilee. Right in the middle of the region was a little place called Samaria, a town that was a mixed breed area. In 720 BC the northern kingdom invaded their privacy and captured all of the noted people and took them away captive. The only people left were illiterate folk, slow learners, sick and handicapped people – people who couldn't keep up. Well, others moved in to try to rebuild the town and they started an interracial marital situation. When Ezra and Nehemiah came to rebuild the temple in 450 BC, a group of Samaritans came and offered their help. However, their help was refused because they were cross-breeds. A feud started in 450 BC and that feud was still going on when Jesus came many years later. So Jews would avoid the little town of Samaria.

However, Jesus had a reason for going through Samaria. He had a divine appointment. But first he had to deal with a racial barrier. Moreover, we still have to break down the racial barriers today. I need to tell us that the God I serve is not just a black man's God. Some think we have special privileges because we are black and because we have suffered. Nor is He just a white man's God or a red man's God. He is our God. If there is any person who is color blind, it is our Heavenly Father. He doesn't look at us from the color of our skin; he looks at us from sin. He is ready, willing and able to forgive all of us of all of our sins. We are going to have to learn as people of God to let down the barriers of the racial separation. It's a shame that we can go play football and basketball side-by-side, we can work on the job side-by-side, but when we get ready to come to worship we go to our own separate places. Jesus went out of his way to take the good news of salvation to a different ethnic group and manifest God's heart.

She Was Wanted

John 4:7
*There cometh a woman of Samaria to draw water: Jesus saith unto her, Give
me to drink.*

Jesus was waiting for a particular woman to come to the well for
water. He knew the woman's record. She had been married five
times and was now living with a man who was not her husband.
We don't know the specifics of her story, but this is what I think could
have happened in her life. I think the very first marriage she had was a
mistake; she did not marry the man based upon a gift from God. She
was attractive and this fellow had a good line. A nice looking cat. Since
looks change, this marriage was soon over. She was hurt over the fact
that this fellow wouldn't stay with her. So she just grabbed the second
fellow to try to heal her wounds and took the bitterness out on him.
The third guy thought he could help her come out of her shell and so
she accepted him on his offer. He tried a couple of years and gave up.
The fourth guy had some money but soon all he saw was the inside of
her hand, so he left. The fifth guy was twenty years younger. It wasn't
very long before he saw an old woman and he put her down. Now it's
the sixth man. She said, "I am through with marriage. I'm just going to
shack it out."

Hence Jesus is sitting on the well—a well sitting on a well. Because
of her bad reputation, this woman came to the well at noon, after
others had already gone. Jesus approached her first and said, "Give
me a drink of water." What I detect about Jesus is that he will always
approach you first. I like that. He doesn't wait until we come to him;
he comes to us. If Jesus had waited for us to come to him, most of us
would never be saved. He makes provisions for us. He sends out the
invitations for us to come to him. Although Jesus really didn't need
any water, he gave the woman an opportunity to feel needed. The
woman was an outcast and lost, but Jesus came looking for her.

A Loser Became A Winner

John 4:10

Jesus answered and said unto her, If thou knew the gift of God, and who it is that saith to thee, Give me to drink; thou would have asked of him, and he would have given thee living water.

The woman had said to Jesus, "How is it that you being a Jew ask me a Samaritan for a drink of water?" Jesus said look your problem is you don't know me or you would ask me for a drink. When I see people backing up on Jesus, I think it is because they don't know him. When people make excuses about serving the Lord or miss prayer service and Bible study, it's because they don't know him. If you know Him, you will rush to serve Him. This woman knew about God. She talked about Jacob, her forefather and the coming Messiah. She knew about the past and the future, death and resurrection, but she did not yet know that the Resurrection was with her that very moment.

So the woman asked Jesus for the kind of water that would not run out. Jesus said, "Go and get your husband." Jesus will always give you an opportunity to confess your sins to him. She said, "I'm sorry sir. I don't have a husband." Then Jesus shocked the woman when He said to her, "You told the truth; that isn't your man. But you have had five husbands." When she realized that she was speaking to the Messiah, she dropped her water pots and headed into town. She said, "Come, see a man, which told me all things that ever I did: is not this the Christ?"

And many of the Samaritans believed on him when they went to hear Him. . This woman had been an outcast and lost. John 3 speaks of Nicodemus, a ruler of the Jews, who came at night to speak to Jesus. He was religious and still lost. Regardless of your state in life, you still need Jesus. If Jesus will save a Nicodemus at the utmost, he will also save the outcast at the guttermost. The Lord took that woman and made her a soul winner. Hallelujah!

Seek The Kingdom

Matthew 6:9-10

After this manner therefore pray ye: Our Father which art in heaven, Hallowed be thy name. Thy kingdom come. Thy will be done in earth, as it is in heaven.

The disciples came to Jesus saying, "Master teach us to pray as John also taught his disciples." Jesus, being an effective teacher and knowing the type of people that He had in His audience, wanted to make sure the lesson was understandable. So He made this prayer in letter-like form. It was addressed to our Father. The actual address where the letter was sent was "which art in heaven." Then there were several requests made in this Letter Prayer. First was that the kingdom would come; second, that the will would be done; and third that we would receive daily bread. The seal of the Letter Prayer was "for thine is the kingdom." The day that it was sent was "this day." The stamp that He used on the Letter Prayer was "Amen." The Pattern Prayer was simple enough for anyone to understand.

This Model Prayer is vertical, but it is also horizontal. It goes up to God, but it also goes out to our brother by saying "Our Father." Jesus says, "Our Father, which art in heaven, hallowed be thy name." He says, I want you to spotlight – put my Name on display, and whatever you do, if you're going to be successful, you must do it in my Name. His name is important. "Thy kingdom come, thy will be done." Too many of us actually believe that it's our kingdom. We act like it's ours because we do what we want to do, say what we want to say and show up when we want to show up. But it's the Lord's kingdom. It is not about us. Sometimes we worry about issues that are none of our business, walking the floor at night over matters we have nothing to do with. God loves His kingdom so He's not going to let His kingdom go down. Matthew 6:33 "But seek ye first the kingdom of God and His righteousness and all of these things will be added unto you." Seek His kingdom!

Our Father

Matthew 6:9-11

After this manner therefore pray ye: Our Father which art in heaven, Hallowed be thy name. Thy kingdom come. Thy will be done in earth, as it is in heaven. Give us this day our daily bread.

Our Father is God. The whole prayer is laid out and has God in view. When Jesus says, "Our Father which art in heaven," He's talking about God's Parental. When he says, "Hallowed by thy name," He's talking about God's priority. When He says, "Thy kingdom come," He's talking about God's program. When He says, "Thy will be done," He's talking about God's plan. When He says, "Give us this day our daily bread," He's talking about God's provision. When he says, "Forgive us of our debts as we forgive our debtors," He's talking about God's pardon. And when He says, "Deliver us from evil," He is talking about God's protection. The focus is God and his kingdom.

So Jesus gave us a wonderful prayer that is appropriate any time. It sets our focus straight and sets the tone for extended prayer. One of the reasons that sometimes we're weak, wounded, and without strength is because we have not taken advantage of a prayer life We need to understand that when we talk to God, He answers our prayers in several ways. Sometimes when you ask him for something He says no, sometimes He says slow, sometimes He says grow and sometimes He says Go! In other words, if you ask for something that you don't need, since you are His child He says no. If you ask for something that you need, but you can't handle it yet, He says slow. If you ask for something and it's already in store for you, He says "before I give it to you, I need to know you can really handle it, because you may stop praising me," so He says grow. And then if you ask for something that you know you need and He knows you can handle it, He says Go. In other words, Go get it! No, Slow, Grow, and then Go!

Thinking God's Way

Romans 12:1-2

I beseech you therefore, brethren, by the mercies of God, that ye present your bodies a living sacrifice, holy, acceptable unto God, which is your reasonable service. And be not conformed to this world: but be ye transformed by the renewing of your mind, that ye may prove what is that good, and acceptable, and perfect, will of God.

How do I know His will? I have a son who is thirty years of age who I believe loves me. He's still obedient to his father. Let's assume I say, "Now Junior, I got something I want you to do; do it before sundown. If you don't, I'm going to box your head." He says, "All right Daddy, since you put it that way, I'll go on and do it." When he asks me to tell him what I want him to do I could say, "I'm not going to tell you, figure it out for yourself!" Now, it wouldn't be right for me to tell my boy that I want him to do something but not to tell him what I want him to do. Well God has more sense than I have. If God wants us to do something, don't you know, God has enough sense to tell us what He wants us to do.

The Bible will show us how to understand God's will. First you must present your body to Him. Your body is near and dear to God. You need to give your body over to the Lord. Next, you must separate yourself from the world's way of thinking. Don't let the world dictate your lifestyle or influence your decisions. Then you must be transformed. Let a change take place in your mind and your life. A tadpole starts off in the mud but through metamorphosis, becomes a frog. The frog likes to hang around clear water and sit on a log singing his own praises to God. Let go of the stagnant environment of gossip envy, and hatred and move into a clean way of living.

After you have presented your body to God, separated yourself from the world, and been transformed with a new way of thinking, then God can reveal His will to you.

The Greatest Day In History

Matthew 28:1
And the end of the Sabbath as it began to dawn toward the first day of the week came Mary Magdalene and the other Mary to see the sepulchre.

Looking back, I must admit that there are many great days now in the archives of history. Great was the day of creation, when God came from nowhere, stood on the platform of nothing, reached back through nowhere, got something while standing on nothing, and slung it all into existence. The S-U-N started shining; the moon began to glow; the stars began glittering; fish started swimming; birds started flying; roses started blooming and blossoming; fruit came on trees. And great was the day when God ended his work and saw that it was good. Great was the day when Abraham finally stood over little Isaac, saw that the child he had waited 100 years for had finally made his arrival. Great was the day when Noah had spent 120 years building an ark for God. When the flood was over and he was able to step out of the ark with his family; great was that day.

Great was the day when Elijah prayed on Mount Carmel and God answered by sending fire from heaven. Great was the day when Jesus the Christ was born of a virgin in Bethlehem of Judea. Great was the day when Jesus went into the temple at the age of twelve and baffled the minds of the professors. He talked like an old man, but had a young body. Great was the day when Jesus responded "I must be about my father's business." Great was the day when He ascended the mountain and met Moses and Elijah after He was transfigured right before the disciples' eyes. Great and dark was the day when Jesus finally arrived at the hill called Calvary to conquer sin, death, and the grave. But the greatest day of them all was resurrection morning, when the tombstone was rolled back and Jesus rose from the grave, the first begotten of the dead. Resurrection morning – that is the day of celebration!

A Private Plan Prevails

Exodus 2:3
And when she could not longer hide him, she took for him an ark of bulrushes, and daubed it with slime and with pitch, and put the child therein; and she laid it in the flags by the river's brink.

Pharaoh had charged that every Hebrew boy be cast into the river. God chose this time for the arrival of Moses. An expectant mother who loves her unborn baby begins thinking about her baby's life long before the due date. She may pray for the health of the child and that she will be a good mother to the child. Can you imagine the mother of Moses? Maybe she prayed for the child to be a girl so she wouldn't have to watch him drown. What a distressing situation! When Moses was born, his mother believed God's hand was on him, so she hid him for three months. If she had been caught, she could have lost her life. She risked the lives of the whole family for just one child. The presence of faith is obvious in the lives of Moses' mother and father.

Faith will cause a person to do things they would not normally do. Hebrews 11:1 says that faith is the substance of things hoped for. Substance is something you stand upon. So Moses' parents made a little ark and hid Moses in the river among the bulrushes. They didn't know what God would do, but they believed He would do something. One day Pharaoh's daughter came to the river and found the baby and took him for her own. Miriam, Moses' sister, ran to her and offered to bring a Hebrew nurse for the baby. So Moses' own mother was able to care for him and influence his life as a child. Moses became a protected child. However, if Moses had been brought up totally in his parents' home, he wouldn't have received formal education and training about the ins and outs of the federal government. Because Moses' parents put their faith in God, obeying God and not man, Moses lived to fulfill that plan.

Impostors Among Us

1 John 2:19
They went out from us, but they were not of us; for if they had been of us, they would no doubt have continued with us: but they went out, that they might be made manifest that they were not all of us.

Since these people went out from the group it means that they had been a part of the fellowship. By leaving, they denied Christ. When you deny him, you not only deny his person you also deny his power. Matthew 28:18 All power is given unto me. He takes his power and places it behind us to give us power. Acts 1:8 Ye shall have power. Also, they deserted the church. If you are going to stay with the Lord do not leave the church. I know there are those that say, "I can make it without the church." You can be saved and not be in church; that is true. But after you are saved you'll want to be in the church. The wise person will stay in the church where lies their strength and help. When you leave the church, you lose fellowship with God.

One of the problems with our church today is that we assume that everybody who attends the church and functions are saved. Consequently, we let our guards down around church folk. Just because somebody responds to you, it does not mean they have been born again Most of our enemies came out of the church. Satan himself was a choir director who decided that he wanted his throne to supersede God's throne. But there's a difference between just being a church member over and against being saved.

Many church members are offensive and act in a manner unbecoming to church folk. Now remember the problems come from church folk, not saved people. There is a big difference between the two. Just because you're in church does not mean you're saved. Just because you sing in the choir doesn't mean you're saved. Because you preach does not mean you're saved. Or just because you can pray eloquently, it does not mean you're saved.

God's Church

3 John 1:5-6

Beloved, thou doest faithfully whatsoever thou doest to the brethren, and to strangers; Which have borne witness of thy charity before the church: whom if thou bring forward on their journey after a godly sort, thou shalt do well.

This is what the church should really be: the church should be a lighthouse shining forth its light upon a dark and stormy world. It should be a restaurant feeding the souls of men with the pure satisfying word of God. The church should perform as a hospital ministering to sick of sin and shame – a lifeboat that rescues victims from the raging sea of life. It should exist as an orchard producing wholesome fruit of the spirit, a baker displaying the bread of life. The church should be a house where souls can find compassion, love, and understanding, a service station where souls can refuel for a journey ahead. The church should be a factory where faithful employers produce godly work. The church should be a dry cleaners where spiritual garments become cleaned and pressed. The church should be an insurance agency giving free assurance against the fires of hell. It should be a lumberyard where the supply could be secured to help build new lives. The church should function as a working water department making the water of life available for whosoever will. The church should act as a travel agency giving directions, a signpost guiding souls to the straight and narrow. Best of all, the church should subsist as a jewelry store where God purchases precious jewels to be placed in safe keeping.

And what I discovered about the church saints is you can not stop it. You can cut the church's head off and it will come back with new heads. Put the church in the water and she will come up cleaner from her washing. Put the church in the fire and she will come up pure from her burn. Starve the church and she will come back with bread in her hands to feed the hungry. The true church of the living God!

An Attack On The Church

Ephesians 3:21
Unto him be glory in the church by Christ Jesus throughout all ages, world without end. Amen.

Satan has many plans to attack the church through his devious designs. But the first thing I must do if I am going to be victorious over this attack on the church is that I must stay with the church of God even if I run into something I do not like. We know the church should become not become a fashion show displaying the garments of self-righteousness. It should not be a convalescent home where people just sit around and wait to die or a motel where people just pass through on their way to somewhere else. A church should not be a vacation spot where people only come once or twice a year. A church should not be a zoo where people are simply amused at everything that happens or a museum where people only remember what it used to be like. The church should not be a factory where the workers do only that for which they get paid and nothing else. The church should not be a storm cellar where people enter only during the time of a storm. Satan also desires for the church to become a social club where members gather to gossip and grumble about everything and everybody.

I made up in my mind that I'm going to stay with something that will last. I'm with something that the world can't harm. Satan would have to pull down all the stars in order to destroy the church because Jesus is a bright and morning star. I don't where I would be if it weren't for the church of the Living God. When I am down and out, barely making it, if I can just make it to the house of the Lord somebody will shake my hand and say, "I'm praying for you Reverend," unaware of what I am going through. Somebody will say we've come this far by faith leaning on the everlasting arms. Jesus said, "Upon this rock I'll build my church, and the gates of hell shall not prevail against it." The devil might shake us, but he can't destroy us.

Prisoners Of The Lord

Acts 16:16

And it came to pass, as we went to prayer, a certain damsel possessed with a spirit of divination met us, which brought her masters much gain by soothsaying.

The scene opened with a young lady. Luke does not give us her name; he just calls her a damsel, a notorious psychic. In our day she would have a 1-900 number. The Bible says she had made much gain for her masters. Evidently it was someone else's business; she was just bringing in the dough. So this girl had a spirit that knew how to deal with people looking for this kind of lore. Then a strange thing happened; she encountered two broke preachers, Paul and Silas, who were on a missionary journey for the Lord. They were on their way to another destination when this unnamed person got caught in the crossfire of the Gospel and her power departed. When her masters saw that the hope of their gains were gone they took Paul and Silas to the marketplace and accused them before the people and placed them in prison.

So Paul and Silas were in jail because of the Bible. Paul said he was in jail so much until he just named himself a prisoner of the Lord. A prisoner doesn't have to worry about a place to stay, because you will have a roof over your head. You don't have worry about a place to eat. Medical coverage is also provided for you. When you are a prisoner for the Lord you have the same benefits, because when you're saved and born again you don't have to worry about a place to lay your head. The God I serve will make sure there's a roof over your head. When you're saved you don't have to worry about food to eat because He will supply your every need. You don't have to worry about security guards walking beside you because Psalm 91:11 says He gives his angels charge over us to keep us in all our ways. Their mission landed them in prison.

Free Prisoners

Acts 16:22

And the multitude rose up together against them: and the magistrates rent off their clothes, and commanded to beat them … they cast them into prison, charging the jailer to keep them safely.

Now the multitude didn't have the faintest idea what was going on, but have you ever noticed how crowds like to follow crowds. Sometime crowds have no idea what's happening, but if it is a crowd they want to be a part of what the crowd is saying. It was the crowd that crucified Jesus. Many times people get in trouble following crowds. Some of you have broken The Ten Commandments because you tried to keep up with the crowd. Paul and Silas were convicted without a trial; there was no evidence to find them guilty, but Satan doesn't need any evidence. You see you're in trouble when you stand for God in the first place. If you take a stand for the Master you're going to run into Satan. Stocks were put on their ankles and hands and they were put in the inner jail; they had them so bound up that they were uncomfortable while being in prison.

Preaching the Gospel can often get you in trouble. Sometimes your own brothers will plot for your downfall. Just because a person is your color or identity doesn't' mean they are with you. Joseph told his brothers his dream and they put him in a pit and left him for dead. You work up enemies when you preach the Gospel.

So Paul and Silas may have been in prison, but they were free because they knew the God they served. I get letters week after week from brothers and sisters behind bars and they say, "Reverend, when I was loose I was running the streets, but now since I been in here I met Jesus. And there's a freedom that I can not explain." And sometimes when you're loose you're really not loose. And when you're bound you're really not bound because being with Jesus is the best freedom a person could have.

The Midnight Prayer

Acts 16:25

And at midnight Paul and Silas prayed, and sang praises unto God: and the prisoners heard them.

I like the way Paul and Silas handled being in jail The Bible says at midnight Paul and Silas prayed and sang praises unto God. You know about midnight don't you? You see midnight is not just the time on the clock. It is that hour when you don't know what move to make next. It is when your family walks away from you. Midnight is when your job lets you go and you're too young to retire and to old to get other employment. That's midnight. Midnight is when the doctor says, "I've done all I could." Midnight is when your best friend turns their back on you.

Paul and Silas didn't complain. They prayed. We're here because we did what you told us to do. We preached and souls were saved. Now Lord we're not asking you to get us out. We just thought we would talk to you anyway. We get great consolation when we talk to you. Sometimes midnight is a good time because Job 35:10 says that God will give songs in the night. Some things in life you've got to pray and sing your way through. I hear them singing, "Let the light from the lighthouse shine on me, do Lord, do Lord do remember me.

Then one of the angels received a message from the Lord. "Gabriel, get me four angels and stand one on each corner of the earth. And when all of you get there I want you to shake the earth." And you see that's what prayer will do. Prayer will shake situations and circumstances. If you've got a son that's gone astray, just start talking to the Lord. Prayer will shake that boy. You've got a daughter that won't listen to reason, just keep on praying. Prayer will shake your home. Prayer will shake your job. Prayer will shake your circumstances. The angels shook the earth. The earth shook the jail. The jail shook the hinges. The shackles fell off. It was the midnight hour and God was there!

Today Is The Day

2 Corinthians 6:2
...Behold, now is the accepted time; behold, now is the day of salvation.

I've been here on planet earth for over half a century. I have observed people daily. Many people are serious about making a living. Most parents tell their children, "You have to study to make sure that you're smart so you can get a good education. Then you can get a good job and make a living for yourselves." And we focus on getting, getting, getting instead of being. I've known people to work hard day and night, trying to get ahead, taking no time for family or friends — living on the edge, half crazy trying to make a living. I say to them many times, "Well what about church?" They say, "Reverend, I don't have time for church, I'm too busy making a living. They are making a living, but failing to make a life.

One day this life will end. It will be over. The steady march of the chariot wheels is on its way to our address even now. I don't know when, but sooner or later it will come. We can't determine our future or how long we are going to live by what we eat, what we drink, or how we exercise, because the man that wrote the book on jogging, died jogging. Some of the healthiest people I know are shot down with guns or killed in automobile accidents. They have a massive heart attack or a stroke. There is no guarantee because we are healthy that we will live forever.

Therefore, we need to make sure that after this life is over, we're going to the right place. Now I must remind you that there are two destinations we will end up at. We will either go to hell or to heaven. And you won't go in a little department and wait six months or ten years or twenty years for God to change his mind. No, he gives us ample time while we're on planet earth to prepare for the next life. God gives us time to get our houses in order, so we in turn can help someone else. The time to do that is now.

The Hour Of Judgment

Revelation 14:7

Saying with a loud voice, Fear God, and give glory to him; for the hour of his judgment is come: and worship him that made heaven, and earth, and the sea, and the fountains of waters.

Many times the Bible will state, "the time is at hand," referring to a certain period of time. Or the Bible will state, "the day is at hand." Here the text says, "the hour," which means that the count down is on. The hour of judgment is hell. We don't want to run into God's judgment because God will judge out of anger. The Lord gets angry with us when he sends his Son to die for us and we reject the Son. The ransom price was paid for every one of us on Calvary and we live as if the debt has not been paid. He is saying with a loud voice, "Fear God and give glory to Him."

So fear God; have some conviction in your life. Every blood washed saint ought to fear God. God is too awesome for us not to fear him. God can do whatever he wants to do whenever He gets ready any way he wants to do it. A man one day stood out in the middle of nowhere and he just hollered, "God, I heard you was so bad and awesome. If it's true, strike me down with lightning." And he just stood there, hollering and cursing. God didn't say a word. He said again, "If you're so bad, strike me down with lightning." While he was hollering, a gnat flew in his mouth and choked him to death. You see God doesn't have to have lightning for us. God doesn't even have to take our lives, he can just stop giving it to us, and we're just as dead.

Give glory to God. The only way a person can give God glory is by being converted. An unconverted person will never give God glory; they will only bring glory to themselves. It is better to worship God while you are able than be forced to do it. The day will come when every knee shall bow. This will be easy for those who continually bow their hearts in prayer on bended knee.

Flirting And Fiddling

Revelation 14:8

And there followed another angel, saying, Babylon is fallen, is fallen, that great city, because she made all nations drink of the wine of the wrath of her fornication.

Babylon is fallen. Whenever the Bible talks about Babylon in the New Testament, it is actually talking about the condemnation of the world. Babylon is considered as being the world. Babylon the great city is fallen because she made all nations drink of the wine of the wrath of fornication which means fiddling and flirting with the world. It is the idea of a street woman or a prostitute walking the street, wearing a short dress, looking in cars, licking out her tongue. Along comes a family man just trying to live a life that will be pleasing in the sight of God, ambushed by the unexpected. This sister sees him and gets his attention, enticing him to turn aside. She starts off by giving him a sip of wine. He gets to grinning and laughing, enjoying the festivity. She pours him a little more wine. He drinks a little more and finally crawls into bed with this prostitute who has already been with thirty or forty other men all of whom had been with other women. And some of them had different diseases. Now since he crawls in the bed with her, he picks up some of the diseases, creating a problem back home. His marriage starts going down and before long there is a divorce with the children going one way and the family going another way. The man gets embarrassed and leaves the church of the living God because he doesn't want to show his face. It all started by flirting and fiddling around with this woman.

Well you see that's what the text is saying. Don't fiddle with the world because the world doesn't like you. The world is carrying some diseases. You can't bow to the world without getting some diseases from somewhere. It starts off with just a sip of wine, but then you start having a relationship with the world. That's fornication!

The Profits Of Patience

Revelation 14:12
Here is the patience of the saints: here are they that keep the commandments of God, and the faith of Jesus.

Luke Chapter 16 gives us an example of patience. Lazarus, a sick beggar full of sores, waited daily at a rich man's gate, desiring to be fed with the crumbs which fell from the rich man's table. He just lay there day after day. The dogs came and licked his sores. Eventually, the beggar died and was carried by the angels into Abraham's bosom, but the rich man died and was sent to hell. Matthew 25:46, declares, "And these shall go away into everlasting punishment: but the righteous into life eternal." But the righteous – those are people that deny themselves, take up the cross and follow Jesus. People who believe that he died one Friday and got up Sunday morning with all power in his hand.

Here is the patience of the saints. Saints you have to have some patience, because everything doesn't happen at once. Sometimes we want to grow faster than we should grow, or accomplish a certain goal overnight. But you must have patience. One good way to learn patience is by being a parent. Before becoming a parent, you could get up anytime you wanted and go to bed when you got ready. But when those children showed up in the house, you got up when they wanted to. A concerned parent waits on their own needs in order to provide for the children. You're not out wearing alligator shoes when your children are bare-footed. And parents when you try to get rid of your children, you're missing what God brought them there for, to teach you patience and to teach you selflessness.

So when God sends things in your life, he's trying to create some patience in you. Verse twelve states, "...here are they that keep the commandments of God." He didn't say it was easy, but He says that they kept them. The righteous will have their patience rewarded with life eternal.

The Blessed R's

Revelation 14:13

...Blessed are the dead which die in the Lord from henceforth: Yea, saith the Spirit, that they may rest from their labours; and their works do follow them.

There is a blessed release for the saints, because when you die, you get rid of this old body. On earth, we are like eagles living in a chicken pen. Once we begin to grow and get our wings, we want to fly up and sit on the fence. Then we want to fly a little higher on up to some tree branches. We want out of the pen. Another eagle comes flying by and we want to soar with it. Well that is really what happens to our body and soul. You see there is a restlessness underneath the skin after you get to a certain point in your life, when you want to leave this old caged body. Your soul wants to get out of it and soar to higher heights.

Then there is also a blessed rest. It is impossible to find true rest while you're here on earth. Even if you have a pillow-top mattress and a downy pillow to lay your head on, true rest will not show up. There's always something around to disturb your mind, a phone call or a person in the other room. The only place you can find true rest is in Jesus Christ.

I also see a blessed resurrection; this old body is going to get up one day and we'll have a brand new body. Sometimes diseases will cause you to lose limbs off your body, but when the Lord gives us a glorified body, we will be completely whole.

You shall rest from your labor and their works do follow them. That is a blessed reward. We are working now. The Lord has recorded things other folks forgot about – that time you stopped by and led a brother to the Lord. In that resurrection morning, the Lord will read off every good deed you did for somebody else. When I get home how happy I will be. When I get home, the Savior's face I'll see. Bells will be ringing, saints will be singing!

Those Last Words

Acts 1:8
But you shall receive power, after that the Holy Ghost is come upon you: and ye shall be witnesses unto me, both in Jerusalem, and in all Judea, and in Samaria, and unto the uttermost part of the earth.

On July 16, 1977 at 8 o'clock in the morning, I received a telephone call while lying in the bed. Someone on the other end said, "Frank, if you want to see your father alive, you need to rush home. He has just had a massive heart attack." You would have to know me and know my father to know how I felt. No one was as near and dear to me as my earthly father. He lived in Arlington, Tennessee at that time and I was living here in Memphis. I got in my car and in twenty minutes I had rushed to Arlington trying to get there to see my father before he left me. I remember it as though it was yesterday. When I pulled up to the house, they had lifted the sheet and were pulling it over my father's head. He had gone without saying good-bye. Without leaving any fatherly instructions for his son, he left. Oh how I wish I had been there to hear him give me some kind of last minute instructions. But I was too late to hear them.

Over 2000 years ago, I had a similar incident occur in my life. I had another brother that was getting ready to go back to be with his Father, our Father. Unlike my earthly father, he did leave last minute instructions. These were the final words he said to me and to you before he caught the cloud and went back to be with his Father. He told us that we will receive power after the Holy Ghost is come upon us and that we will be witnesses for him wherever we are. I cherish those words. They were His final words. You always cherish the last; the last means so much. Jesus had to go because He said, "If I don't go, the Comforter will not come." And I'm glad I've got a Comforter who walks by my side. He'll be there for me. Those precious last words.

Natural Yet Very Un-Natural

Hebrews 9:27
And as it is appointed unto men once to die...

Jesus' life was so unusual. On one side He was tired, but on the other side, He says to you, "Come unto me, all you that labor and are heavy laden and I will give you rest." He was human, but He was also divine. He was so human that He walked through doors, but so divine that He said, "I am the Door." So human that He played with rocks, but so divine that He said, "I am the Rock of Ages." So human that He drank water, but so divine that He said, "In me is a well of Living Water." So human that He died, but so divine that He said, "I am the Resurrection and the Life." So human that He ate bread, but so divine that He said, "I am the Bread of Life."

Jesus was an unusual character in His life. Nobody suffered like Jesus. Jesus suffered so much, until even the Father turned His back. I heard Him say, "My God why has thou forsaken me?" He suffered so until He didn't want us to see how much He actually suffered. While He was on Calvary's cross, He touched the sun and put it out. Isaiah is the only prophet that came close to telling us what really happened. He said, (Isaiah 53:5) "He was wounded for our transgressions. He was bruised for our iniquities. The chastisement of our peace was upon Him, but with His stripes we are healed." Nobody suffered like Him.

Nobody died like Jesus. His death was natural, unnatural, pretold natural, and supernatural. It was natural because He died. It's natural for any man to die. It was unnatural because He died without committing a sin. And that's unnatural because the wages of sin is death. So it's unnatural to die and never commit sin. It was pre-told natural because it was pre-determined before He was born. We were born to live, but Jesus was actually born to die. But His death was supernatural because even though He died, He got up without any effort on His part!

The Benediction

Acts 1:9
And when he had spoken these things, while they beheld, he was taken up; and a cloud received him out of their sight.

Jesus came to the Mount of Olives. Mount Olive is where Jesus would go and pray all night. Mount Olive is where Jesus preached his installation sermon to his disciples and where Jesus continued to teach them. So Mount Olive was the classroom of Jesus, the closet where He prayed, and the pulpit where He preached. It was more than fitting for Him to leave from Mount Olive. Luke closes his book with Jesus giving the Benediction. You should not run from the Benediction. Benedictions are important. Benedictions are designed to bless the saints of God until we meet again. You don't know what might happen between one worship service and the next. So many things can happen in that time. So we need the prayer of the Benediction.

A lot of important things happened on a lot of mountains. For instance, it was Mount Ararat where the ark landed when the flood was over. It was Mount Sinai where Moses received the written law. It was Mount Pisgah where God showed Moses the Promised Land. It was Mount Nebo where God buried Moses. It was Mount Carmel where Elijah went and challenged the God that answers by fire. It was Mount Herman where Jesus was transfigured, where His divinity out shined his humanity. It was Mount Calvary where He died and said, "It is finished."

Jesus' hands were lifted. Then clouds hovered low to serve as his chariot. When He was through talking, He was taken up. Then angels stood by the disciples and said, "Ye men of Galilee, why stand ye gazing up into heaven? This same Jesus, which is taken up from you into heaven, shall so come in like manner as ye have seen him go into heaven." (Acts 1:11) It is good to wait around for the benediction.

From Sorrow To Praise

Psalms 150:1

Praise ye the Lord...

This is the final Psalm in the Book of Psalms. This would really be called the Deuteronomy of the Psalms. The Psalms are divided into five categories like the Pentateuch in the Bible – The Genesis, The Exodus, The Leviticus, The Numbers, The Deuteronomy. Notice the last Psalm begins differently than the first Psalm. The first Psalm opens with man being blessed by God, but the last Psalm opens with man blessing God. Psalm 1 says, "Blessed is the man." The last Psalm says, "Praise ye the Lord." Now between Psalm 1 and 150 a whole lot of things have happened.

I hear echoes in the field from Psalms prior to this saying, "Fret not thyself because of evildoers," meaning that the Psalmist had run into some crooked folk, difficult dilemmas, and trying situations. Psalms prior to this say, "Weeping may endure for a night," letting us know the Psalmist had run into tough times and that his eyes had focused upon the calendar of time; he was counting the hours at night looking forward to the morning. The Psalmist said, "I lifted up mine eyes unto the hills from whence cometh my help," indicating he ran into something he couldn't get out of. He couldn't think his way out, pay his way out, or trick his way out. I listened to the Psalmist as he seemed to say to us at one time he had been isolated from the church of God. Because I heard him say, "I was glad when they said unto me let us go to the house of the Lord." He went to the sanctuary to praise God.

And so from Psalm 1 to 150, the Psalmist had run into sorrow. He had experienced sadness, suffering, and sin. He had been in sour situations, but this Psalm says that in spite of what you have gone through, it's time to praise the Lord. Just being here is an indication that God has brought you through.

The Sanctuary Above

Psalms 150:1

Praise ye the Lord. Praise God in his sanctuary: praise him in the firmament of his power.

raise him in the firmament of his power. God has another church that's not on earth. He says He has one in heaven. There are some folk already up there that you used to know. They didn't stop shouting just because they left here. Momma is somewhere shouting now. Grandpapa is over there shouting today. God wants to connect His heavenly church with His earthly church. I am referring to Hebrews 12:1 which states, "Wherefore seeing we also are compassed about with so great a cloud of witnesses." In other words he's saying the folk in heaven are watching us. Since the folk in heaven are praising Him, He wants them to be connected to the folks on earth that are praising Him.

God says, I've got some folk on earth who are praising me. "I've got some folk down here who know they've been washed in the blood of the Lamb. They know they've been sanctified, set aside for a special purpose." And the only difference between you and the folk up there is that we just haven't made the transfer. The ones down here are just as saved as the ones up there, because you have accepted Christ as your savior. John 5:24 says he that believes on him as the scriptures have said has everlasting life. So that means I'm walking down here, but I've got everlasting life and the only thing that's holding me back is this old body. And sooner or later it's going back to the dust. And when it goes back to the dust, I'll be free to shout all day and all night and all day again.

So he says, "I've got a sanctuary below. And I have a sanctuary above. I want to connect the folk down here with the ones up there. I want a unified worship. I want the folk in heaven to join those on earth and praise me together." Psalm 19:1 tells us the heavens declare the glory of God; and the firmament shows his handy work.

The Mighty Act Of Creation

Psalms 150:2
Praise him for his mighty acts: praise him according to his excellent greatness.

You ought to praise him for his mighty acts. You can start with creation. That's a mighty act. God created. That means he took nothing and made something. When you take nothing and make something, that's a tremendous action. Now man can say, "I made," but we can't say, "I created." We can say, "I'm creative, but we can't say, "I created something," because we have to use stuff that's already there. Twenty years ago man took a seed of a man and the seed of a woman, put it in a test tube and brought forth a little girl and they named her Louise. But man had to take the stuff that was already here. Many years ago two Wright brothers came together and invented and iron bird, called it an airplane. They fixed it so you can eat breakfast in Memphis, lunch in New York City, and attend an evening concert in Paris, France but they had to use the things that were already here.

Man went out one day and caught lightening and changed it into electricity so now you can touch a button and be warm in the winter and cool in the summer, but he had to utilize the matter that was already here. Man found a substitute for butter, a synthetic for rubber, a replacement for sugar, but he had to use substances that were already here. However, God took nothing in that he walked out and stood in the middle of nowhere and just spoke and worlds without end came into existence; waters came forth He spoke the lightening. The sun started shining, the moon began to glow, and stars started glittering. He spoke and the earth began to rotate on its axis; vegetation came up. Beasts began to roam the earth. Fish started swimming and birds began to fly. ...the everlasting God, the Lord, the Creator of the ends of the earth, fainteth not, neither is weary. There is no searching of his understanding. Isaiah 40:28

God's Orchestra

Psalm 150:3

Praise him with the sound of the trumpet: praise him with the psaltery and harp. Praise him with the timbrel and dance: praise him with stringed instruments and organs. Praise him upon the loud cymbals: praise him upon the high sounding cymbals.

Trumpets, or animal's horns (shofar), were very important in Old Testament times. The watchman on the wall would blow the trumpet to give out a message to the people. When a warrior was marching the street, he would blow the trumpet. And when a worshipper would come to church he would blow the trumpet. And if you haven't got a trumpet, Isaiah 58:1 says to lift your voice like a trumpet. When the Lord comes back, He's going to blow the trumpet.

And then it says to praise him with a psaltery. A psaltery could be played like a drum. And you can't play the drums without getting dancing in your feet. When the drum starts playing your feet get light. Next the Psalmist says to praise him with the timbrel. A timbrel is the same thing as a tambourine. That means you ought to shake it and get involved. So now we've got our voice. We've got our dance. We're moving our hands.

We are also supposed to praise him with the stringed instruments and the organ. The organs in that day they were pipe organs and you didn't play pipe organs; you blew the organ. Breath or wind, a form of energy caused the organ to work. And then the Bible says to praise him with a loud cymbal and a high cymbal. One was loud; the other was high. When you put them together, they bring melody to the orchestra. What the Lord is saying is, "I want you to praise me right. I want the sound to come out right."

The orchestra is now in place. Praising time is just about ready. God says, "I've got all my instruments, they're ready to roll. I've got my solo singers; they're all in place." If you have breath, use it to praise the Lord.

Born To Praise

Psalms 150:6
Let every thing that hath breath praise the Lord. Praise ye the Lord.

It's amazing how God can take a little of nothing and do so much with so little. Mathematics is made up of ten numbers: 1, 2, 3, 4, 5, 6, 7, 8, 9, 0. If you can master these ten numbers you can handle geometry, trigonometry, and algebra. As matter of fact anything you calculate deals with these ten numbers. I didn't know what my teacher was doing when she started me off counting 1 to 10, but if I can master these ten numbers, I can master the rest of them. Even in the realm of music there are only 12 notes – five black notes and seven white notes – and with these notes you can literally revolutionize planet earth through the arena of music. In literature we have 26 letters in our English alphabet. Only 26, but with these 26 letters we can build libraries. We can train minds and open schools. We can read the word of God with just 26 letters.

He used 10 numbers and 26 letters and he joined the music and brought together two worlds for one reason and that is to praise God. Our number one purpose on planet earth is to praise God. Regardless of what you think you're here for, the first thing he wants us to get clear is that we have to learn how to praise him. The word tailors the truth for us to help us learn what praise is all about and why we should praise the Lord. And of course if we don't praise on our own, God will fix it so we will. I heard him say that there will be a time when "every knee shall bow and every tongue shall confess." He said He has some rocks prepared with some special tongues that will cry out praises to Him. I don't know how you feel about, but I don't need a rock to cry for me. God has done enough for me and I am aware of what he has done to make me mindful of the fact that I need to spend time praising him. Just thank him for waking you this morning and giving you a place to praise Him.

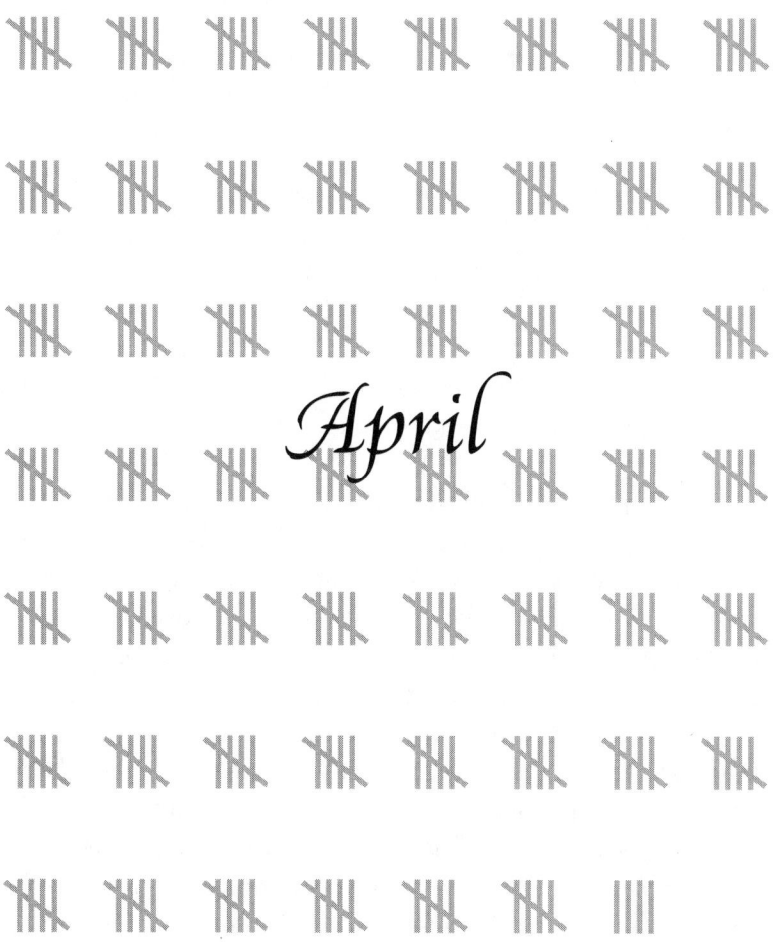

April

From Royalty To Riff-Raff

Genesis 46:34
...for every shepherd is an abomination unto the Egyptians.

Moses had received a demotion. Most of us expect promotions, but sometimes God demotes us in order to promote us. Yes, God does that sometimes. Moses had spent forty years in Pharaoh's house as Pharaoh's grandson. And Moses had everything that any prince or king would want to have. Moses was faring well. He was doing good, but at the age of forty he chose to suffer the afflictions of God's people rather than enjoy the pleasure of sin for a season. Somehow he detected that the stuff he was doing wouldn't last. And if you are going to survive in life, you need to get a hold of something and somebody that will last. So Moses moved from the bright city lights to the dim quiet nights on the backside of the desert.

It's not hard to be riding a city bus and continue to ride it, but it's difficult when you have to lose a Lexus, a Jaguar, or a Lincoln and have to move to riding the city buses. It's not as easy as it would be if you had never been used to a Lexus before. It's not hard to move from neck bones to T-bones, but it's kind of hard to give up T-bones for neck bones. It isn't easy to be demoted. Maybe we could handle the neck bones instead of T-bones, because they are both red meat. But we begin to worry about what people will say just because of the fact that people will shake their heads sadly saying, "Look how far they came."

So God pulled Moses away from Pharaoh's house and put him on the backside of the desert where he stayed for forty years. I mean he moved from a street address to a box number. He moved to the backside – to the desert where they had no cell phones, moving from comforts of a home to living out in the open. His job status of shepherd was at the bottom of the list, and even at that he didn't own his own sheep. He was watching his father-law's sheep. Moses was in a tough spot. But God was watching Moses.

God Uses Busy People

Exodus 3:1
Now Moses kept the flock of Jethro his father in law, the priest of Midian: and he led the flock to the backside of the desert, and came to the mountain of God, even to Horeb.

When God calls a person, that person is usually already busy doing something. Very seldom does God select a person that is merely sitting by day dreaming and building mansions in the sky. Moses kept the flock of Jethro, meaning that he was extremely busy. Merely watching sheep may sound like a very easy job, but in Psalm 25, David says the shepherd's job is a very sensitive one. The first thing a shepherd must do is to make the sheep lie down in green pastures. Shepherds know that sheep will not lie down if there are things disturbing the sheep such as parasites and insects. If a sheep is hungry, he will not lie down. So the shepherd had to prepare the pasture for the sheep. Also, sheep must be lead beside still water because they cannot drink running water. A good shepherd leads his sheep in the path of righteousness; he has to put the sheep on the right track.

God majors in calling people that are already doing something. When God called Abraham, he was busy taking care of his father. When He called Joshua and Caleb, they were busy working with Moses. When He called Peter, James, John, and Andrew, they were busy fishing. When He called Matthew, he was busy collecting taxes. If you're lazy and doing nothing, you're not much good for anything. You can actually go to hell just for doing nothing. The rich man spoken of in Luke chapter 16 wasn't doing wrong. He fared sumptuously every day and walked around dressed in purple and fine linen. But he died and went to hell for doing nothing.

God is looking for busy people who are willing to do something for the Lord. Moses was busy keeping the flock.

The Fire Encounter

Exodus 3:2
And the angel of the Lord appeared unto him in a flame of fire out of the midst of a bush: and he looked, and, behold, the bush burned with fire, and the bush was not consumed.

If you're going to go forward with the Lord you need to at least have a fire experience. Sometimes the reason you don't see us move any more than we do is because we have not had an encounter with fire. There is something about fire that takes the coldness out of our lives and helps us move when we don't feel like moving. There is something about fire that makes you shout when you don't feel like it. It makes you run when there isn't anybody behind you. It makes you laugh when nothing seems funny. It makes you cry when nobody bothers you. And anytime you see fire in the Bible it is symbolic of the presence of the Lord. Elijah said, "I want the real God to answer by fire." And fire came down from heaven and licked up all of the water. Jeremiah wanted to quit preaching one day; and he discovered that his license was not on paper, but like fire shut up in his bones. And on the day of Pentecost, tongues, like live coals of fire, came and sat upon each of them indicating "the presence of the Lord."

Likewise, I'm glad that I've had a fire encounter, because it's amazing what happens when the Holy Ghost fire comes upon you. Fire accomplishes many things. Fire purifies; whatever impurities are on the inside are burned out. Also fire makes you move. The Bible says the angel of the Lord appeared unto him in a flame of fire out of the midst of the bush. Now most of the time if we get ready to get a message to somebody, we want to use a Ph.D. to get the message to the person. We don't want an ignorant person carrying a message, but look at what God used. He took a bush to get a man's attention. Not a majestic tree or a huge oak, but just a plain old bush and put some fire in it. On that occasion Moses had his fire encounter.

Turning Aside

Exodus 3:3
And Moses said, I will now turn aside, and see this great sight, why the bush is not burnt.

The bush didn't burn; it had sticking power. It did not weaken under pressure. It was really symbolic of the children of Israel. In spite of all the stuff they had gone through, they were still making it. That's the way it is with God's people; they can take so much. The average person might call it quits. But in spite of the pressure, God's child can go right on through. Listen to Philippians 4:13, "I can do all things through Christ which strengthens me." I keep getting strength every day. The bush did not burn it up. It's similar to the word of God. We've had snoopers, snappers and snipers from everywhere trying to destroy the Bible, trying to change the language, trying to destroy it. But in spite of all the negative things that have happened, the Word still stands. God says before one jot or tittle of His word shall fall, heaven and earth will pass away. God is a consuming fire, Himself. God will never burn up.

Moses says, "I will now turn aside." I could expound upon this one statement for quite some time, because most of us are too busy to turn aside. We see God talking but we won't listen. God is speaking to us everyday, but we won't turn aside. We're too busy doing our own thing. We are still trying to sow our wild oats, and the Lord is trying to get our attention. Notice that God didn't talk to Moses until he first got Moses' attention. Some people say. "I read the Bible and don't get any understanding." It is because they haven't turned aside yet. When you turn aside, God is ready to speak. You can read His book from cover to cover and never understand a thing you are reading until you first turn aside because it is God that opens your understanding. We must turn aside and say, "Speak Lord, thy servant is listening." Moses stopped and turned aside.

A Divine Diversion

Exodus 3:4
And when the Lord saw that he turned aside to see, God called unto him out of the midst of the bush, and said, Moses, Moses. And he said, Here am I.

The Bible says Moses turned. This could mean that Moses was inquisitive, that he saw something he had never seen before, but I really think that Moses was focused on God. Most of us are too busy to turn aside. God is speaking to us every day, but we don't turn aside. We're busy doing our own thing. You see when you get by yourself you have time to focus on God. Sometimes we have too many people around us for God to talk to us. Or we stay on the phone all day and half the night. Sometimes you should hang up your phone and turn off the television. Put the dog out of the house and have a chance to turn aside and let God talk to you. The Bible says Moses turned aside.

When the Lord saw that he turned aside to see, God called unto him out of the midst of the bush. God didn't talk until Moses decided to listen. God isn't going to just throw his Word out for no reason at all. He's too busy to just throw his Word away. You can't have thirty minutes and say, "I'm going to see what I can pick up in these thirty minutes and then I'll take it and live by it." No, it must be a full time business. Either you're with the Lord or you're not with the Lord. Either you are going to serve him or you aren't going to serve him. You can't do God like you do a sandwich, drive by and pick you up one in a hurry. You've got to take time. As a matter of fact, you need to meditate day and night. If you aren't praying, you ought to be reading, if you're not reading, you ought you to be praying. If you're working two or three jobs and don't have time for the Lord, you need to cut back something and give God some time, because one of these days the stuff you're working for is not going to make any difference. God will be the only one that will really count in life.

Bare Feet

Exodus 3:5
And he said, Draw not nigh hither: put off thy shoes from off thy feet, for the place whereon thou standest is holy ground.

When the Lord saw that Moses had turned aside, God called to him out of the midst of the bush. In other words this is a serious call as are all of God's calls. I know Moses got ready to run to the Lord, but God said, "Hold it Moses; don't come another step closer. Stop right where you are. Before you come to me you've got some things you've got to do. The first thing I want you to do is take off your shoes." Why would the Lord want Moses to take off his shoes? What is wrong with Moses' shoes?

You see shoes represent whatever you have walked on. Moses walked on trash and dirt and filth. But God wanted Moses to know he was on Holy ground. Why was it so Holy around that burning bush? The reason it was Holy is because the Lord was there. And wherever the Lord is, that's Holy Ground. And right now, anything that God has something to do with, that's Holy. Don't mistreat anything that God has set aside to be Holy and treat it as if it is unholy. So God let Moses know that he the ground he was standing on was Holy ground because of the Lord's presence.

The Lord also wanted to teach Moses that there are some restrictions in His program. People are so used to doing what they want to do in their own way and when they are ready. But God says, "You can't do what you want to do when you decide to follow me." Moses had to make some changes. First, he had to learn obedience. When God told him to stop, he had to stop. Then he had to learn respect. Taking off his shoes were a sign of respect the same way as a man removing his hat. A man dishonors the house by walking in with his big old hat on. By the act of removing his shoes, Moses acknowledged God's presence.

Moses Meets The I AM

Exodus 3:6

Moreover he said, I am the God of thy father, the God of Abraham, the God of Isaac, and the God of Jacob. And Moses hid his face; for he was afraid to look upon God.

I am God. Not I was, but I am. Not I will be, but I am. Just that alone is enough for me to sit down with, because He seems to say that whatever your needs are, "I am that." In other words, if you're sick I am a doctor. If you're in the dark, I am the light. If you're hungry I am the bread of life. If you're a lost sheep, I am the good shepherd. If you can't go through a place, I am the door. If you don't know where you're going, I am the way. If you've been hanging around lies all your life, I am the truth. He says, "I AM."

The thing about God is that yesterday He could say I am, today He can say I am, and tomorrow He can still say I am. He said, "I am the God of your father, the God of Abraham." Although Abraham had been dead 400 years, God spoke of him in the present. When a saint dies, he's an is, not a was. When a saint dies, he's really not dead; he's still living. The Lord looks at saints as just being a sleep. Listen to John 11:25, I am the resurrection and the life, he that believeth in me, though he were dead; yet shall he live, and whosoever liveth and believeth in me, shall never die. In other words Abraham is still living.

Moses hid his face for he was afraid to look upon God. Moses had reverence for God. And you ought to have reverence for the God you serve. Don't treat God as though he's nobody. God is a holy God. God is omnipotent. God is omniscient. God is omnipresent. He's got all power. He knows everything. He's everywhere at the same time. You don't just treat a God that can speak heaven and earth into existence any kind of way. He speaks and a man dies. He speaks and the man gets up and rises again. Moses experienced this awesome power and hid his face.

Suffering And Sorrows

Exodus 3:7

And the Lord said, I have surely seen the affliction of my people which are in Egypt, and have heard their cry by reason of their taskmasters; for I know their sorrows.

I like my God because nothing goes by him without him seeing it. You say, "Well, I'm suffering preacher and nobody knows it." The Bible says that God sees it. Your family may not know what you're going through. But God says he has surely seen the affliction of His people. You don't go through things without God seeing. God sees and hears our cry. When you weep at night after the family goes to sleep, God hears that cry. When you moan late at night and think nobody else knows it, God hears every moan and every groan. He not only hears my cry, but he hear the cries of people that have been deserted, people that have been put away. He knows. He hears."

God had allowed His people to go into Egypt for a period of time, 400 years. There were only a few of them when they went in but they had multiplied into a great nation. However, they had now become slaves in a foreign land. The Israelites were in agony. God saw their struggles and He had a plan for them. God wanted to bring them out and give them a land of their own and prosper them and bless them.

"I know their sorrow." God knows everything you do and every time you stumble. And the good part about it is that He knows you completely – from the inside out and the outside in. Sometimes when people misunderstand you, they think you're low down. They think you're hateful; but they don't understand you're trying to do the best you can with what you've got. I heard the Lord say, "I know. I know." We are our heavenly Father's children; we all know that he love us one and all, yet there times we find we'll answer another voice and call, but if we're willing, the Lord will teach us all, because he knows.

When God Shows Up

Genesis 18:1
And the Lord appeared unto him in the plains of Mamre: and he sat in the tent door in the heat of the day.

The scene opens with God visiting Abraham. Abraham was a hero. He was a giant. He was a role model. The Lord appeared unto Abraham in the plains of Mamre while he sat in the tent door in the heat of the day. Abraham wasn't expecting God, he just showed up. Abraham was sitting in the door. If somebody had been walking up or coming up to him in the distance, he would have noticed, but when he looked up there He was. It is amazing how quick God can show up. He comes without you expecting him. And sometimes you don't see him when he's on the way. Abraham lifted his eyes and three men instantly stood by him. When he saw them he ran to meet them from the tent door and bowed himself toward the ground. You can tell these were not ordinary men, because whenever a superior walks up and you're present men stand, but when God shows up, we bow.

But in chapter 16 something had happened in his life that smeared his name. Abraham took a woman that was in the house that was not his wife; however, she was given to him by his wife. He lay with her and had a son named Ishmael. That was an ugly chapter in his life. And of course all of us have ugly chapters. But thank God for being a God of a second chance. Sometimes your family won't give you another chance, but God will. Your boss on the job may not give you another chance. But the God I serve is a God of a second chance. As a matter of fact, He will go beyond the second chance; I'm up in the thousands now. He keeps on giving me chance after chance after chance after chance. Where would I be if God didn't give me another chance? God was solid with Abraham for fourteen years. After he messed up, God didn't say a word to him from the age of eighty-five until he became ninety-nine. Then the Lord came and spoke to him.

The Lord And His Angels

Genesis 18:3
And said, My Lord, if now I have found favour in thy sight, pass not away, I pray thee, from thy servant.

This incident took place in the plains of Mamre when three men appeared to Abraham. As you read through the text, you will discover that two were angels and one was Jesus. Thank God, he uses angels. I need to tell you that each of you has an angel assigned to you. Psalms 91:11 says he gives his angels charge to keep watch over you. I guess that's why the old folk used to sing the song all day and all night about angels keep watching over me.

Let me illustrate. An old lady who had been living by herself became frightened because two men were following her. However, they would vanish when the police showed up. She told her pastor about it. The reverend said, "Oh I know those fellows. Psalm 23:6 calls them goodness and mercy, the angels that God has assigned to keep watch over you."

Abraham was glad to see the Lord and his angels. The word LORD in all caps in the Old Testament is Jehovah, but in the New Testament it is Jesus. And so really this text is actually saying that Jesus himself made an appearance to Abraham in the Old Testament. You must know that Jesus did show up in the Old Testament just like in the New Testament. He's hidden in every book of the Old Testament. In Genesis he's the seed of the woman. In Exodus he's the Passover Lamb; in Leviticus he's the sacrificial one; Numbers the uplifted one; Deuteronomy the true prophet; Joshua the captain of our salvation; Judges the delivering judge; Ruth our kinsman redeemer; Samuel, Kings, and Chronicles the promised king; Ezra and Nehemiah our restorer; Job my redeemer; Psalms my all in all; Proverbs our wisdom; Ecclesiastes our pattern; the Songs of Solomon the lover of our soul; Proverbs our wisdom and in the Prophets, he's the promised Messiah.

God's Hidden Plans

Genesis 18:17
And the Lord said, Shall I hide from Abraham that thing which I do?

The Lord had two reasons for visiting Abraham that day. First, He spoke to Abraham about Isaac who had already been promised, letting him know Isaac would arrive in less than a year. You see God may not come when you want Him to, but you can rest assured that he will always be on time. Abraham and Sarah had problems like most couples have problems. They wanted to help God out and get a child some other way. But God has reasons for delaying His coming. Your soul may not be strong enough to handle what your mind is requesting. You may be looking for something on the first, but He has it penned in for the fifteenth. After setting this matter straight, the men rose up and looked toward Sodom.

Abraham went with them to bring them on the way similar to what used to happen when I was at home living out in Arlington, Tennessee. We stayed a mile or two from everybody and whenever a person decided to come to our home and visit us we didn't just stand at the door and say bye. We would go a piece of the way back home with them. Abraham was so excited that these heavenly visitors came to see him that when they got ready to leave he went a piece of the way back with them. City folk would compare this to taking a person to the airport, parking your car and walking up to sit and wait until time for them to leave.

Then Abraham heard the Lord whisper to the angels, "Shall I hide from Abraham that thing which I do?" You can be so tuned in to the word of God that when God speaks, you will hear. And every child of God, if you've got stuff in you and on your mind that's distracting you from hearing the voice of God, get rid of it and get off to yourself and listen. When God talks to you, you'll have a good conversation. He never uses wasted words.

Radiant Lights

Genesis 18:18
Seeing that Abraham shall surely become a great and mighty nation, and all the nations of the earth shall be blessed in him.

We need to let the world know who we are and Whose we are. He says in Matthew 5:16, "Let your light so shine," which means your light ought to shine publicly. It should not be a shock to the folk you work with to know that you attend church. It shouldn't surprise them when they see you on television sitting up in church. Your light ought to also shine privately. Let your light so shine privately that men might see it publicly and glorify your Father purposefully. You shouldn't have to have a cross around your neck for folk to know you're saved. You shouldn't have to walk around with a big old Bible saying, "Thank you Jesus, praise the Lord, praise the Lord, thank you Jesus, thank you Lord," every time you open your mouth for folk to know you've been with God. It ought to show up in your walk. It ought to show up in your talk. It ought to show up in your character. If you're mistreated at the cash register, don't act ugly. You belong to somebody. If they give you too much money, don't walk out talking about this is a blessing from God; that isn't no blessing from God. They just made a mistake. Return the money because if nothing else catches you, your conscience ought to disturb you.

When you mistreat somebody your conscience ought to go to bed with you at night. You know your conscience is the greatest preacher you've ever met. You may never invite me to your house for dinner, but every time you eat, conscience has a seat. I may never ride in your car, but every time you ride, conscience is riding beside you. And before you know it, conscience will walk down your hall and start writing on your walls. We are lights. You can't hide lights. If it is a light it's going to show up shining. A good conscience helps produce a radiant light.

Rules And Regulations

Genesis 18:19

For I know him, that he will command his children and his household after him, and they shall keep the way of the Lord, to do justice and judgment; that the Lord may bring upon Abraham that which he hath spoken of him.

For I know him. This is God talking about Abraham. I wonder how many of you know that God knows you. God wants to lift you to a higher height. Then God says, "that he will command his children." Too many of us think that the way you handle your children is just to talk to them. You say, "Well my child is intelligent. All I need to do is talk to him; he'll understand." That's why we have ten, twelve, thirteen and fourteen year-old kids in the house whose parents say they can't do anything with them. Can you imagine a child living in your house with you paying the mortgage, eating your food, sleeping in your bed and you can't do anything with him? He comes in when he gets ready in your house, turning the key on your door, and turning on your light.

I heard about a young fellow who was trying to talk back to his daddy about why he had to live by the orders. Daddy says, "I didn't say you have to live by these orders. If you don't want to obey, hit the door. Pay your own rent. Buy your own groceries. Sleep in your own bed and you can do what you want. But you must follow the rules to live in this house." You will live longer and better if you obey your parents. Learn how to respect the folk you live with.

Then God said that He knew Abraham would command his entire household. He's the daddy of the whole house. Whenever the father is not in order with God, more than likely the wife won't be in order with the father and more than likely the children won't be in order with either one of them. But when the father follows God, the wife will follow the father, and the children will have to line up with mommy and daddy. And when that happens we can empty the jail houses because God's ways are kept.

Senseless Sodomites

Genesis 18:20
And the Lord said, Because the cry of Sodom and Gomorrah is great, and because their sin is very grievous.

The sin of Sodom and Gomorrah was very grievous to the Lord. The word grievous means heavy. The whole town of Sodom was filled with homosexuals. The Bible calls this an abomination, not a way of life. Calling it sin is also missing the mark. For instance, if the mark is that door straight in front of you, and you commit sin you might bear to the right or to the left; that is missing the mark. But abomination would be if you aimed in the total opposite direction. Romans 1:24-32 describes the state of unclean men dishonoring their own bodies between themselves. God gave them up unto vile affection for even their women changed the natural use into that which is against nature. Men burned in their lust one toward another, men with men, working that which is unseemly and receiving in themselves the recompense of their error. Even as they did not like to retain God in their knowledge, God gave them over to a reprobate mind. Romans 1:26 says that God gave them up, which meant they still had a chance. But in verse 28 it says that He gave them over, which meant they had gone beyond the point of no return.

Leviticus 18:22 says, Thou shall not lie with mankind as with womankind. It is abomination. Leviticus 18:29 tells us that whosoever shall commit any of these abominations even the soul that committed them shall be cut off from among their people. Leviticus 20:13 says if a man also lie with mankind as he lies with a woman, both of them have committed an abomination and they shall surely be put to death. Their blood shall be upon them. Are you to dislike homosexuals? No. They are people that we should love, but don't love the sin. Hate the sin, but not the sinner. It is the Lord who will determine the condition of people. He decided it was time to judge Sodom and Gomorrah.

The Value Of The Virtuous

Genesis 18:23
And Abraham drew near, and said, Wilt thou also destroy the righteous with the wicked?

Abraham had a nephew named Lot who had pitched his tent on the out skirts of Sodom. He fell in love with a Sodomite woman and she convinced him to buy a home in Sodom. Now Lot was saved but worldly. When the Lord told Abraham He was going to destroy the city, Abraham decided to have a prayer meeting with God. He asked God if he could do some evangelistic work before God made His final decision.

We cannot discount the righteous folk. You hear these old rumors that the church world is doing nothing. What you're trying to do is count what the church is doing in dollar and cents. But you can't put what the church is doing in commercial appeal because sometimes the church doesn't even know all the church is doing. For example, a person went to church getting ready to commit suicide but when they walked in the word got in them and changed their mind and they went back and became a decent husband and a lovable father. How you are going to put that in the paper? Things happen at church that you can't explain, because when you try to tell somebody they don't believe you.

You paid your tithes and afterwards God opened a door and you had five jobs waiting for you after being unemployed for six months. When you go to the doctor and he says you have terminal cancer and the man of God prays over you and you go back and the doctor examines you and can't find anything wrong you discover that God is still a healer. The church brings strength and encouragement when you feel low and don't know how you will make it. But God is working it out.

Thank God for the righteous. Lot was a righteous man living in a very unrighteous place. But it was time to move.

For Their Sake

Genesis 18:26
And the Lord said, If I find in Sodom fifty righteous within the city, then I will spare all the place for their sake.

braham worried about the fifty righteous men and thought he had better check with the Lord a second time. "What if there are only forty-five righteous in the city?" Notice how patient God is. He says, "Well if there are forty-five, I'll spare the city for forty-five." Sometimes you think that the church must be huge to make a difference. However, just one or two saints can be carrying the whole city. You just might be making a difference in your own neighborhood. You're not knocking on doors or out canvassing the neighborhood, but you're praying in the community. A storm came by the other day and hit up the block from you but it jumped over your neighborhood. Somebody down the street said they were lucky, but no, it was a saint in the neighborhood that knew God and had asked God for that house a long time ago. So God spared the whole section.

Abraham continued to speak with God about the destruction until he asked God if He would spare the city for just ten righteous, hoping that Lot's entire family would be living for the Lord. If Lot had been the kind of father he should have been, his whole house would have been saved. But when Lot went to get his sons-in-law out of town, the Bible says they thought he was joking. You know you have to be careful how you walk when things are going well, because if you haven't lived right at first, you won't get the support you need at the end. There were not ten righteous.

So the angels went to rescue Lot. Lot asked them to dinner. The angels declined and said they would wait out in the street. But Lot urged them into his home because of the wickedness outside. The homosexuals tried to break down the door in their anger. Finally, the angels blinded their eyes until they gave up and went home. Are you righteous to impact your community?

Cover Your Community

Genesis 19:22

Haste thee, escape thither; for I cannot do any thing till thou be come thither.

God was getting ready to destroy the whole city, but he would not destroy the city until Lot got out of town. The Bible says the same hour that Lot left was when God destroyed the city. What power a child of God has. Have you known of a family with a praying mother in the house? As long as she is living, there is peace in the family. But as soon as she died trouble broke out. Sister stopped talking to sister. Brother stopped talking to brother. Grandson raped granddaughter. All that stuff started happening because the praying warrior is not in the house. Whatever you do, don't forsake the church of the living God. If you don't get anything physically out of it, show up any way. Rub shoulders with somebody that's talking to God and loves the Lord. The angels said, "Lot, take your family and leave here running. And whatever you do, don't look back.

The angels tried to hurry Lot; yet Lot still lingered. Mrs. Lot started thinking about the designer drapery and custom made furniture she had in the house in Sodom. She thought about the jewelry she had in her jewelry case and how she would miss all her party friends. So out of God's mercy, the angels grabbed them and set them outside the city. But Mrs. Lot had to take just one look back. "Just one look won't hurt," she thought. But when she turned back the Bible says she became a pillar of salt. If only she had obeyed. Lot and his two daughters kept running until they came to a city called Zoar. Now Zoar was on the map to be destroyed with Sodom and Gomorrah, but because Lot made it to Zoar, God spared that city.

Your neighborhood might still be standing, child of God, because every morning you get on your knees and say, "Lord bless this home, this neighborhood, and this community. Stay faithful in prayer and righteousness!

An Altered Attitude

John 20:28
And Thomas answered and said unto him, My Lord and my God.

Something happened between Calvary and Pentecost. There were only fifty days between Calvary and Pentecost – Calvary for us, Pentecost in us. In that fifty day period, Jesus allowed himself to be seen fourteen different times with fourteen different groups. The first one that saw him was Mary Magdalene. The second group was certain women. The third one that saw him was Simon Peter. The fourth one that saw him were the men on their way to a place called Emmaus. And the fifth group was the ten that Jesus allowed to see him after he got up. They were in the upper room frightened and afraid with the doors closed and windows down. Jesus walked in the room without opening a door, without coming through a window and breathed on these disciples and said, "Receive ye the Holy Ghost."

The next time he was seen was with the eleven and Thomas had showed up. Critical scholars say that when the ten saw him that first Resurrection Sunday, they ran back and told Thomas. "We've seen the Lord." Thomas said, "I don't believe nothing any of you are saying. Peter, you know I don't believe you. You cursed and swore and said you didn't know the man. James and John, you have been bucking for the top seats in the Kingdom. Philip, you were with Jesus three years and still didn't know who he was. Matthew, you were a tax collector and you majored in lying to folk about their taxes. So I really don't believe any of you." But when a person tells you something about Jesus that sounds good, you want to come back and check it out for yourself. And you can tell when a person has been with the Lord because their attitude changes. They are on a higher level. When a person is serious about the Lord, that from the heart will reach the heart. When Thomas saw the Lord, he responded with a changed attitude.

Seeing The Saviour

Acts 7:55
But he, being full of the Holy Ghost, looked up stedfastly into heaven, and saw the glory of God, and Jesus standing on the right hand of God.

And then he came back and decided to show himself to Stephen, that good deacon that decided to follow the Lord. Stephen, the one that would not deny Christ under crisis. Some of us will follow him as long as we don't have to go through anything, but if we have hard times, we'll tell Jesus, "See you later." Stephen allowed himself to be stoned to death. He would not deny Christ, but while he was dying he looked up and saw Jesus.

Jesus understood that Thomas had a doubting problem. Jesus will do a lot of things to help us to know who He is. He will go out of his way to help us to understand that there is a reality in serving a true and a living God. He said to Thomas, "You know that I'm who I say I am. Look at my hands. I have the evidence of Calvary on my hands. Look at my feet, I have the marks on my feet. Look at my side. Look at my forehead, you see the marks. As a matter of fact, Thomas, take your finger and thrust it into my side." Jesus loved Thomas and wanted him to experience the reality of seeing Jesus face to face. Also, the Bible says that Jesus showed himself to five hundred brethren at one time.

Then Jesus showed himself to James, the brother of Jesus. You know James didn't believe Jesus while He was living. And sometimes your biological family has a problem believing where you stand with God. Sometimes your own family has to go through some things before they will recognize that you are really serious about the work of the Lord. That's why you should never give up on your family. They may not see it now, but if you keep living right, if you keep praying and keep living a life that will be pleasing in the sight of God, soon or later they will see your light but glorify your father which is in heaven.

Looking With Expectancy

Titus 2:13
Looking for that blessed hope, and the glorious appearing of the great God and our Saviour Jesus Christ.

Jesus was a person. It is good to look at Him. Jude 1:21 says, Keep yourselves in the love of God, looking for the mercy of our Lord Jesus Christ unto eternal life. If you just look at Him your life will change. He will change your attitude. He will change your disposition. For some mysterious reason, Jesus wanted His disciples to see Him leave. If they didn't see Him, it's no telling what they would say. They watched Him go. While He left, the disciples were gaping with their mouths open. They were standing with their eyes bucked, with their hearts fluttering, to the extent that they were gazing as Jesus is slowly going away. They were seriously looking at what was happening, amazed and yet with a longing for Him to remain.

Now He is gone. I see the disciples still gazing. Their way maker has just disappeared, and they are gazing. Who will they talk to now because Jesus is gone? Jesus was not only a God that cares, but He was also a God that is able. Hebrews 12:2 says, "Looking unto Jesus the author and finisher of our faith; who for the joy that was set before him endured the cross, despising the shame, and is set down at the right hand of the throne of God." It's all right to look at Jesus. What does it mean to gaze? It means that you aren't doing anything but gazing. The angel was telling them not to spend all of their time watching Jesus leave. They had a job to do. And you have a job to do while He is gone. That is why we show up Sunday after for worship. You worship a true and a living God. He is worthy of our worship and our praise. John 4:24, "God is a spirit and they that worship Him must worship Him in spirit and truth." The same Jesus that the disciples saw ascending into heaven is coming back again. That's a promise. Is your house in order? Are you ready for the Lord's return?

The Reward For Waiting

Acts 1:4

And, being assembled together with them, commanded them that they should not depart from Jerusalem, but wait for the promise of the Father, which, saith he, ye have heard of me.

Wait on the Lord; you must wait on him. I'm reminded of a story I heard. A young man went to town with his daddy. His daddy had to take care of some business. He said, "Son, sit on the step and wait here; Daddy's got a lot to do, so you sit here and wait until Daddy comes back." Daddy went to work and got kind of busy. It started raining on the boy. Folk down the street said, "Young man, you want to come in?" He said, "I can't come in; my daddy told me to wait right here. It started to get dark on the boy and somebody else came by and asked the young man if he wasn't getting scared a little bit? They tried to get him to come on in. He said, "No, my daddy told me to wait right here." Dogs came by and started barking at the boy. But the boy wouldn't leave.

The father, being a human, forgot the boy was there. He left the store out the back way and went on to the house. He didn't think any more about Jr. until time to eat dinner. The wife said, "Where is Jr.? He said, "Oh, I forgot. I left him up town sitting on the step at the store." The father rode back up there and the boy was still there; rain coming down, he was still there; darkness had set in, he was still there; dogs were barking and he was still there. You may be in a situation where it's raining on you; storms of adversity are coming down on you, but wait. I know it gets dark sometimes in your life. Sometimes you can't see your way, but the Lord told me to tell you to wait. Enemies sometimes bark at you and scandalize your name, but oh don't give up. Wait! One of these days when the weary will be at rest you will be able to walk up to the Lord and say, "Lord I thank you. You told me to wait, here I am."

40, 40, 40

2 Chronicles 7:14
If my people, which are called by my name, shall humble themselves, and pray, and seek my face, and turn from their wicked ways; then will I hear from heaven, and will forgive their sin, and will heal their land.

I have been reciting this passage for over twenty years, yet it stirs me every time I read it. This passage is like a fountain bubbling over with water; every time you take a dip, there is more left than what you drew out. I could preach from this passage all the year long and when I finish, the verse will still be crying, "Say more!" because it sets before us principles to practice as we plan to prosper on our spiritual pilgrimage.

Whenever you see the number 40 in the Bible, it indicates there is a period of probation, a period of testing, or a period of trials. This verse contains 40 words. The number 40 is scattered throughout the Old and New Testaments. Samuel, Solomon, and David each had a 40 year reign. Moses spent 40 years in Egypt, 40 years in Midian, and 40 years in the wilderness. Jacob waited until he was 40 years old before he took a bride. Jonah went to Nineveh and gave the Ninevites a 40-day probation period to repent of their sins. Ezekiel lay on his right side 40 days as protest against Judah. Jesus spent 40 days in the wilderness and afterward He was tempted by the devil. He died, rose, and spent another 40 days on planet Earth before He caught the cloud to go back home.

The verse begins with If; that is possibility. My people; that is personal. Which are called by my name; that's paternal. Shall humble themselves; that's preparation. Pray; that's power. Seek my face; that's a privilege. Turn from their wicked ways; that's progress. Then will I hear from heaven; that's procedure. Forgive their sins; that's pardon. Heal their land; that's prosperity. Forty days, forty years, forty words packed into one verse.

Fringe Benefits

2 Chronicles 7:14

If my people, which are called by my name, shall humble themselves, and pray, and seek my face, and turn from their wicked ways; then will I hear from heaven, and will forgive their sin, and will heal their land.

If stands for choice or chance. You have the choice to accept Christ as your personal Savior or you stand the chance of being swallowed up by the wrath of God. Notice the i-f in the middle of the word l-i-f-e. The old people used to say this, "I will see you next Sunday if it's the Lord's will." It seems to say that if "if" is in the middle of life, it stands for uncertainty. Life is uncertain. We would do well to get it together while we have life. Life is not sure, but death is sure. We are here today and gone today. We are here this morning and gone this evening. We are here this minute and gone the next minute.

The only way you can have real life is to have the real life. John 10:10 says, "The thief cometh not, but for to steal and to destroy. I am come that they might have life, and that they might have it more abundantly." You don't have to spend the rest of your life on welfare when you can fare well. You don't have to spend all of your time at the complaint window when you can move to the claims department. Life becomes much more certain with Christ.

"If my people." How did I get to be in the God family, because everybody is not His child? Just because God made you does not make you His child. He also made the skunk, snake, and baboon. They are not his children; they are His by creation. The only way you can be His child is to be His by redemption. The Lord somehow allows us to be born into the God family and adopted at the same time. You can be born into a family and have the father's nature but not his name. When you're adopted, you can have the name and not the nature. But when you are His child, you look like Him, act like Him, and receive the fringe benefits.

Not Any Name

2 Chronicles 7:14

If my people, which are called by my name, shall humble themselves, and pray, and seek my face, and turn from their wicked ways; then will I hear from heaven, and will forgive their sin, and will heal their land.

If my people. The Lord didn't use the word my too often. When He got ready to build His church, He said, "Upon this rock I will build my church." When He got ready to talk to His father, He said, "I am praying to my father." Psalm 100 speaks about the children of God, "Ye are my people; the sheep of my pasture." I don't know how you feel about, but to me it's a joy to be in this family. It is the greatest family a person could ever be in. This family is a royal family. You have been called. Called by whom? Called by God. Called from darkness to light; called from death to life; called from sin to salvation; called from hopelessness to hopefulness; called from dust to divinity. You have been called.

"If my people which are called by name…" You may get upset because folk call you out of your name. When they call you a Christian, that is not the name that God gave you. We received the name Christian from our enemies. We were first called disciples. Then we were called the people of the way. We were then called Galileans, and finally we were called Christians. It was not as an honor, but as a criticism by the people of Antioch. They were using the term as a reproach to the church of the Living God. It's good to be identified with the right name. His name is like no other name. In his name is salvation and healing of body and soul.

Today, are we still being called out of our name. Are we really Christians? Are we following Christ? If we were taken to court and put on trial, would we be found guilty of being a Christian or would they have trouble finding enough evidence to convict us?

Humility Has Its Perks

2 Chronicles 7:14
If my people, which are called by my name, shall humble themselves, and pray, and seek my face, and turn from their wicked ways; then will I hear from heaven, and will forgive their sin, and will heal their land.

It is hard to believe that God has some folk that are not humble. It just doesn't sound right. If I am a child of God, I ought to be humble. If I am humble, I should have the characteristics of a child of God. Sometimes one of our problems is that we get lifted in what we call spiritual pride. You see some folk are so holy until they are no earthly good. Jesus would go to seaports and find sin sick folk and lay His hands on them. He would let a sinful woman touch the hem of His garment. Shame on any person that becomes too holy to speak. After all, we are just dust that has been saved by grace. There is nothing on our part; we are what He made us. What I know, He taught me; where I am, He brought me. The reason I'm still here is because He kept me.

Humbling yourself is something you can do. It is not something you have to wait on. You can't help but humble yourself when you look back and see where you came from and then look and see where you are. I know some folk that have more sense than I have who didn't make it. All I have is faith and a true and living God. Stop walking around with your head up in the air acting so special; humble yourself. I would rather be poor and be in the presence of the Lord broke than to be rich hanging out with the devil. When you know who you are and whose you are, you don't have to be afraid of losing what you've got.

And pray. It is only when I am humble that I am in a position to pray. We are not to come before the Lord telling him how good and faithful we are or we may not receive answers to our prayers. If you pray enough, you will learn how to pray effectively. Pray always and stay humble.

A Proper Prophet

Ezekiel 37:1
The hand of the Lord was upon me, and carried me out in the spirit of the Lord, and set me down in the midst of the valley which was full of bones,

Ezekiel was a prophet of the Lord. A prophet is a preacher and a preacher ought to be a prophet. I don't mean the kind of prophet that believes you should keep a rabbit's foot in your pocket for good luck. Just having the foot alone is a reminder that it's not good luck. Ask the rabbit. I'm not talking about a prophet that believes you should sprinkle salt over your right shoulder or tells you to wear a dime around your ankle or put a horseshoe above your door, but a real prophet. A prophet is a man with sight, insight and foresight. With sight he looks on things; with insight, he looks into things; and with foresight, he looks beyond things. A prophet is a man that understands the past and knows how to live in the present. With his knowledge of the past and his insight into the present, he's able to predict the future. Such a man was Ezekiel.

Ezekiel had witnessed captivity. He had been part of Israel that had been carried away captive. He knew what it was to be isolated and left alone with nowhere to go and nothing to do. Things had gotten pretty bad for Ezekiel. No longer had God visited him during the day and the night with smoke from the altar indicating his presence with the people. Ezekiel was a long ways from home. He was with the crowd that said, "How can we sing the Lord's song in a strange land?" However, in the midst of his dilemma, he tuned in to the Lord. You never know where God will lead you, but if the Lord leads you, thank God for where he's leading you. The Lord set Ezekiel down in the midst of a valley full of bones. Now most folk don't like to vacation in the valley; they want to go to the hills and mountains. But if Lord put you in a valley, stay there because He placed you there for a reason.

Dry, Dry Bones

Ezekiel 37:2

And caused me to pass by them round about: and, behold, there were very many in the open valley; and, lo, they were very dry.

Ezekiel had been led into a place that was full of bones, not life, but bones. He saw spiritual lifelessness. He saw some thing that looked like hope, but wasn't; the bones were lifeless. We live in a world full of lifeless folk. Life exists when the body, soul, and spirit are together. Physical life is life without the presence of God. You can function, but you are dead. You can move around, but have no spirit on the inside. There are many folk that have physical life, but spiritually they are dead. They can't feel the presence of the Lord; everybody's shouting at them.

Spiritually dead people don't like the people of God getting emotional. Yet God saved us and lifted us up out of the muck and morrow, and set us on a good path. We were on the way to a burning hell and God snatched us out right in the nick of time. Spiritually dead people think it is okay to get emotional when their hand is hit with a hammer or when somebody slaps them. Then they jump. But when you think about what God has done, how God has brought us, and what God is doing in our lives, it's shouting time!

I see in this valley of dry bones choir members that are not singing, scattered all out in the audience. I see ushers not on their post, outside smoking and laughing and joking. I see deacons asleep on the front pew. There were very many bones in the open valley. The church was full, but they were very dry. The crowd was there, but they weren't saying anything. They weren't giving anything. The choir wasn't singing anything. There were no amens going on. They were not just dry; they were very dry. A new pastor got excited when he first saw the bones because he had a church. But when he passed by and got a really good look, he saw they were very, very dry.

A Curious Question

Ezekiel 37:3

And he said unto me, Son of man, can these bones live? And I answered, O Lord God, thou knowest.

It seems like Ezekiel should have been asking the Lord, but the Lord asked Ezekiel, "Can these bones live?" Think it not strange for God to ask questions. God often asks questions. When He walked and saw Adam in the garden hiding behind a bush, covering himself with fig leaves, God asked, "Adam, where art thou?" When the woman pressed her way through the crowd and touched the "h-e-m" that was wrapped around the "H-i-m" Jesus asked, "Who touched me?" I discovered that when God asks questions, He already knows the answer.

I'm a little different than Ezekiel. If God had asked me that question, I would have said, "Lord, if you give me a chance, I think I can put these bones together. I can get in my lab and find a way." But Ezekiel was smarter than I am. Ezekiel said, "Lord, thou knowest." There are some things in life we just don't know, and we need to admit it. If you don't know, don't mess it up and act like you do know.

I have observed the way God does everything in order. For instance, a potato bug hatches its eggs in seven days. A canary will hatch her eggs in 14 days. A hen will hatch her eggs in 35 days. An eagle hatches her eggs in 42 days. A snake hatches her eggs in 49 days. They all are multiples of seven. A watermelon will always have even stripes on it. An orange will have even segments. A tiny tree will have enough 2X4s to build half a house. He is a mighty God. And some people are so presumptuous to think they have more sense than Him. Most of us are so smart, but let me ask you a few questions. How high is up? How low is down? How far is across? Where does darkness hide when daylight appears? In contrast, God is all knowing. He knows my heart and my heart's desire. Nobody can stop my God. You can't quiet him down; you can't shut him up.

Ugly Bones No More

Ezekiel 37:4, 5

Again he said unto me, Prophesy upon these bones, and say unto them, O ye dry bones, hear the word of the Lord...I will cause breath to enter into you, and ye shall live.

*P*rophesy to these bones. Don't get caught up in politics; just go on and preach. Don't worry about results; just preach. Don't worry about how much you know and how much don't know; just go on and preach. Say unto the dry bones, "Hear the word of the Lord." The word is so powerful that you don't have to add to it. Adding to the word is like trying to add sweetness to honey when it's already sweet. It is like adding whiteness to snow.

Maybe there are some things in the word that you would like to change. But God said, "Don't do that." Just go on and preach the word. There's power in the word. The word is like a double-edged sword; it will cut at and back. It will cut going and coming. It will cut the accused and the accuser, the convicted and the convicting. The word will cut the person in the pew as well as the preacher in the pulpit. The parishioners may leave bloody sometimes, but the preacher will also be cut up and need bandages. The word hurts and heals at the same time. Hebrews 4:12 For the word of God is quick, and powerful, and sharper than any two-edged sword, piercing even to the dividing asunder of soul and spirit, and of the joints and marrow, and is a discerner of the thoughts and intents of the heart.

God told Ezekiel to let the people know that even though things look bleak, it was not hopeless. There is a lesson for us today. Take hold of the promises of God. Believe that He is the God of restoration. Breath and life will come back into these bones and they will be covered with skin and flesh. No longer will there be an ugly skeleton without body and soul. If you have lost the vibrancy of life and you feel like dry bones, begin to trust in the One who has the power to make you whole again.

Quaking And Shaking

Ezekiel 37:7

So I prophesied as I was commanded: and as I prophesied, there was a noise, and behold a shaking, and the bones came together, bone to his bone.

There is noise in the valley because a lot of folk are thankful for what God has done for them. The person who was healed of cancer is telling their story. Another person who God saved out of the muck and the mire has a report to give. And when people start giving their testimonies, it is going to get noisy. There will be a lot of singing and praising going on.

Then came the shaking. There were head bones too headstrong to listen; neck bones too stiff in sin to turn from wrong to right; back bones that had been lying in the bed of adultery; thigh bones that had been sitting in the seat of the scornful; knee bones that had been bowing to idle gods; leg bones that had been standing in the way of sinners; and toe bones that had been tip-toeing in and out of other folks' back doors.

Then God told Ezekiel to prophesy to the four winds to come and breathe into these bodies. The Hebrew word for wind and breath is Ruwach, which means spirit. The Lord was saying to Ezekiel, "They are alive, but they still don't have any spirit in them." You may attend church and have your name on the rolls, but you must be filled with the Spirit. If you are going to minister and win lost souls, it is imperative to be filled up with the spirit of God. So when he preached that word, the head bones started listening. The neck bone started turning from wrong to right. The back bone picked up its cross and started following the Lord. The thigh bone got up off its behind. Knee bones started praising God. Foot bones started dancing in the spirit. I am thankful that I was a dry bone one day, but I heard the preacher say, "Come ye that love the Lord and let your joy be known!"

May

Getting It Right

Genesis 5:23
And all the days of Enoch were three hundred sixty and five years.

I'm always fascinated with important characters in the Bible that accomplished a great deal, yet about whom the Bible says so little. Even though Enoch is a role model, he is not mentioned nearly as much as Adam and Eve or Abraham, Isaac, Jacob, Noah, Joseph, Moses and Joshua. He's not mentioned as much as Ruth or Esther. He isn't discussed as much as Isaiah, Daniel, Ezekiel or Jeremiah or even Hosea, Joel, Amos, Obadiah, Jonah, Micah, Nahum, Habakkuk, Zephaniah, Haggai and Zechariah. There are only about 5 places in the Bible that say anything at all about Enoch. Sometimes we believe that when a person is not talked about much, that person doesn't mean that much, but not so in the eyesight of God. You may play a greater role than the folk that are mentioned all of the time.

Enoch's life was short compared to the lives of others that lived in his day. Genesis 5:5 tells us that Adam lived 930 years before he died. Seth lived 912 years before he died. Enos was 905 years old when he died. Jared lived 962 years before he died. Methuselah, Enoch's son, lived to be 969 years old. The Bible says in Genesis 5:21 that Enoch was sixty five years old when Methuselah was born. And after he begat Methuselah he walked with God. He then lived three hundred years and begat sons and daughters. And he walked with God. You would think that the text would conclude by saying, "And he died," as with others. Instead, it says, "And he was not, for God took him." He is only 365 years old compared to 969 years. Sometimes we value a person's life and success based upon the length of their life. We think that because a person lives to be a certain age that they're doing everything right. It could be just the opposite. You could be doing everything wrong and God keeps giving you another chance to get it right.

Hidden Treasure

Genesis 5:24
And Enoch walked with God: and he was no;, for God took him.

I discovered it really does not matter how long one lives; the important thing is what you do while you are living. Your life should be a role model, an example for others to follow and to pattern after. Every person needs at least three people in his or her life. First of all, they need a Paul – a person that's been where they are trying to go. Secondly, they need a Barnabas – a person that when you're wrong will be honest with you and try to get you back on the right track. They will help us to see our blunders. Thirdly, they need a Timothy – a person that's coming on behind them, that's watching you and wants to be like you. All of us, if we're honest with ourselves, need a role model that we can follow. So here is Enoch. Even though not much is said about Enoch, he's a character that all of us should take notice of.

Enoch was a very unusual, mystifying character and person in that for some mysterious reason he did not see death. Death is always a frightening factor for most of us. We have difficulties handling death. Also, whatever we have accumulated must be left behind. It behooves us to get ourselves together, knowing that we will have to leave here. But for some mysterious reason, Enoch did not see death. He was able to get to heaven without dying.

One of the authors of one of the great dictionaries happened to become a millionaire because he found several million dollars in an old abandoned house. As the outside walls began to deteriorate, the inside treasure began to expose itself. Money was hidden in the walls; when the outside started falling apart the treasure showed up. There's a treasure in every one of us. But it is hidden with walls of flesh. Once the walls of flesh deteriorate, then the hidden treasure shows up. Enoch was a man of hidden treasure.

The Real Team

Amos 3:3
Can two walk together, except they be agreed?

The text keeps repeating the phrase, he walked with God so that must be the number one key to why Enoch did not have to face death. But how can a finite walk with infinite? How can dust be in harmony with divinity? How can a human walk with a divine? How can a man that's measured with time walk with a person that's measured with eternity? How can a person that has a box number or an address walk with a person that's from everlasting to everlasting? How can that take place? Well, I've discovered that there are several ways that I can walk with God. Amos 3:3 says if two are going to walk together they must agree. So if I'm going to walk with God I must be on his side. Instead of trying to get him to get on my side, I need to be on His side. Too many times we ask the Lord to be on our side. But if you'll notice, we change so much. You see us today and we're happy go lucky. Tomorrow, we bite your head off. We speak one day, don't speak the next day. We are up today, down tomorrow. We are going this way today, but tomorrow we are going in another direction.

It's difficult for God to be on our side, since we change so much. We ought to be on his side, because Malachi 3:6 says, I am the Lord God, I change not. Hebrew 13:8 said, Jesus Christ the same yesterday and today and forever. He doesn't change the way I change so I need to move to His side. Another reason I need to move to his side is because he's older and wiser than I am. There's a birthday assigned to me but not one assigned to God. For Genesis 1:1 says, In the beginning God. When the beginning first began its beginning, God was already here. God had no beginning nor does He have an ending. He is omnipotent; He is omniscient; He is omnipresent. He knows everything; He sees everything. He's everywhere at the same time. And with that kind of a God I need to get on His team!

140

Walking In Fellowship

1 John 1:6

If we say that we have fellowship with him, and walk in darkness, we lie, and do not the truth.

Walking with God means being in fellowship with Him. Now when I'm having fellowship with God that means I'm holy like God is holy. God calls upon us to be holy and to live holy lives. I beseech you therefore brethren by the mercies of God that you present your body a living sacrifice, holy, acceptable unto God. Without holiness no man can see God. He gave us the necessary means to be holy. Through Jesus, my sins are forgiven. The Holy Spirit dwells within me, and guardian angels are around me. Consequently, I ought to be able to live a life that will be pleasing in the sight of God.

Walking with God also means exercise. Whenever you walk you exercise. Many of us need to do a little more walking in the spiritual realm. Here again, the Bible tells us how to exercise the members of our bodies, so we can be pleasing in the sight of God. With my eyes I take Psalms 121:1 and lift them toward the hills from whence cometh my help, my help comes from the Lord. With my ears I take Matthew 11:15 He that has ears to hear, let him hear. With my mind I take Philippians 2:5 Let this mind be in you which was also in Christ Jesus. With my mouth and heart I take Romans 10:10 For with the heart man believeth unto righteousness and with the mouth confession is made unto salvation. With my hands I take Ecclesiastes 9:10 Whatsoever thy hand find to do, do it with thy might for there is no work, nor device, nor wisdom, nor knowledge in the grave where thou goest. With my knees I take Philippians 2:10 At the name of Jesus every knee should bow and every tongue should confess. And with my feet I take Hebrews 12:2 Laying aside every weight and sin which does so easily beset us and let us run with patience the race that is set before us. Do your spiritual exercises.

Beneficial Motivation

Genesis 5:21

And Enoch lived sixty and five years, and begat Methuselah. And Enoch walked with God after he begat Methuselah three hundred years, and begat sons and daughters.

What was it that motivated Enoch to walk with God? All of us need motivations. When you're motivated right, you can do a lot of things you never dreamed you could do. You can accomplish goals you thought were impossible. The first thing that motivated Enoch to walk with God was family. And say what you will, family will motivate you to walk with God. If you don't walk with Him before you get a family, Lord knows you need to walk with Him after you get one. A lot of our prayers are centered around family. If you've got a good husband or wife you're constantly praying to the Lord saying, "Thank you for my spouse." If you got one ain't so good, you say, "Lord straighten him up. If he really ain't too good at all, you say, "Lord help me to keep me from killing him." You are constantly praying for your family. If you've got good children, you thank God for them everyday. If your children ain't so good, you be asking God to help you handle the situation at your house. As parents age, we pray for them. Every family needs to have a straight line to God. It just makes good sense to be close to the Lord as a family because research shows that a family that prays together will stay together.

When you walk with God you will be leaving some folk behind. If you aren't going with me, don't hinder me because I'm on my way somewhere and I've got a certain time to get there and I can't have extra baggage holding me back while I'm on my way to heaven. I'm going to the place where the streets are paved with gold and where the walls are jasper. Everybody that associates with you isn't going to that place. So you ought not allow them to hinder you from going. Don't let folk take away your motivation.

Longsuffering With A Purpose

Genesis 5:27

And all the days of Methuselah were nine hundred sixty and nine years: and he died.

Each one of us is here for a purpose. You may not yet know what your purpose in life is. You're wandering around now like a wild goose. You say, "Well I don't know about me because I was an accident; my momma and daddy wasn't aiming to have me." Most of them weren't aiming to have us, but we got here anyway because it really wasn't up to momma and daddy. God had a hand in this just as with Methuselah.

The name Methuselah means, 'when he is gone, it will be sent.' What a strange name to name your little child. Amos 3:7 tells us that there is nothing revealed under the sun that God does not reveal to his servant the prophet. And Jude 14 says that Enoch was a prophet. God talked to Enoch one day, and said, "Look I'm going to destroy the world. When Methuselah is gone, it will come." However, Methuselah lived a long time. When Methuselah was 187 years old, Lamech was born. Lamech was 182 years old when his son, Noah, was born. That's 369 years. Noah was 600 years old when the flood came just after Methusalah's death. But he didn't live 969 years just to live. His life span demonstrated the lo-o-o-ng-suffering of God. What his life really fulfilled was 2 Peter 3:9 which says, The Lord is not slack concerning his promise as some men count slackness, but is long-suffering to us, not willing that any should perish, but that all should come to repentance.

The reason the Lord hadn't come back yet is because He is waiting to get more folks saved. That's the only reason he hasn't come back. The world is ready. God is ready to wipe us off the map right now, but he's still waiting on some more folk to come to know Him. And you can say what you will or may. He will come back. Just as with Methuselah, He will keep His promise.

Firm Foundational Faith

Hebrews 11:5
By faith Enoch was translated that he should not see death; and was not found, because God had translated him: for before his translation he had this testimony, that he pleased God.

Enoch was motivated by faith. Hebrews 11:6 says it is impossible to please God without faith. You can feed all the hungry folk you want, but if you don't have faith, God is not pleased. When you don't live by faith, you're living by sight. And sight will mess you up. Sight will wonder what tomorrow is going to bring. But faith will rejoice in tomorrow's victory. Sight starts looking for food, whereas faith give thanks before it show up. What is faith? You may have faith in an old car, but you don't even know the folk that made it. You get in it. You've already scheduled your appointment at 10:15 and you leave the house at 10:05 because faith tells you that you can get there in 10 minutes. We have faith in everything except God. And all the stuff that you do have faith in will sooner or later fail on you. Cars can explode. But I've never known God to back up on us. This God is a God you ought to have faith in because when he tells you something, you can trust it.

You don't know how scared I was at the age of twenty-two when the Lord called me to preach. I joked and played for three years trying to get out of it. And at age twenty-five, I couldn't take it any longer. I just surrendered, Lord here I am. Growing up in the country, I didn't even like Memphis. But when the Lord called me, within three months he sent me to New Salem. He sent me here with thirty-five folk and eighteen of them were deacons – mean and lowdown deacons! And here I am, twenty-five years of age, straight from the country. I said, "I don't know how I'm gonna be able to do this." But that still small voice said, "I called you and I wouldn't send you if I wasn't gonnna be with ya." And thirty plus years later, I'm able to say that when you trust in Him, He will keep his word. Faith!

A Prophet Was Not

Jude 1:14

And Enoch also, the seventh from Adam, prophesied of these, saying, Behold, the Lord cometh with ten thousands of his saints to execute judgment upon them all...

Enoch spent time with God. God shared things with Enoch – things of the future. Having a relationship like that and having the call of a prophet requires spending time alone with God. You see sometimes we'll walk a while and then quit a while. We'll start a while and sit down a while when things begin to get rough. But keep on walking. The Bible says that Enoch walked with God three hundred years. I like that because he had endurance.

The Bible says that he was not. What does this mean? What the Bible is really saying is that when Enoch disappeared, somebody went looking for him and they could not find him. Please allow my imagination to help explain. When he didn't show up for church, some of the deacons went down and said, "Methuselah, your daddy didn't come to church today. It ain't like him to miss church. Where is he?" Methuselah answered, "The last time I saw daddy, he was out yonder walking with God." They went and found his grandson, Noah. "Say Noah, we've been looking for several days, trying to find Enoch. Can you tell me where he is?" Noah said, "Well, the last time I saw my great granddaddy, he was out walking with God."

And you know, when you're doing something you enjoy doing, doesn't time just fly? You start off early in the morning, but when you look up, the sun is going down. If you want your day to pass well, get up in the morning and start a walk with God. Get up early and start having conversation with God. Have you ever tried walking with him? Isn't it a sweet journey? One of these days, you're going to pull up to my address and ring the doorbell and I won't be able to answer. But don't you get upset if I don't come to the door; I've just moved to another place.

No Where To Hide

Genesis 3:7
And the eyes of them both were opened, and they knew that they were naked;
and they sewed fig leaves together, and made themselves aprons.

Picture in your mind that you've just gone to a movie theater. You've found your seat, and you have your popcorn in one hand and your drink in the other. It is a love scene with a man and a woman just leaving their wedding. They did not have normal bridesmaids or best men. The bridesmaids were cows, sheep, and camels. The best man was a lion, a tiger. Such was the scene of Adam and Eve. In the early stage of their marriage they had the fellowship of God. They looked forward to God visiting with them every evening. He would sit and talk and share with Adam and Eve.

But one day Eve decided to have dialogue with the devil. It was down hill from there on. This was a shaky moment in their marriage because instead of coming to church, they started hiding. They made fig leaves and covered themselves. The Bible says they left God's presence, meaning they quit church. It is amazing how when you get weighted down with sin, the first thing you do is to quit church. Church has not done anything to you; you just can't feel the spirit. And so you blame the church.

I thank God that even when you do him wrong, He will come after you. I like it because he doesn't come with an eye of envy; he comes with a heart of compassion. Adam and Eve were on the run. But God tracked them down. It is so dangerous to be on the run from God. The Psalmist asked one day if you are running where can you hide? If you make your bed in hell, He's there. He says even if you take the wings of the morning and fly to the uttermost parts of the world, when you get there, He's already there. He's everywhere at the same time. And when God caught up with him, he asked a question, "Adam where art thou?"

Do You Know Where You Are?

Genesis 3:9
And the Lord God called unto Adam, and said unto him, Where art thou?

I was puzzled when I first read that because we all are aware that God knows everything. And so I called God and asked Him about this. He explained to me that He knew exactly where Adam was, but it was Adam who didn't know where Adam was. Many times we think we know where we are, but we're going so far out in left field. When you measure yourself by yourself, you'll give yourself a grade too high. If you are the only one in the mirror looking at you, you'll always be beautiful. Let someone else critique you once in a while. You might have some areas you need to straighten up and particles to clean off. When you grade your own paper, you could easily give yourself too high a score.

God said to Adam, "you're on the wrong side. You've become my enemy now and you have covered yourself with fig leaves and you have made yourself aprons." However, an apron covers only the front end. And God could be coming from any direction. So God preached the first gospel message ever by symbolizing, by precept and example because the Bible says he took coats of skin and covered their nakedness. That may not say much to you, but when you dissect it and let the Holy Ghost breathe on it, it says a lot. They had already been covered by the fig leaves they were wearing. But God said, "What you did for you, won't work." You see you can not save yourself by your own righteousness. It's going to take more than you to get you out of the mess you are in. You can scheme; you can connive; you can read; you can study; you can go to counseling sessions; you can go to rehab, but you can not clean yourself up. It takes somebody greater than you to get the job done. So God said that dressing yourself won't do. I will have to put the right clothes on you.

Parents Are Priests

1 Timothy 2:14
And Adam was not deceived, but the woman being deceived was in the transgression.

I believe that Adam was the priest in his house and that he took time alone with Eve to take care of their two boys. I admire Adam and Eve for doing a good job in taking care of their children. I know that she had great expectations for Cain because of the name she gave Cain. The name Cain means, "gotten from the Lord." She really expected Cain to be the promised Messiah. Thank God for that. Every parent should have high expectations for their child. As a parent, you should do everything in your power to make your child as great as you possibly can. I thank God for day care centers and baby sitters, but nobody can raise your child like you. You may need to back up on some things, maybe get a house a little smaller and car just a little smaller in order to spend a more time with your child. Nobody is going to love your child like you or discipline your child like you. But when you see them only at bedtime and early in the morning, you don't know what you're raising. You should spend time with the child.

Even before the baby is born, you should discipline your own body. Be careful how you curse while you're carrying the baby, because the baby inside you is picking up your spirit. If you've been drinking, lay down your bottle. If you've been smoking, put up your cigarettes. Father or mother, if you're on dope, leave it alone. God has invested within you a treasure. He has put in you a diamond and it is up to you to get that diamond where God would have the diamond to be. If you're not ready and you've got a baby, memorize the 23rd Psalm. Let them know that the Lord is my shepherd and I shall not want. Get with the Lord and get with the church. Others can help, but you are the primary caretaker of the child's life. Learn to depend on the Lord and be the priest of your own family.

Perseverance Produces Prosperity

Proverbs 22:6
Train up a child in the way he should go: and when he is old, he will not depart from it.

There was a sister who shouted in church all the time; when the scripture was read, she'd shout; during prayer, singing, and preaching she would shout. Two sisters saw this lady out in the mall and decided to tell her to stop keeping up all that noise in church. So they eased up to her and said, "Excuse me, say I think we go to church with you; aren't you the lady that shouts all the time? Why do you shout so much?" She said, Well I do get pretty emotional. It's a long story. I had a good husband and I thanked God for him; he was a great provider; he loved the children and me. But one night he went to bed and didn't wake up. And we didn't have any insurance on him and we didn't have any money saved up and I had no trade myself. When he died I had five little boys that I had to struggle and raise by myself. I had to take jobs I didn't want, scrubbing floors and washing windows."

But let me tell you about my boys. All of them went to school. My oldest boy is a doctor; the one under him is an attorney; my third boy is an engineer; my fourth boy is an accountant; my fifth boy was just elected to public office. I thank God for my five boys. They all got together and built and furnished a nice house for their momma. And you see the little car sitting right in front of this store? My boys got that for their momma. My boys take turns each week buying groceries for me. Now you ladies know why I shout so much. I've got so much to thank God for! It is good to train your children to know love and a disciplined life.

Be careful how you look under eyed at people because you don't know where they've been or what they had to go through. You don't know how long it took them to get to where they are. Oh, don't bother anybody if you see them shouting; you should try to join them.

A Set Time For Worship

Genesis 4:3
And in process of time it came to pass, that Cain brought of the fruit of the ground an offering unto the Lord.

Adam and Eve brought forth a child and called his name Cain, which means gotten of the Lord. And then she brought forth another and called his name Abel, which means vanity or waste. She believed that Cain was going to be the right one and Abel was going to be the loose one. You must be careful when you start trying to judge which child is going to be the right one, because you will miss it most of the time since God is the one in charge. The one you think is a troubled child now may just be going through stuff. They'll get through it after a while; some children learn some sense at twelve or thirteen and others don't get it until forty. So don't give up on your child. If he acts a little silly and strange now, just keep on bowing. Let them see you praising and magnifying the Lord. Train your children that church is a priority. If they are living under your roof, they should not be given a choice about church attendance. And hanging outside during worship is not acceptable. After church, don't rush out ahead of the crowd in a big hurry to do something else.

Cain and Abel were trained to honor worship. The word worship actually means to drop prostrate on the ground; kiss the ground. In the New Testament the word worship means to kiss the hand. When you come to worship you discover whom it is you're worshipping. Cain and Abel had a set time that they came to worship. The Bible says, in the process of time they came to worship. All of us should have a time for worship. We know that Satan and society are trying hard to interfere with our time of worship. Super bowl comes on Sunday. Graduation is on Sunday – anything to rob you. Or they'll advertise enough junk for you to buy so that you end up working when you should be worshipping. Set aside your worship time.

Timely Worship

Genesis 4:3
And in process of time it came to pass, that Cain brought of the fruit of the ground an offering unto the Lord.

God did something different for each of you. So you can't worship just like the person next to you. That person might have gone all the week and didn't even stump their toe. But you're sitting right there and just had a massive heart attack and the Lord brought you through. You can't sit there like the person God hasn't done anything for. The person in front of you may have been living foot loose and fancy free, never had a worry in the world and you just came through a divorce and you've still got your right mind. Your son is getting ready to go to court and your daughter is getting ready to do time. You can't sit like a person that has never had anything happen. Because you can say to yourself, I need my God; He's a mind regulator.

So don't try to worship like somebody else. You see somebody else saying Amen and you say Amen; or somebody else waving their hands, so you say it's a good time to wave mine. If no one else says a word, but you want to see a child that's blessed, just look at me. I don't care if nobody says a word or they don't wave their hands; it will not bother me. No one is going to take my joy from me. I know what God has done for me. God watches how you worship. God doesn't just look at you coming in with pretty hats, pretty dresses and see how you sit and how you act and see if you say Amen every once in a while; he is interested in your worship.

You may not know that you have a baby in you called the soul. And if you're not careful, you can smother your soul with junk all around you like the lady who laid her baby on the bed during a party while her friends came with their minks and furs, piling them on the bed, smothering the baby to death. Don't let your possessions or busy life interfere with your worship.

No Sanction, No Action

Genesis 4:4
*And Abel, he also brought of the firstlings of his flock and of the fat thereof.
And the Lord had respect unto Abel and to his offering.*

Cain brought an offering to the Lord and Abel also brought an offering to the Lord. Both Cain and Abel were church people. They both came to worship. They had been trained that when you show up at church, give something. They both gave, but one gave what God asked for. The other gave what he wanted to give. If God can give us instructions on raising children; if God can give us instructions on marriage; if God can give us instructions on salvation; he can also give us instructions on how to give. After all, he knows us. He knows what's best for us.

Cain gave of the fruit of the ground. What was wrong with that? Evidently something wrong with it because God rejected his offering. I think what really happened is that when they came to make their presentations to the Lord, they had some place set aside where they would put the offering. And when they would leave, God would respond by burning it. That fire would come down to indicate that He had accepted the gift. And if he didn't accept the gift, He would leave it alone. Cain built his little spot there and put his corn, cabbage, peaches, pears, and plums on the altar. Abel came with his first lamb; he laid him on the altar. Then they waited for the Lord.

When they backed up, fire came and burned up Abel's gift. However, it didn't touch Cain's offering. The Bible says that God rejected Cain and his offering, but he accepted Abel's offering. Now it looks like God is partial there. But you see if God doesn't accept what you want to give him, there's no need of you giving it. There's no need in trying to pacify God by saying, "I know what you want, Lord, but I don't want to give that." I'm going to give him what I want to give him. No, God requires obedience.

A Furious Face

Genesis 4:5
But unto Cain and to his offering he had not respect. And Cain was very wroth, and his countenance fell.

Hebrews 11:4 says that by faith Abel offered unto God a more excellent sacrifice than Cain, by which he obtained witness that he was righteous. God testifying of his gifts and by it he being dead yet speaketh. He said that when Abel gave his gift, it was a testimony of his righteousness. Oh my goodness. In other words Abel was saying, "Look I know who I am. I know I am a sinner and I deserve death and destruction. And so what I'm going to do is give God what he asked for and when I do that, then God will impute his righteousness upon me."

In 1 John 3:12 the Bible says Not as Cain who was of that wicked one and slew his brother and wherefore slew he him because his own works were evil and his brother's righteous. When you don't respond in your giving like God requested it, the Bible calls you evil.

Then Lord asked Cain, Why are you wroth and why is your countenance fallen?" You see when you are reminded of your wrongness, it's hard to keep a straight face. When you've been getting away with something or getting by with it and then the word exposes you, it's not easy anymore. Look Cain, your whole expression has changed. You're not smiling anymore; you have a semi frown on your face. If thou doeth well, shalt thou not be accepted? In other words, you brought it on yourself by not following instructions. God says, "I'm a just God. I'm a righteous God. I know what to do. I know how to do it." But watch what God says next: "and if thou doeth not well, sin lieth at the door." In the Hebrew language, the word lieth, means crouch. It is like an animal, a lion, or a tiger sitting right in your front door bending, waiting for you to come out so he can attack you. The text is saying if you're not doing well, sin is right outside your door waiting to attack you.

God's Rejection List

Genesis 4:8
And Cain talked with Abel his brother: and it came to pass, when they were in the field, that Cain rose up against Abel his brother, and slew him

Cain talked with Abel his brother. The thing about sin, especially when you mistreat God, is that you start falling out with God's people. As long as you're doing what you're supposed to do, it doesn't matter what anybody says or does around you. You can handle it fine. They can lie on you, well that's all right. They can mistreat you. But when you get caught up in sin, you can't stand anything, not even the truth, and you sure can't stand other people that God has blessed. YOU GET REAL UPSET WITH PEOPLE who God keeps on blessing.

Now I don't know what Cain talked to Abel about but I can guess he might have said, "Look, you're the second child and I'm really supposed to be the one blessed rather than you. I don't know what kind of things you did to get God to bless you and not me, but you won't get away with it, Abel. When people get upset with you, they always have a lot to talk about. Not only did he talk with him, but he killed Abel, his own brother. "Lord have mercy." Old people used to say if a child will lie, they will steal; and if they steal, they will kill. Cain killed his own brother. He went walking around as though nothing had happened. Don't you know your sin will find you out? Cain thought he had quieted Abel down. He thought, "I won't be having anymore trouble out of him. Now I can get what would have been his."

I'm really trying to convince us that you don't want to be on God's Rejection List. I can tell you what will happen. You will be in line for a promotion and they'll cut it off right before they get to you. Every time you turn around something will go wrong. Your roof will fall in; your credit card interest will increase. Get on the good list!

Buried But Not Hidden

Genesis 4:10
And he said, What hast thou done? the voice of thy brother's blood crieth unto me from the ground.

Cain stopped Abel's mouth but he couldn't quiet his blood down, because his blood started crying from the ground. Psalm 116:15 says, Precious in the sight of God is the death of his saints. Every time a saint dies, the Lord is there. He said, "Cain I heard your brother's blood crying from the ground. Not only will you be cursed, but also the ground you travel on is going to be cursed." It's hard for you to grow prosperous on ground that's already cursed. You can be accepted in the house and have a rejected living with you, and a curse will be hanging over your house. Every time you think you're going to make it, something else will happen to pull you right back down.

And then the Lord said, "Cain, I'm going to put a mark on you so every where you go people will stay away from you. Can't you see Cain coming to some church asking for an offering so he can be sent out? But somebody noticed the mark on him. I'm sorry Brother Cain; we can't help you here. You see brothers and sisters, when God curses you, man can't bless you. You thought you could live from hand out to hand out, but when God takes his hands off of you, can't anybody put their hands on you.

Cain had to run the rest of his life because God rejected him. Have you ever been rejected by God's will? If so, you should straighten it up today. Don't try to live in God's world out of God's will. When you fail to support God in the ministry of giving, you are causing a lot of people to miss the gospel. He wants his gospel to spread across the world. While you have alligators, some soul that could be saved will never hear the gospel. However, when you are in his will, whatever your needs are, He will supply. If you will recognize who he is, He wants to bless you. After Abel died, he kept on talking through his life.

Hand Over Your Load

Matthew 11:30
For my yoke is easy, and my burden is light.

One would think that once you accept Christ as your personal Savior, you would be exempt from burdens, stress, trials, heartaches and disappointments. But it seems that the burdens continue to show up. Many times Satan does his best to discourage us from living a life that will be pleasing in the sight of God. But the Lord never told us that we would not have problems. He never told us that difficult days would not come or that we wouldn't have burdens. He did say, "My yoke is easy and my burden is light."

One of the crises we face as believers in Christ is that when these things come we really don't know how to handle it. We don't mean to be depressed, to quit, to back up, to slow down, or to weep and cry and moan. However, it is the human part of us. We ask the questions, "Why?" and "What do I do next?" I am trying to go by the book. I read my Bible every morning; I talk to God at night before I go to bed; I take care of my obligations; I come to church on a regular basis; I even visit the sick and help people when I can. Why is it that my load is so heavy? What am I doing wrong? Where am I going wrong? What mistakes am I making? I believe God loves me, but when I call, he seems to take so long to come. There seems to be a void. I seem to have to bear this heavy load by myself.

If you are in this predicament I need to tell you that you are not alone. There are others bearing loads that are heavier than yours. When the load gets heavy, just ask for strength and keep on toiling. Don't be like the man walking down the road with his pack on and was offered a ride on a wagon passing by. He jumped on, keeping the pack on his back. The driver asked, "Sir, why are you not resting your sack?" He said, "Well, sir, it's enough for you to carry me. I don't want you to have to carry my load also." The driver said, "The wagon handles it the same, on or off your back."

Chillin' Out

Psalm 23:2
He maketh me to lie down in green pastures...

The Lord refers to His people as sheep. Sheep are a different kind of creature than any other animal on earth. Other animals can be trained and trained well, but not sheep. You can train dogs or cats to jump through hoops and leap; you can train snakes; you can train elephants and lions; but it is difficult to train a sheep. As a matter of fact, you can take your dog or cat on a trip and let him out a hundred miles away; if you have stopped a few times and let him out, he can make his way home. But you can get a sheep and he will wander in the back yard and won't have enough sense to come back to the front. The sheep is a dumb creature. And yet the Bible calls us sheep. Ye are my people, the sheep of my pasture.

God makes us, as sheep, to lie down. A sheep will not lie down if it is frightened. Fear is a terrible emotion. Fear keeps us from resting. Many of us have a lot of fear in the back of our minds. Old folk are afraid that time is running out; young people are afraid that too much is confronting them while they are young without having life experience to handle those things. Some people won't go to the doctor for fear he will detect something and they don't want to know about it. Sick folk are afraid there is not a medicine to heal them of their disease. Married folk are afraid they may find out their spouse is unfaithful. Single people are afraid they may not get a spouse. Parents are afraid the child might mess up. Children are afraid that parents may not understand them when they do mess up.

So fear is in the minds of a whole lot of people, but the Lord wants you to know that he knows how to handle your fears. The green pastures spoken of here refer to safe areas with little huts for the shepherds and pens and food for the sheep. God takes your fears away and makes you cozy and comfortable in a beautiful green pasture.

What's Bugging You?

Ezekiel 34:14
I will feed them in a good pasture...

A sheep will not lie down if there is friction in the fold, if he cannot get along with other sheep. The same thing happens in the body of Christ. It's difficult for you to rest when somebody is upset with you or you're upset with somebody else in the body. In John 13:35 Jesus says, "By this shall all men know that ye are my disciples, if ye have love one to another." That is the Christian's identification card – that you have godly love for each other. It is important to eliminate the friction between us. If you are upset with somebody, settle it before sundown. Don't go around with grudges and hold them week after week, month after month because you are the one that is damaged. The person you are mad at may not even know it and if they do they often don't really care. Even your giving is no good if you are upset with your brother. It is more important to God that we have harmony. Division will affect our rest.

Moreover, a sheep will not lie down if he has problems with flies, fleas, and parasites. These small creatures got in the nose and ears and laid eggs that turned into worms, bugging the sheep and making it miserable. If you have something bugging you, you can't sleep. Little things will keep you awake, a problem on the job you can't solve or a little problem with a friend. When stuff starts bugging, you begin to have problems with the folk around you. You can't talk to people about your problem because you don't want them to go and tell everyone. You feel cut off.

There may be problems with parasites, little blood suckers similar to some people you may know. A parasite is a person who won't work. He has no car of his own, but is always driving someone else's vehicle, eats other's food, wears their clothes, stays in their house. The Lord wants us to be free of flies and fleas so that we can freely rest.

Chew On It

Psalm 23:3

He restoreth my soul.

The green pasture is the Word of God and the still water is the Spirit of God. When you have the Word and the Spirit, you have everything you need. You are talking about a real good diet when you have the Word. The Word promises rest to those that wait upon the Lord. They shall renew their strength. Job's load got heavy. But he said, "Though God slay me, yet will I trust him. I'm going to wait until my change comes." Don't complain when you find yourself in green pastures beside still waters. Grass has all the proteins, minerals, and vitamins a sheep needs to be his best. And the Word has all the spiritual proteins, vitamins and nourishment for strength to fight the battle.

A sheep has two stomachs. When he eats, the food passes to the first stomach, then to the second stomach. After the sheep lies down, the food comes back to stomach number one and that is when the sheep really enjoys his food. He is able to lie there and chew on it and digest it properly. This is the way with the Word of God. Sunday morning is not long enough to really digest the Word. You need to find some time during the week to get by yourself and let it regurgitate and come back up and let the Word speak to you as an individual.

The shepherd has His eye on you. He knows if you are fatigued and when you need some quiet time alone. Often we work too much; we watch too much television; we look at too many games. Sometimes people are just downright too busy for God to speak to them. But all of the great Sons were born out of quiet time. Poets wrote great poems when they were quiet. Sometimes you need to isolate yourself and let God speak to you. Say, "Speak Lord for your servant is listening." Let the Lord restore your soul. Don't allow too many jobs and too many possessions rob you of your time alone with God.

Fruitful, Fragrant Oil

Psalm 23:5

Thou preparest a table before me in the presence of mine enemies: thou anointest my head with oil; my cup runneth over.

We do have enemies. But enemies can not defeat you if the Lord is your shepherd. Enemies lose their strong hold when the shepherd is available to supply your needs. Recently, I looked at this shepherd matter in John 10:11, I am the good shepherd. I give my life for my sheep. John 10:9 I am the door. John 10:7 I am the door of the sheepfold. I asked the Lord, "Are you the shepherd, the door or are you the door of the sheepfold?" He said, "I am all of it. What I do is I gather my sheep and I bring them into the sheepfold. Once I get them on the inside I lay down at the door and I then become the door, which means the enemy can not come in without coming in by me and the sheep can not get out without going out by me." What a swell job my shepherd is doing with his sheep.

But I was interested in knowing why would he make such a statement as Thou anointest my head with oil. This is a compassionate aspect of the character of the shepherd. Think about it now. Here he is, as busy as can be, yet he takes time to lay his hand on my head. How special that God is in the business of touching his children. It is a compassionate touch to the extent that with this anointing he supplies my every need.

Go with me for a few moments to Palestine to the Bible land to discover what the shepherd or David was actually saying when he said he anointed my head with oil. He would put oil mixed with sulfur and spices into the sheep's nose and on their eyes and heads so the flies would no longer hang around. You can't do your job right being bugged. You can't live a comfortable, decent, thought provoking life being bugged. He has already anointed you and the anointing that's on you should be bug-resistant. He wants you to be happy, comfortable, productive sheep.

An Anointed Mind

Psalm 23:5
...thou anointest my head with oil; my cup runneth over.

The Hebrew word for anointed here means be greasy. I heard that Skin-So-Soft now has something that you can let your dog swallow. It gets on the inside and produces some type of odor that comes out through the body that keeps flies, ticks and fleas off of you. I understand that just a few days ago someone had an accident and was killed because some bug got in the car. I have seen folk spill a glass of water trying to hit at a bug, turn over plates and pots. You will destroy something that is important fooling around with a bug. If you take your eyes off the target and focus on bug situations, it can get the best of you. In the Old Testament that oil signifies the Holy Ghost. There is something about the Holy Ghost that will keep you content when bugs are all around you trying to take your eyes off the prize. There is a certain amount of spiritual grease placed in your life to soothe and keep you.

Bugs also caused sheep to have scalp problems; sores and boils would break out on the sheep's head. It was contagious. When the sheep would butt heads with each other, they would pick up this scalp disease. This same disease is here today and we get it by butting heads. You know, mind-to-mind talk, minds meeting minds, listening to talk shows. We should be very careful when we allow minds to meet with our minds when the person doesn't know Jesus. A person unsaved should not advise you on how you should be living your life. They are living life based upon what they see. We are living our lives based upon who's living in us. We move by faith, not by sight. We want to be careful who we open our minds to. So the shepherd, "anointed my head with oil" because the problem started with the head. Most of our problems start in the head. Some folk will miss Heaven 18 inches because they have not accepted Christ from the neck up.

Anointed For A Purpose

Exodus 29:7

Then shalt thou take the anointing oil, and pour it upon his head, and anoint him.

Another problem occurs with sheep during mating season. As long as it is not mating time, they all get along fine. But as soon as mating time comes around the male sheep begin fighting. They start butting heads with each other. All during the night you will hear them hitting one another. They are trying to fight for the champion, the boss in the spot. Sometimes they even kill each other over the female sheep. So how does the shepherd handle that?

The shepherd goes out and does the same as fighters do. Fighters are intentionally all greasy when they get in the ring. They put heavy grease on their body so when the opponent hits them the blow will slide off. That's the way the shepherd does the sheep. He takes the sheep and anoints his head with axle grease all over so when he butts the other sheep's head, it will slide off. After they butt each other two or three times and can't get a good hold, they see they have done no damage and they just stop fighting altogether. He anointed my head with oil to protect me.

What all does it mean when he says he anointed my head with oil? One purpose for the anointing is separation. If I have been anointed, I have been separated from the world. You want to be careful when folk call you regular, because when they say you are a regular person, you are just like everybody else. But you are not regular; you are separated. The Bible says, "Be ye separated. Come ye out from among them. Be ye transformed by the renewing of your mind." We have been separated. We have been set apart for a holy use. God doesn't anoint everybody; He anoints only his children. He gives us a special anointing in order to fulfill our purpose in his kingdom. The anointing helps prepare us for the storms of life. The anointing is an indication that we have been accepted by Him.

New Wine Changes You

Ephesians 5:18
And be not drunk with wine, wherein is excess; but be filled with the Spirit.

The Bible compares being filled with the Spirit to being drunk. On the day of Pentecost, those on the outside said, These men are drunk on new wine." Peter replied, "They are not drunk as you suppose but this is that spoken of by the prophet Joel that one day my Father will pour out His Spirit upon all flesh. Let me illustrate the comparison. When I was young, I had an uncle named Bob. Uncle Bob, when he was sober, was stingy. I would go to him and say, "Uncle Bob give me a quarter." "Get away from here. All you do is beg." But then when he came by drunk, he would say "Hello my nephew. How you doing, boy?" He would hand me a dollar and say, "Go and spend it." When he was sober he was cheap, but when he was drunk he was kind. The Holy Ghost affects you that way. When you are not filled with the Holy Ghost you are tight, you don't want to give, or share with anybody. But when you are filled with the Spirit, you will give your last dime to the Lord and for the cause of Christ and go home happy bout it because you are Spirit-filled.

When you are sober, you are so clean. I'm not going to drink out of this. But when you are drunk, two or three people stand around the liquor store passing the bottle. If they clean it off, they will use the back of an old coat and wipe it off. We are scared to get on our knees and pray. When you are filled with the Holy Spirit, not only will you get on your knees, you will wallow on the floor if the Holy Ghost works on you right; you don't care if someone laughs at you or talks about you. We must recognize that the anointing is on the child of God. We have been separated. We have been called out to be a peculiar people, a chosen generation. So if somebody says you are different, you can say, "Thank you." Because you are.

The Earnest Money

John 3:6-7
That which is born of the flesh is flesh; and that which is born of the Spirit is spirit. Marvel not that I said unto thee, Ye must be born again.

When does the Holy Ghost show up in my life? Some folk say He comes after you are saved, down the road after you tarry and wait on Him. He really shows up before you are saved. John 16:8 says that when He has come He will reprove the world. The word reprove can also be translated as convict. So before you are saved, the Holy Ghost brings conviction in your life. You don't come looking for Jesus on your own. You come looking for Jesus because the Holy Ghost has already convicted you that you need a savior in your life. A sinner won't anymore come to church looking for a savior than a criminal will flag down a police officer. But when the Holy Ghost starts working in your life, He convicts you and tells you that you need to be converted. So he begins before you are saved.

Then John 3:6 says, That which is born of the flesh is flesh and that which is born of the Spirit is spirit. To be in Christ you must be born of the Spirit. In 1 Corinthians 12:13 the Bible says, By one spirit are we all baptized into one body. Therefore, joining the church does not make you part of the church; you must be baptized into the family of God by the Holy Ghost. Afterward, we are sealed with that holy Spirit of promise, which is the earnest of our inheritance according to Ephesians 1:13. This earnest money tells me that since I'm saved every time I feel the Holy Ghost, it is a down payment reminding me of a down payment of what I am going to get. So I am convicted on the Spirit; I am converted by the Spirit; I am baptized by the Spirit; I am sealed with the Spirit; and then I am filled with the Spirit. The baptism happens only once, the sealing happens only once, the receiving takes place only once, but the filling is over and over and over again.

The Approval Stamp

Ephesians 1:6
To the praise of the glory of his grace, wherein he hath made us accepted in the beloved.

The anointing tells me that my life is not only a separated life but also it is an accepted life. I have been accepted in the Beloved. What do I mean by that? Let me give an illustration. If I want to speak to the Queen of England, I can't just walk up to the door and announce," I want to see the Queen." Protocol requires me to have an introduction; a qualified person must tell the Queen who I am. As with God, I can't walk up to Him and say, "Look here, I am one of your children." No, I have to be accepted by his Son. It is His Son that carries me to the Father. Jesus said, "You can't get to the Father except you come by me." As a matter of fact, if you want to write the Father a letter you've got to send it to Jesus' address. You've got to talk to the Father in the name of the Son. When He lays his hands on me and anoints me, it means I have been accepted in the Beloved. Thank God! Let me share a story with you.

You remember David early in his life when Samuel planned to anoint someone as king. Samuel went down to Jesse's house. He had all these big boys and they all went under the cup and the oil didn't run. Samuel said, "It must be somebody else in the camp." David's father said he did have one more son, David, but that he was just a child out watching the flock. David was sent for and when he passed under the cup, the oil ran. When the oil ran, it was a symbol that God had anointed him to be king of Israel. When the Holy Ghost fills my life, it is an indication that I have been accepted in the Beloved.

I hear folk say you can be saved and then lost. Have you ever wondered why the Bible never speaks at all about any person who was saved and lost and saved again? I know if I lost my salvation, I would try to get it back. The reason is because you can't lose it to begin with.

A Satisfied Saucer

Psalm 23:5

...my cup runneth over.

In the winter the shepherd has to keep a close watch over the sheep because sometime it gets cold and they will freeze to death. The shepherd brings the sheep. He gets oil and mixes a little wine in the oil. Then he gets the sheep to open his mouth while he pours in the liquid. That gives the sheep enough on the inside to keep him warm, to keep him from freezing to death. In other words, the shepherd prepares the sheep for storms. Well, the anointing prepares us for the storms. Storms will come, saints. I don't care how much sense you have. Every one of us is either in a storm now or just coming out of a storm or you could be on your way to a storm. We know people can get into some predicaments that money can't get pay their way out of. You can get into some predicaments that even your connections can't get save you from. But we know somebody who can get us out of any given situation. The God I serve is a deliverer.

When I was young, my daddy, brought up in the country, had his own ideas about things. Daddy believed that children should not drink coffee. What Daddy would do is fill the cup with coffee and then place the cup into a saucer. When he would fill the cup, sometimes coffee would spill over into the saucer. Even though he would not allow me to drink out of the cup, I could sip coffee out of the saucer. What a spiritual lesson for me later in life.

When I was twenty-two years of age, I was crowned as a deacon of the church. I was one of those deacons that loved his pastor. I would carry his briefcase and drive for him. I was the saucer; my pastor was the cup. Whenever his cup would get full, I would get some of the spillover. That means God did not just give me what I needed. He gave me more than I had room to store. He anointed my head with oil. My cup is running over.

Too Anointed To Be Disappointed

Romans 15:13

Now the God of hope fill you with all joy and peace in believing, that ye may abound in hope, through the power of the Holy Ghost.

He won't only give you joy, but he will give you joy unspeakable. He won't just give you love, he will give you more love than you can store. If you know somebody that has more than you think they need, don't become jealous of them, but get under them. Rub shoulders with them. Hang out with them and tell them, "Go on child." Keep on letting the Lord bless you and keep hanging out with them. After a while, a few drops will fall your way. Before you know it, your cup will become full, also. Even more importantly, stay close to the spiritual cup.

When I was a deacon, what if I had backed off my pastor and decided I didn't want to be his saucer. Let me tell you where I would be. I would be out there somewhere picking cotton, plowing behind Mike and Jim, still mad because he was getting all of the blessings. But I got under him. Every time I got on my knees, I said, "Now Lord, you can't see me, but you can see him. Fill his cup every Sunday morning and every Sunday night. Fill his cup." I even stopped asking the Lord for anything for myself; just fill his cup. Hallelujah! One Sunday morning, the second Sunday in September 1971, I heard God say, "You have been a saucer long enough. I am going to make a cup out of you. Now, saucers are all around me. So all you do is just tell the Lord to keep on filling the cup and keep getting close because God is still in the cup-making business. Is he all right? I know he is all right. Ain't nothing wrong with being a saucer because when God shows up, He will give you more than you've got room to hold. That's why I'm too anointed to get disappointed. When one says something bad, someone else will say something good. I may not have everything I want, but I have more than I need.

A Cure For A Troubled Heart

John 14:1-3

Let not your heart be troubled: ye believe in God, believe also in me. In my Father's house are many mansions: if it were not so, I would have told you. I go to prepare a place for you. And if I go and prepare a place for you, I will come again, and receive you unto myself; that where I am, there ye may be also.

This passage seems to touch all. This passage has visited more hospitals, sojourned at more funeral homes, stood by more graveyards and gone by more homes than any one passage in the Bible. It seems to give you strength in the hour of weakness. It is like going to the Atlantic Ocean; once you dip, you have hardly touched the surface. It is like going to a mine getting a teaspoonful of diamonds when there are truckloads that are left. This passage is deep enough for scholars to dive in and never reach the bottom, yet it is shallow enough for babies to swim in and never drown. It works like a pack of handkerchiefs, drying away tears. This passage is like an in-house surgeon, mending broken hearts.

This passage is a head lifter when you walk in certain places with your head down. When other things send you down stream, this passage will help you go upstream. It's a way of lifting heavy burdens. It's a way of giving ease to a trouble mind; there is something in this passage that your medical doctor can't discover. There is a comfort you can receive without money; you can get without price. You can be ignorant or you can be a professor; you can be rich or poor; learned or illiterate, it makes no difference. This passage will work with any person of any race, any creed, or any color; this size fits all. It works when nothing else will work, handling life by itself without anything else. You can take this passage and carry it from time to eternity. What a powerful piece are these three verses. They have great force behind them.

June

Bad News Brings Good News

John 14:18
I will not leave you comfortless: I will come to you.

The scene opens with Jesus and his disciples sitting around a table. They had received bad news. The news was that it was time for Jesus to leave. He had been with them for over three years now, supplying all their needs. If they were hungry, he would get two fish and five loaves of bread and feed everybody that followed him and would reward the servants by giving them an extra basket. If they ran into demons, he could cast them out. If their mother-in-law had fever, he would go to the house and speak a word and fevers would flee. If they ran into a storm he would just awaken out of sleep and walk to the edge of the ship and say, "Peace, be still," bringing about great calm. Whatever their needs were, he could and would supply.

Jesus made the disciples look good because He lifted them up. He made something out of nothing because when Jesus found them they were fishers and farmers and tax collectors and publicans and sinners. He took nobody and made somebody. He lifted me from behind a plow and set me in the pulpit. Jesus gives you sense; he takes the bend out of your back; he puts a smile on your face; he puts joy in your heart; he puts a glow in your eyes; he makes you feel like you something. And then when somebody tries to say you're nothing, he'll shout out, you are a royal priest hood. You are a chosen generation. You are a peculiar people.

Jesus had left his trail every where he went; he would make statements such as, "If the son of man be lifted up, he shall draw all men unto himself." "The time has come when the son of man should be offered into the hands of sinful men, be crucified, die but rise again on the third day." "As a grain of seed falling to the ground it must first die before it can live." Now it was time for Jesus to go, just as He had been telling them. But He left them with hope!

A Foolish Transaction

John 13:21
When Jesus had thus said, he was troubled in spirit, and testified, and said,
Verily, verily, I say unto you, that one of you shall betray me.

Jesus was saying that He had a crook in church. He was letting the disciples know that one of them would betray him. One of them would try to get rid of him. They began asking, "Who is it?" Jesus said "Look at the one with his hand in the dish." Everybody that grins at you doesn't love you. Everybody that holds you doesn't mean you good. Smiling faces tells lies.

It is impossible to understand why Judas would even attempt to sell a man like Jesus, and at that, to sell him so cheaply. How many times do we have a good thing, yet we are unaware of it. Judas had no idea he was going to get sick, but here is a sick man selling his only doctor for thirty pieces of silver. Here Judas was a dying man, selling his dying bed maker for thirty pieces of silver. Here Judas was a hungry man, selling bread in a starving land for thirty pieces of silver. Here Judas was a thirsty man, selling water in the well for thirty pieces of silver. Here Judas was outdoors selling his shelter in the time of a storm for thirty pieces of silver; he sold him too cheaply.

How often we do the same thing, when we walk around with our heads down after we just got through telling somebody how we are a child of God and that our Father is rich in houses and in land. But we act like we haven't got a dime in the world. If your father's rich and you know how to talk to your daddy, He will supply. David said, "I've been young and right now I'm old, but I have never seen the righteous forsaken or their seed begging for bread." I was alone and idle, I was a sinner too, but I heard the voice of Jesus saying, "There is work to do." I took my Master's hand and I joined the Christian band; I'm on the battlefield. Don't sell your Source.

Defeated Disciples

John 14:1
Let not your heart be troubled: ye believe in God, believe also in me.

So the disciples were upset; they were nervous and they were baffled. Jesus looked at them and saw them sitting around him with a hung down head. However, it was Jesus who was on the way to Calvary. There were nails waiting for Jesus' hand. There was a spike waiting for Jesus' side. There was a crown of thorns waiting for the head of Jesus. He was the one that was going to be tortured and beaten and whipped until blood gushed from his back. It looked like somebody should have been encouraging him. But he turned around to his disciples and said, "Let not your heart be troubled."

Now Jesus is concerned with the heart; he deals with the emotions of man. And when your emotions get out of whack, nothing else works right. If your heart starts messing up, your head doesn't think right, your feet don't move right. Your ears don't hear right; hands won't work right. You can have a troubled heart and lie down and sleep won't come. You can have a Rolls Royce in your garage and not feel like driving. You can get on your knees and it seems like you can't get a prayer through. Your friends want to talk to you, but you don't want to talk to anybody. There's no need in anybody trying to say, "Baby, I understand." If they haven't been where you are, they don't understand. If they haven't worn your shoes, they need to stop talking because they don't know what you are going through and the anxiety you feel.

You can go to the doctor and he can't find anything wrong with you. He'll send you back home, but you know you're hurting somewhere. The drug store has remedies for lots of other ailments, but not heart trouble. Only Jesus can cure heart trouble. Only Jesus can bring peace to troubled emotions and an afflicted heart.

Permit His Presence

John 14:27
Peace I leave with you, my peace I give unto you: not as the world giveth, give I unto you. Let not your heart be troubled, neither let it be afraid.

Jesus implied, "Now for you to be helped, you're going to have to meet me half way." Jesus could just demand that you be healed. But the word let tells you that you must do your part. Revelation 3:20 Behold, I stand at the door, and knock: if any man hear my voice, and open the door, I will come in to him, and will sup with him, and he with me. But for me to get in, you've got to let me in. If you go somewhere and you are strung out on drugs and you're trying to get help, you can't be helped you if you don't let them help you. You can be right here in church today while the word is going forth, but the word will do you no good if you don't let the word work on you on the inside.

Let not your heart; don't worry about the neighbor's heart, you work on your heart. When you are hurting, you ought to remember at least three things: (1) Whatever you're hurt over, don't curse it, because when you curse it you get mad. And if you get mad at something it just linger on and on and on and on. (2) Don't nurse it. If you nurse it, you become attached to it. You won't be able to let it go. (3) Don't rehearse it. When you rehearse something, it's the same as having a wound trying to heal and you scratch the scab off. It begins to bleed all over again.

So Jesus said, "Let not your heart be troubled." There is a lot of stuff around you that will trouble your heart. You've got to be almost blind not to see stuff that will trouble you. Everywhere you look, there's strange stuff going on. You hear strange stuff; you dream about strange stuff. How can I keep from being troubled? Here is the answer Jesus gave, "You believe in God, believe also in me." Believe means to put your trust in God.

Magnificent Mansions

John 14:2-3

In my Father's house are many mansions: if it were not so, I would have told you. I go to prepare a place for you. And if I go and prepare a place for you, I will come again, and receive you unto myself; that where I am, there ye may be also.

Jesus said, "I'm going away to prepare a place for you." Then Jesus promised that He will come back again. Now there are some things when the Lord gets ready to do, he sends other folk. When he got ready to lead Israel out of Egypt, he sent Moses. When he got ready for Israel to march across Jordan, he sent Joshua. When he got ready to build his first temple, he sent Solomon. When he wanted to give a man a vision, he sent Isaiah. When he wanted us to have patience, he sent Job. When he wanted us to get baptized, he sent John the Baptist. When he needed a preacher, he sent up Paul. But I heard him say, "This job is too big for them, I don't want to send Moses, he might get mad before he got the last saint. I don't want to send Solomon; a pretty woman might get his attention. I don't want to send David, because David's too busy blowing his horn. I've got to go myself.

We see the phrase, in my Father's house. You see heaven is called a house, but heaven is also called a city. Heaven is called a country; heaven is called a kingdom; heaven is called a paradise. It's called a country because of its vastness. It's called a city because of its huge population; it's called a kingdom because it's in order; its called paradise because it's a place to rejoice.

So we know that Jesus Himself went to prepare a beautiful place for each of us where there is plenty of room and a special home for all those who have accepted Him. He says, "I'll come again and receive you." Isn't that good news? Because one of these days, oh, I don't know when, but he's coming back.

Proper Preparation

John 14:4
And whither I go ye know, and the way ye know.

When I look at this text, I look at it with a touch of sadness, but also with a taste of gladness. I look at it with a broken heart, but also when I look at it, I experience a heart of eagerness and anxiousness. Those that are ready to go have a heart of joy. But there are those who are not ready. That brings a heart of sadness. It's often true we want to be able to stay here forever. Our mansions are built, but the stuff it's made out of is not eternal. It is here for just awhile. Some of you are looking for a place where you can spend eternity on earth, but even outside conditions won't let you stay. If you move to Florida the floods will get you. Earthquakes shake you in California. Storms will get you in Texas. The winter will get you out east. Conditions of the weather won't let us stay here forever. But if you do happen to find a place that's just right, don't get too comfortable because your body will stop functioning. The average life span of a man is three score years and ten.

We can compare the human life span to four quarters of a football game. From age one to seventeen is the first quarter. That's the time you develop your life. You start working, training your brain, and conditioning your body. If you mistreat your body from one to seventeen, you'll hear about it later. From 18 to 34 is the second quarter. This is the quarter to be settling down. You ought to be finished sowing your wild oats. You have to treat the second quarter right because there is a third quarter which goes from 35 to 54. And the fourth is from 55 to 73. There is no other quarter unless you have to go into overtime. Time will not allow us to stay here. Eventually we will have to check out of this place. Since we must go, we need to have a place prepared ahead of time. Moving is all right if you made previous arrangements. Make sure you have appropriate reservations for the next life.

Jesus Anticipates Our Arrival

Matthew 7:11

If ye then, being evil, know how to give good gifts unto your children, how much more shall your Father which is in heaven give good things to them that ask him?

My brother Louis went off to the Army. When Louis wrote back and said he was coming home on a furlough, Mama got excited and began making provision for his homecoming. She said, "Frank, Louis likes sweet potato pie. Go out and you'll see the ground bursting. Dig up two or three nice sized potatoes; I'm gonna fix a pie for Louis." Louis also liked fried corn and so I had to go out and pull corn and prepare it for Louis. We also had some nice sized watermelons in the patch. However, Daddy had a way of hiding the really big watermelons in the fields that he wouldn't let anybody touch. But when Louis wrote and said he was coming home for a furlough, Daddy went out and brought in that huge watermelon. He wouldn't let anybody touch it. He wouldn't let us cut it until Louis got there because Louis was special to the house.

Well Jesus is saying something like this. "I have some special people on planet earth and I don't want you to come to the house unprepared." Have you ever been invited to a place and when you got there the hosts still had to clean up after you got there? They invited you, but they had to do housekeeping once you got there. They say, "I didn't know you were coming this soon." So they are vacuuming the floor and washing the dishes. They are still cooking while you are sitting and waiting until you aren't hungry no more. But Jesus said, "I don't want to have you waiting when you come. I'm going away to prepare a place for you." You may not realize how special you are to the Lord; you're very special. You're so special that he died for you. You 're so special that he made provision for you ahead of time. He is anxiously anticipating our arrival with many wonderful preparations that we can only imagine.

Dedicate Yourself

Luke 8:15
But that on the good ground are they, which in an honest and good heart, having heard the word, keep it, and bring forth fruit with patience.

So what do I do since I know he's preparing a place for me? What you ought to do is prepare yourself for the place, because if a place is prepared, unprepared folk won't be able to get in there. You can't just go to heaven on your own. Even though God is merciful, he's just. Although God is forgiving, he must not change. And so this place is first of all a place for a holy people. Romans 12:1 I beseech you therefore brethren by the mercies of God that you present your bodies a living sacrifice, holy, acceptable unto God, which is your reasonable service. The Lord wants total and complete surrender, which involves not only the giving over of our physical body, but also the surrender of our heart. The flesh and the lusts of the flesh must die the same as a sacrifice offered on the altar and consumed. Since God is holy, if I am his child, then I need to be holy.

While we are waiting, we must make sure we are standing on his promises rather than sitting on his premises. Since we know that He is going away to prepare a place for us, we need to go out and round up as many folk as we can and tell them Jesus is coming back. Let people know they will not always be here and they need to think about moving day. Let them know how they can live forever and how their lives can be holy through God's mercies.

But it is also a place for happy people. There will be no sad folk in heaven. He eliminates all the stuff that makes you cry before you get there because He has told us there will be no more sorrow. There will be no more pain. There will be no more death. Just thinking about the goodness of God and what he has done for us seems to cause the sadness to just roll away anyway. Happy, holy people will inhabit the kingdom of heaven.

A Fine Family

1 Corinthians 12:25
That there should be no schism in the body; but that the members should have the same care one for another.

There will be no division and strife among the brethren once we leave here. And that's why we ought to try to practice living in harmony while we are here. We spend too much time cutting each other down. As a matter of fact we almost lose the war in the barracks. We spend all of our ammunition shooting each other and talking each other down, acting like dogs and cats. Now folk, we are sisters and brothers. We're in the same family. It was the same blood that washed us. It was the same Jesus that saved us, the same Holy Spirit that keeps us. For His sake, let us be in harmony with each other.

This family we are now a part of is an undying family. In other words, once you're saved, you don't die any more. The old folk had it right: done died one time; ain't gonna die no more. Now there are two ways of looking at it. When you are saved, there is one death and that's the end of it. And that death is just a taking off and a putting on a new body, like the one Jesus had after the resurrection. Jesus came to see about the disciples without them opening a window or a door; He just walked right through. No one had to move the stone for him to get out of the tomb. The stone had to be rolled away for the people to get in to see what had already happened. Sickness can come in your house without you opening a window. Death can come in your house without you opening a door. And Jesus has conquered sickness and death.

What a special family we are. This family keeps on growing. When you think you have gotten the last person saved, another person comes to receive their Savior. It is an ever-increasing family, a number that no man can know. What a wonderful family to be a part of. This family will live on through eternity, praising and worshipping Jesus.

He Will Arrive

John 14:3

And if I go and prepare a place for you, I will come again, and receive you unto myself; that where I am, there ye may be also.

The word come is mentioned 682 times in the word of God. Can you imagine what would happen if this one word was removed? Listen to Isaiah 1:18. Come let us reason together, though your sins be as scarlet, I will make them white as snow. Or Matthew 16:24, Then said Jesus if any man come unto me let him first deny himself, take up us his cross and follow me. Matthew 11:28; Come unto me all ye that labor and are heavy laden and I will give you rest. In Luke 14:23, Jesus said, Go out into the highways and hedges, and compel them to come in, that my house may be filled. As Peter saw Jesus walking on the water, he said, "If it's you, let me come to you." Jesus spoke just one word, "Come." What if this word was removed from the text?

If this word come were eliminated, we would have to carry our burdens alone. Our invitation for salvation would be canceled. He said, "Now, not only do I want you to come, but I'm going to come unto you and receive you unto myself that where I am you may be also." Have you ever asked, "Jesus, where are you?" How can I locate you now? The last time Stephen saw him he was standing on the right hand side of his Father according to Luke in Acts 1:10-11. The last time Peter saw him, He was on a Mt. Olive cloud heading back to heaven. Paul was in such a trance that he didn't know if he was in or out of his body.

How can I get to where he is? Jesus said not to worry about trying to come to where He is. He is coming to receive us unto himself. Have you ever been so glad to see someone that you parked your car and went up to the gate at the airport and waited for their arrival? Jesus will do something like this. But instead of Him waiting at the gate for us, He will leave heaven and come to where we are.

Know The Way

John 14:4
And whither I go ye know, and the way ye know.

Jesus just assumed that the ones closely following him would at least know the way. But every once in a while there's somebody in the crowd that misses the statement. Thomas raised his little Baptist finger and said, "Excuse me. Some of us don't know the way, and how can we know the way? Jesus said, "I'm glad you asked me that because I didn't want to leave if it was not clear with you.

Then Jesus said, "I AM. Not some way, but I AM the way. A friend of mine that's also a professor at a theological seminary told me that he spent time in Africa and even lived there for awhile. He decided to tour some of the African soil and so he wouldn't get lost, one of the chiefs sent a guide to lead him through uncharted territory. They traveled long and far, cutting their way with a bush ax through dense areas. He hollered to the guide, "Say sir, are you sure you know the way?" The guide turned around and looked at him and said, "Yes, I know the way. I've traveled this road many times. Do you see these marks on the trees? I made those marks. Do you see the scars on my body? I scarred myself making this trail. I am the way."

I think if you asked Jesus today, "Jesus are you sure you know the way?" Jesus would respond by saying, "Me, know the way?" He would say, "Do you see the nail prints in my hand? Do you see the scars from a thorny crown on my head? Do you see the spear hole in my side? Do you see the prints in my feet?" He would say, "Do I know the way? I am the way. I am the only way." In everything in life most times you can find different directions, different routes to get to different places. But when it comes to heaven, there's only one way. The way to heaven is not a street, freeway, or trail. It is not through the teachings of a prophet of some religion. It is not religious beliefs. The way is a person and that person is Jesus.

Genuine Joy

John 14:6

Jesus saith unto him, I am the way, the truth, and the life: no man cometh unto the Father, but by me.

Jesus is the truth. Now the truth is not something you put in a bottle and put a cork over. Nor is the truth is something you try to locate in a book or on the internet. The truth is not something you go to school and try to discover. The truth is a person. And Jesus said, "That's who I am; I am the truth about everything." As a matter of fact, he is the one that told us the truth about heaven. You see nobody else really told us what heaven was like except for Jesus. Abraham brought it up by saying he was looking for a city whose builder and maker is God. Paul says all of us will be changed in a moment, in the twinkling of an eye. We will be caught up to meet the Lord in the air.

And you know it ought to be a breath of fresh air to know that you are associated with the truth, because almost everything you get your hands on is a lie or artificial. Sometimes you don't know what is or isn't real. You can look at something and you think it's the real thing, but it's a substitute, a phony. But it's a breath of fresh air to know that I can associate with the real person who is the way, the truth, and the life.

You cannot have real life if you don't have Jesus. He said in John 10:10 I come that you might have life. So that means that you can be living and not really have life. You are existing; you may have two legs functioning well; you might have 20/20 vision; you can be looking pretty walking right, shaped just right, and still be dead. If you don't have Christ in your life, you are really a corpse. But Jesus wants to remedy that situation. He says, "But I come that you might have life. And I don't want to just give you life, I want you to have it more abundantly; I don't want you to just have a cupful, I want your cup to run over. I want you to have joy unspeakable!" Full of life and truth.

The Light Of Life

John 8:12

Then spake Jesus again unto them, saying, I am the light of the world: he that followeth me shall not walk in darkness, but shall have the light of life.

In him was life and the life was the light of men. When you have life, you have light. When Jesus is in you there's a light around you. You don't have to tell anyone that you've been born again, because the light on the inside will show up on the outside. You don't have to walk around with a big old Bible tucked under your arm. If you open your mouth, somebody will know you have life. If you sing somebody will know it; if you pray somebody will know it, because what you have, the world didn't give it to you and the world can't take it away. John 11:25-26 I am the resurrection and the life; he that believeth in me though he were dead yet shall he live; and whosoever liveth and believeth in me shall never die.

You may say, "But, you're still stumbling." Can I let you in on a little secret? God ain't through with me yet. He's still molding me and still shaping me. He's still cutting off some stuff; he's till pruning me. One of these mornings, he's going to present me a perfect vessel. How about you? Is he through with you yet? Is he still working on you? Do you still need to drop off a little stuff? Do you still have a little envy in you, a little malice, a little jealousy? If you feel a little weak, wounded, weary, and without strength, steal away somewhere and say, "Precious Lord take my hand lead me on and let me stand; I'm tired; I'm weak and I'm worn, but through the storm, through the night, oh lead me on. Lead me on to the light." Look people straight in the eye and say, "Child, I've been through it, but I'm still holding on." Don't be afraid to tell them. "Child, I've come through the storm and rain but I still made it. Because every one of us have done enough wrong to be wiped off of this map. But he gave us another chance.

One Of Which Bunch

Matthew 25:1
Then shall the kingdom of heaven be likened unto ten virgins, which took their lamps, and went forth to meet the bridegroom.

The scene opens with the text using the word then. All Jesus had talked about is now on the horizon. Jesus spent a lot of time talking about the kingdom. As a matter of fact, when he taught us the model prayer, He said one of the things that you need to do is to pray for the coming of the kingdom. Anything you pray for, you will work to get it done. There are several ways of looking at the kingdom. You could say the kingdom has already come. And you could say the kingdom is here. And you could very easily say the kingdom is coming, which means it was yesterday and today it is on it way. The kingdom is so important that Jesus said in Matthew 24:14 And this gospel of the kingdom shall be preached in all the world for a witness unto all nations; and then shall the end come.

So the kingdom will come. The kingdom is connected with a will, for He said when you pray that the kingdom would come and the will would be done. Now if there is a kingdom, there must be a king. And if there is a king and a kingdom, then there must be a will. If there is a will, then the will must be done. If the will is going to be done, kingdom builders must do it.

Jesus introduces three categories of people. First of all He brings the focus on the Jewish people. Then He reminds us of the Gentiles. Next he lets us know He wants us to be familiar with the church. Within these categories, there are groups of people. One group is wise; one group is foolish. Some groups are like wheat while others are as tares. Some are like goats and others resemble sheep. Some spend time at the straight gate while others spend time on the broad way. What Jesus was telling us is that either you're saved or you're lost. You are a part of one of the groups.

Adamant Anticipation

Matthew 25:1
Then shall the kingdom of heaven be likened unto ten virgins, which took their lamps, and went forth to meet the bridegroom.

The bridegroom spoken of here is Jesus. And if there is a bridegroom, there must be a bride. The bride spoken of in this verse is hidden. The bride is actually the church under cover. Then Jesus speaks of the two different kinds of virgins, the wise and the foolish. The wise virgins represent true believers while the foolish virgins denote pretending practitioners of the faith. The oil is symbolic of the Holy Spirit. The lamp actually represents the Bible. Psalm 119:105 Thy word is a lamp unto my feet and a light unto my path. The oil in the lamp represents the illumination of the Holy Spirit once it has embodied itself in the life of the believer. The vessel represents the individual.

The wise virgins were anticipating the bridegroom. They were looking for something to occur. I think one reason people leave from church in the same frame of mind as when they arrived is because they did not come expecting anything. If you come looking for something, you will receive; you must anticipate.

A preacher once complained to Charles Spurgeon that after preaching his sermon, he always gave an invitation to the unsaved, but no one ever responded. Mr. Spurgeon asked, "Do you expect anybody to come when you extend the invitation?" "Not really," answered the preacher. And Spurgeon said, "That's your problem." If you don't anticipate being successful, it will never happen. You must look forward to accomplishing goals in your life. If you think you're nothing, then you are nothing. If you think you're going to fail, then you will. If you think folks are after you, they will be. If you think you're being talked about, then people will talk about you. Success doesn't run you down; you must anticipate success!

A Wrong Robe

Matthew 22:2

The kingdom of heaven is like unto a certain king, which made a marriage for his son.

A wedding is usually a momentous event. A Jewish wedding was a very important event. A great deal of time and planning went into the preparation for the wedding. The young lady and young man really had almost nothing to do with selecting each other. The parents made the selection of a mate for their children and managed the wedding arrangements. The future bride and bridegroom would be engaged for a year. During this time, elaborate plans were made for the wedding. Everybody in the neighborhood and the community had a standing invitation to go. The wedding was a great celebration, often lasting for many days with feasts and music.

Even so, there were very strict rules and regulations concerning weddings. For instance, in Matthew 22:2-7, the king expected all those who attended the wedding to wear a special wedding garment. One fellow decided to crash the party by showing up without his garment. The man was thrown out because he had neglected to put on the proper garment. No exceptions were made. Luke 15:8-9 speaks of a woman who lost one of her ten pieces of silver. This was a crisis because if she did not have ten pieces, her wedding would be canceled. The ten silver pieces were part of the wedding apparel. They would be worn around the tail end of the wedding garment or the coins would be used as a necklace at the wedding. Losing just one piece meant her wedding was canceled; that is why she swept all day and all night. She lit her lights, looking and sweeping the house until she found that lost piece of silver.

The Lord places great importance concerning details and requires our obedience to His ways. The man without the wedding garment represents a person who tries to be part of the kingdom of God without receiving Christ.

Check Your Light

Matthew 25:4
But the wise took oil in their vessels with their lamps.

The virgins took their lamps and went to meet the bridegroom. Now it is believed that these were not actual lamps, but that they were torches. These were merely torches that would keep a light on the path for the bride and groom to walk down the hallway on their way to the altar. If these lights were not lit, then the wedding would have to be postponed. You see God anticipates every one of us having a light. Before God did anything with creation, He took care to get the light straight first. Before he made the trees, before he allowed the birds to fly, the fish to swim, the beast to roam or man to live, God said, "Let there be light." And He liked light because God is light himself. Not only is he light, his Son is the light of the world. And all those who follow him are lights.

Let your light. This means your light should shine privately. It's your light. Your light should shine and shine. In other words, the folk around you need to know you know the Lord. You shouldn't have to walk around with a cross around your neck to let folk know you're born again. You shouldn't have to walk around with a Bible under your arm for folk to know you have been with the Lord. It ought to be in your light. Lights don't have to have any advertising. No, lights don't have to walk up and say, "I'm a light." Anything and anybody knows it's a light. It is its own advertiser. A light does its work without keeping up any noise. No, a light doesn't have to holler, but a light will do its own work by itself. Many of us are lights but sometimes we get our lights mixed up. Instead of being headlights, we're tail-lights. The world is the tail, we are the head. Clearly, we shouldn't follow the world; the world should follow us. Most of us look for the lights of other folks, but we never check our own lights. Is your light on and shining for those around?

Personal Preparation

Matthew 26:41
Watch and pray, that ye enter not into temptation: the spirit indeed is willing, but the flesh is weak.

One of these days there's going to be a great wedding. The bridegroom is on the way. It doesn't make good sense to know He's coming without being prepared for him to come. Everywhere we look, there are signs that say he's coming back again. Although we've had many false prophets lately who predict the time of his coming, we don't know the date. Matthew 24:36 But of that day and hour knoweth no man, no, not the angels of heaven, but my Father only. Matthew 24:42 Watch therefore: for ye know not what hour your Lord doth come. The Lord said, "What I want you to do is spend some time watching. He says in 24:44 Therefore be ye also ready for in such an hour as ye think not the Son of Man cometh. It will be a time when you least expect him. While we're hanging around fussing, arguing, and complaining, the Lord is on his way.

Notice what he says in 24:50 The Lord of that servant shall come at a day when he looketh not for Him and in that hour that he is not aware of. He could show up any time. We must be continually looking for the coming of the Lord. We must actively prepare for His coming by staying true to the faith, actively working for the Lord, keeping our hearts and minds right, and doing good. 1 Corinthians 15:51-52 Behold I show you a mystery. We shall not all sleep, but we shall all be changed, in a moment, in the twinkling of an eye. We must keep the hope fresh that He will come back again. 1 Thessalonians 4:16-17, For the Lord himself shall descend from heaven, with a shout, with a voice of the archangel, and with the trump of God and the dead in Christ shall rise first. Then we which are alive, and remain shall be caught up together with them in the cloud to meet the Lord in the air, and so shall we ever be with the Lord. There must be personal preparation.

Evaluation Time

Matthew 25:5
While the bridegroom tarried, they all slumbered and slept.

These virgins all appeared to be alive. But at the showdown, the difference will be known. We may all look alike just now; we all act like Christians; we all sit like we've been born again. The old folk used to say cream, real cream would rise to the top. And the Lord is the One who will do the separating. Jesus said, "Let the wheat and the tares grow together." Why does He allow that? When the plants are young and tender, they all look just alike. But once they get grown, the wheat ears get heavy and the wheat starts bowing down. The heavier the wheat gets the lower it bows. But the tare, the older it gets the more it lifts its head. In other words, it shows off more the older it gets. The wheat starts hiding itself. Let them both grow together; Jesus will evaluate the situation. So the ten virgins slumbered and slept.

Now there were two different kinds of sleepiness going on. The foolish virgins were sleeping ignorantly, like sinners sleep ignorantly. They brag about what they possess without realizing that they're walking around on a spider web that could break at any moment, possibly two seconds from eternal damnation. I don't see where no body that's unsaved ought to be happy because you could go to hell at any moment. Not only did the foolish slumber and sleep but the wise also slept. Did you know the church is sleeping too? Let's look to Jonah as a witness. Jonah went down in the ship and went to sleep. The storm came and everybody on board was praying to their gods, but their gods couldn't stop the storm because their gods had eyes and couldn't see; their gods had ears and could not hear. The only one on ship that could get a prayer through was Jonah and he was down in the ship asleep. I'm afraid today the only ones that can get a prayer through just might be asleep, maybe sitting on a pew with their eyes open.

Midnight And No Oil

Matthew 25:8
And the foolish said unto the wise, Give us of your oil; for our lamps are gone out.

The Bible says that when the foolish virgins discovered they didn't have any oil, they knew they couldn't be in the wedding. They cleaned their globe; that wasn't the problem. They tested their wicks; that wasn't the problem. They turned the light on, but it wouldn't stay on. The problem was not in the lamp; the problem was not in the wick; the problem was not in the globe; their problem was they had run out of oil. Oil is symbolic of the Holy Spirit; you can't go very far without the Holy Ghost. You might be able to sing and tear up the church; you might be a great speaker and shout folk all over the place. But if you don't have Him when it gets dark in your room, you won't have any light to shine.

The foolish said to the wise, "Come here and let me talk to you; I need to borrow something from you. Can you lend me a little of your oil?" The wise said, "I'm sorry, I wish we could help you, but some things in life you can not borrow. Well you can borrow some churches and have all the weddings you want, but you can't borrow salvation. You can borrow the musical instruments, but you can't borrow joy. You can borrow food if you want, but you can not borrow an appetite. Some things are for you only.

The virgins with oil told the others to go out and buy some oil for themselves. Evidently, what they needed was right in the neighborhood. They went and purchased their oil and were on their way back but the door was shut. The bridegroom had come while they were gone. Some were shut in and some had been shut out. And one of these days the real door is going to be shut I'll be on the inside along with love, joy, and peace. Sickness and death will be shut out. Weeping, wailing, and moaning will be shut out. All my enemies will be shut out as well as the devil, himself!

Beating All Odds

Daniel 6:10

Now when Daniel knew that the writing was signed, he went into his house; and his windows being open in his chamber toward Jerusalem, he kneeled upon his knees three times a day, and prayed, and gave thanks before his God, as he did aforetime.

Many people begin life with the deck stacked against them. An X was placed by your name and you were given little chance of ever accomplishing anything. For a while you believed it yourself. In the school that I attended they had a book going around and they put stars by the people that were most likely to succeed. I was not in that crowd that was to succeed. These students dressed well, made good grades, and came from families who were known in the community. They were set aside to make it. But God knows the end from the beginning and has His own plans for the one who's on the other side of the track and was overlooked. You would have to put me in that category.

Daniel is the central figure of this passage. Daniel now is not a young man; he is in his eighties. When you look at his life and his record, he beat all the odds. When he was sixteen, he was captured and carried to the land of the Chaldeans. They brought him there because he had a brilliant mind; he was one of the upstart Jewish kids in the community. They saw Daniel and planned to take him and de-program him. However, Daniel's parents had already implanted in his heart and mind the word of God with its truths and principles. Good parents will spend time teaching and training their children in the ways of the Lord so that someday the enemy will not be able to overtake them when they leave home and the enemy wants to de-program them. Daniel knew right from wrong. He also knew his God was a might God and was the one, true God. Daniel knew He was the only God worthy of worship. Daniel had courage enough to stand against the odds.

The Reward Of Faithfulness

Daniel 6:3

Then this Daniel was preferred above the presidents and princes, because an excellent spirit was in him; and the king thought to set him over the whole realm.

At the age of sixteen, Daniel was forced to sit at the King's table; however Daniel refused to eat the King's meat. Daniel's parents had taught him the foods to eat for good health and a sound mind. Daniel wanted vegetables and water instead of meat and wine. He did not want the meat that had been offered to idols. Daniel convinced the king to allow him to eat his own way and to evaluate his condition in ten days. In ten days, Daniel looked better than the king's young men. Later Daniel and his friends faced another test when the King decided that everybody in the camp had to bow to an image. Daniel was one that refused to bow along with with Shadrach, Meshach and Abednego, but he was able to live through it. Daniel had the right stuff. Isn't it amazing how you can be in a strange position but when you take a stand for God, He will see you through? You don't have to do wrong because everybody else is doing wrong. You can take a stand if you have to stand by yourself. God will bring you out more than a conquerer.

Daniel was also called on during the reign of King Belshazzar who used holy vessels during a drunken party. He poured wine into one of the holy vessels and attempted to give a toast to a false god. The same hour there came forth the finger of a man's hand and wrote on the wall. Of course, none of his sooth sayers, philosophers, or magicians could read the writing because God wrote it. And when God writes something, his children are the ones that do the interpreting. So they sent for Daniel who told the king that God had weighed the king in the balance and he had been found wanting. That very night the king died. Daniel did not know how the king would respond, but Daniel spoke the word of the Lord. This was his way of life.

Envy, An Evil Enemy

Daniel 6:5

Then said these men, We shall not find any occasion against this Daniel,
except we find it against him concerning the law of his God.

Daniel was put in charge of the three presidents who were over
the kingdom of Darius. Daniel's position was the same as that
of a Prime Minister. Now people have a serious problem when
you get promoted, especially when you are promoted over them. So
when Daniel received his promotion, his enemies started gathering.
They searched to find fault with Daniel. But his enemies could find
no fault. Now that's rare. You don't have to be my enemy to find fault
with me. I've made so many mistakes until I'm really a mistake myself.
I've heard people say, "I'm not ashamed of nothing I've done." Not me,
I'm ashamed of everything I've done. The only thing I'm not ashamed
of is the gospel. Thank God I'm serving a God that knows how to
take his spiritual eraser and erase my past and straighten it up for the
present and walk with me through the future.

But Daniel's enemies, driven by envy, determined to cause trouble
for Daniel. Since they could find no fault in him, they hired private
investigators to watch his habits in order to make up something against
him. They began to notice that every morning before he got ready to go
to work, he would raise the window in the direction of Jerusalem and
kneel down and pray. At lunch, he did the same thing. In the evening
when he got home, he raised the window, knelt down, and prayed.
They said, "We've got him," because they knew that the King was lifted
in pride. They put together a devious plan in the form of a law that
people would have to bow down to the king and no other for thirty
days. If a person disobeyed, he would be thrown into the lion's den.
They convinced Darius to sign the decree. However, this envy would
be their own enemy in the end.

Kneel So You Can Stand

Daniel 6:7

Whosoever shall ask a petition of any God or man for thirty days, save of thee, O king, he shall be cast into the den of lions.

When Daniel knew that the writing was signed he went home, climbed up stairs and raised the window in the direction of Jerusalem. Then he knelt down and prayed the same as he always did. He continued praying morning, noon, and night as was his custom. And while he was kneeling, his enemies caught him. Kneeling in prayer is a good place to get caught. Now Daniel could probably have avoided being caught praying. There are many ways to pray and no one even knows. I talk to God while I am in my car driving down the road. Nobody knows I'm praying and speaking to my Lord. I talk to God in the bed when I'm lying down and can't sleep. I just lie there and have a prayer meeting in the bed. I talk to God in the airplane 28,000 feet in the air. So I wanted to ask Daniel, "You knew the decree had been signed by the king and that you would go to the lion's den if you got caught praying, so why didn't you get in some corner where no one could see you? Why didn't you go in your closet and talk to God?"

I can hear Daniel's answer. He says, "One reason I didn't hide in a corner was because I didn't meet God in a corner. I didn't meet Him in the closet. I met God out in the open. I don't have a closet religion. I don't have a behind the scenes Christianity." If you are ashamed to own Him before men, the Lord will be ashamed to own you before his father in heaven.

Daniel was not afraid to go to the lion's den. He refused to allow a few self-centered men full of envy rule his life and hinder his relationship with God. His faith had brought him too far; he had seen God work in too many ways to turn aside now. Daniel triumphed in each test of his faith and stood strong in the time of testing. We can also.

Don't Disregard Devotions

Daniel 6:11

Then these men assembled, and found Daniel praying and making supplication before his God.

Since Daniel prayed visibly three times each day, it was not difficult for his enemies to find him praying. It makes good sense to pray morning, noon, and evening. It is good to pray in the morning before you become busy with the day's activities. Talk to God before you leave home and he will direct your course. Now Lord I don't know what the day is going to bring, but since you own the day tell me which way to go. It's too late after you get caught in the stuff; you should have talked to God about it. No, talk to him first. The steps of a good man are ordered by the Lord. Psalm 91:11 says He gives his angels charge over you to keep you in all your ways. So take a few moments first and have a little talk with God.

If you come to the middle of the day and nothing has happened, you should tell Him thank you. If something has happened you should say, "God, I believe that you and I can handle this." It is also important to talk to Him in the evening. My goodness, if God gives you a whole day without an accident, certainly you should tell him thank you. If you come home in the evening and your husband or wife shows up and your children made it home from school and you call Mama and she's all right, shouldn't you stop to say thank you? Especially when you think of all things that could have happened.

Daniel had a posture for prayer. When I was young coming up, women would come to revival services wearing cotton stockings. They didn't come to be dressed up looking sharp. They came because they were going to the house of prayer. Men would come with kneepads on. An old deacon used to start like this, "Now Lord, here we are, one more time, our knees are bent and our body is bowed." They knew how to talk to God. Daniel prayed faithfully.

Walking The Floor

Daniel 6:18

Then the king went to his palace, and passed the night fasting: neither were instruments of music brought before him: and his sleep went from him.

Daniel was taken before the king and then he was put down in the lion's den. That doesn't sound like God is answering prayer. The man is still in the den. But that isn't the end of this story. After King Darius sent him away, he was disturbed because he liked Daniel. However, there was nothing the King could do. He couldn't even violate his own law. Have you ever been in a situation where there isn't anything you can do and there isn't anything anybody else can do. The ones that started it can't get you out of it.

All night long, the king was walking the floor; he couldn't sleep. If you have a strong prayer life, this is what your enemies are doing. While you are trying to figure them out, God has them upset; God has your enemies where they can't sleep at night. They have lobster and crab, but they can't eat a bite. They aren't enjoying the music. King Darius was fasting. Isn't that something? God will work on both ends. Daniel is in the den with hungry lions. The authorities placed a heavy stone over the door. But the lions are just lying there. Daniel stretched out on one lion while the other lion used his tail to fan the flies off Daniel.

Before you ask God for something, thank him for it. That's the way we do when we get ready to eat. We haven't even seen the food yet, but we say, "Lord we thank you for the food we are about to receive." If you want a blessing from God, you should before you ask him for it, say, "Now Lord, I've got something in mind and before I make my request I want to tell you thank you for it." Let me tell you why you should say thank you–because you will receive more from God with a grateful heart than you do with a begging heart. If you learn how to tell him thank you for the little bit you do have, God knows how to make it more.

Prayer Fulfilled

Daniel 6:22

My God hath sent his angel, and hath shut the lions' mouths, that they have not hurt me: forasmuch as before him innocency was found in me; and also before thee, O king, have I done no hurt.

And early that morning the King got up and ran to the den and shouted," O Daniel are you still in there?" And Daniel got up and stretched himself and said, "Well I hear somebody calling my name." Daniel hollered back through the mouth of the den, "O King, live forever." Then the King ordered his men to open the mouth of the den. Those same people that put Daniel in the den of lions were themselves thrown in along with their families and God allowed Daniel's enemies to be devoured. Be careful how you cook up negative stuff because sometimes it will backfire on you.

The king said, "Daniel, tell me what happened." Then Daniel said, "You know when you all put me in the den, I wasn't disturbed because I prayed ahead of time. If you pray before trouble comes, you won't have to pray when trouble comes. If you pray in the car, you want have to panic in the storm. Daniel said, last night a visitor showed up in the middle of the lion's den. Once in a while when you think you won't make it, a visitor will show up. Who was that visitor? That visitor in the night was the seed of the woman. He was the Passover lamb. That visitor in the night was Joshua's bail man; He was Ezekiel's wheel in the middle of a wheel, He was Amos' plumb line. That visitor in the night was that fourth man in the fiery furnace. His name was Jesus.

Have you ever been in a situation where the odds were against you? You weren't supposed to make it but here you did. Even your own family and friends thought you would never make it. Not because of what you knew but because somebody showed up. Jesus came and saved the day!

The Other Side

Mark 4:35
And the same day, when the even was come, he saith unto them, 'Let us pass over unto the other side.

Jesus had been with his disciples for quite a while, giving them the comfort of His presence. Whenever there was a crisis, he was there. But Jesus needed to take them to a new turf. He needed to carry them into an environment they had not been in before. That evening, Jesus extended an invitation to his disciples and said, "Let us go over unto the other side." I'm glad I received that invitation from him when I was fourteen years of age to go with him to the other side. I discovered a long time ago that this is not my home; this is just a temporary dwelling place. Stop wasting your worries today about tomorrow. Let today take care of today. And let tomorrow take care of tomorrow when tomorrow gets here. When I was young coming up, the older church people would keep our minds on where we were going. If you fail to recognize where you're going, you might forget where you are. Songs would remind us of where we were headed. They would sing, I'm on my journey and I can't turn around; River Jordan, I've got one more river to cross.

So He invited them to go with him to the other side. Now Jesus didn't tell us what we were going to run into on our way to the other side. I see people all the time going to psychics and calling 1-900 numbers trying to find out about the future. Some things are better not known, because if you knew some things you wouldn't try. If the children of Israel had known when they left Egypt that a red sea was waiting on them, they never would have left. But when they made it to the Red Sea they had come too far to turn around and they were able to cross that Red Sea. Sometimes God says to us, "I need to just give you a little at a time." You see, if you take life by the yard it's hard; but when you take it by the inch it's a cinch.

Exclude The Crowd

Mark 4:36
And when they had sent away the multitude, they took him even as he was in the ship. And there were also with him other little ships.

The first thing Jesus did after He invited the disciples to go with him to the other side was to dismiss the crowd. He sent away the multitude, If you're going and you're in the storm, learn how to eliminate and dismiss the skeptics. Some people will hinder you from going, because every time you talk to them you hear negative talk. When you meet up with them, there's something that's not right; every time you talk with them, it's nothing but criticism. You must eliminate and dismiss the skeptics, because they will have you crying when you don't need to cry. They will have you complaining when you don't have anything to complain about. They will have you grumbling even though you have a loaf of bread under your arm. People who criticize and complain all the time will tarnish your spirit. They will have you walking around looking down. They will have you saying, "I don't know why God hasn't done anything for me."

Jesus had twelve disciples, but he didn't carry all twelve with him everywhere he went. When he got ready to go up Mt. Herman, He left nine at the foot of the mountain. When he got ready to heal Jairus' daughter, he left nine on the outside and took Peter, James, and John inside. Why didn't He carry everybody? He said when I get ready to do something special, I can't have everybody around me. He said, "I can't have everybody around me." Negativity will mess you up so leave negative people behind. I don't care who they are, if it's your son, or daughter, husband or wife, daddy or mamma, if they are always negative, say, "I love you, but I can't keep you around me all the time." I'm on my way somewhere. I've got to learn how to eliminate and dismiss skeptics.

A Perfecting Storm

Mark 4:37

And there arose a great storm of wind, and the waves beat into the ship, so that it was now full.

He sent the multitude away and when they got in the ship, they hadn't made it very far before a storm showed up. They were in Galilee Lake, which is eight miles wide at it's widest and thirteen miles long at it's longest; it's made like a bowl. Those of you who have gone there know there are hills and pockets up in the mountains. When the cold air from the mountains comes down and collides with the warm air from the lake, it creates a storm. You can leave the shore and it can be calm and mild with a cool wind, yet in a matter of moments, you can be in a storm.

Storms can come suddenly and unexpectedly. You can be minding your own business sitting at a red light and someone can run right into you, tearing up your car that your policy lapsed on yesterday. All of a sudden you're in a storm. You go to the doctor just to get a physical and you don't think anything is wrong. You seem to be healthy. The doctor rushes you to the hospital and they do emergency surgery on you the same day. You got up that morning all right, but before sun down you were in a storm. You lost your job after thirty years but you're a little too young to retire and a little too old to start a new job. You're too young for Medicare, but too old for men to care. You're in a storm. You kissed your spouse this morning and said, "I love you," and they said they love you back. You thought everything was going well, but when you came home that evening, everything was gone. You discovered they had walked off and left you and took everything with them.

Storms will come. Look at the storm for what it is. The Lord allows perfecting storms to come our way. They shape us and mold us bringing spiritual maturity. You may not know the strength of your faith if you have not been in a storm. Hold on through the storm. Jesus is there!

July

A Correcting Storm

Nahum 1:3

...the Lord hath his way in the whirlwind and in the storm, and the clouds are the dust of his feet.

A little boy once made himself a little sailboat. And he took the boat out to the water and the little boat got on some waves and it just floated on out in the deep water. The boy tried to wade out to get it, but it was too far and the water was too deep. But he had made the boat with his own hands. So he looked around and collected for himself a pile of rocks. He picked one up and threw it just on the other side of the little boat. Every time a rock would hit the water, it would create ripples. And every time it would create a ripple, it would send the boat back to his direction. The boy kept throwing rocks, creating ripples until the little boat floated right back in his hands.

Well, God made us and sometimes we get satisfied where we are. We begin to skip Bible class. We get to the place where we start going to bed without praying. We reach a point where we'll show up on some Sundays and miss other Sundays. God will whip up a little wave on the other side of us. The Lord brings us back into a safe harbor. And when God gets through with you, you'll find yourself saying, "Father, I stretch my hand to thee, no other help I know; If thou withdraw thyself from me, whither shall I go."

Even while we're in the storm, God is still smoothing us; He's still working on us. When I was in elementary school, my teacher told us that whenever there is a comma, the writer is giving you breathing room. 2 Corinthians 4:8 We are troubled on every side, (comma: breathing room) yet not in distress; we are perplexed, (comma) but not in despair, we are persecuted, (comma) but not forsaken: we are cast down, (comma) but we aren't destroyed. So in the midst of my storm, He gives me breathing room. I like that about God, because what he's doing is correcting me.

Divine Design

Romans 8:29

For whom he did foreknow, he also did predestinate to be conformed to the image of his Son, that he might be the firstborn among many brethren.

For whom he did foreknow. The Greek word for foreknow is the word prognosis from which we get the word prognosticator, a person that can know now what's going to happen tomorrow. Our weathermen give us a prognosis of what's going to happen on a five day forecast. Well if your think the weatherman is all right, check out God, because God doesn't make mistakes. He knows. And that's why I love him so well. Because even when I mess up, I have to say, he knew it before he saved me and he still saved me in spite of my future record. He knew when he saved me that I would stumble; that I was going to fall, and he saved me anyway. He foreknows.

Whom the Lord did foreknow, them he also did predestinate. The Greek word for predestination is the word purseo. In the Greek it means to mark off a boundary. God has set a place for you to go. Have you ever tried to get something and couldn't get it? You went shopping for houses and time after time the deal fell through. But God knew the one you needed where you could make a home. Sometimes we don't understand what He's doing. Every time we try to go through a door we don't need to go in, He closes the door. God says, "I know what I'm trying to do; I'm keeping you from killing your crazy self so I'll close the door on you. But the door I want you to go in, I'll leave wide open so you can walk right through. That's what I love about the God I serve. He is there all the time. That's good news to me. That's why you should let him lead you. You say I don't know where I'm going or what I'm going to do when I get there, but the God I serve, is our heavenly Father. He's over us, looking down on us. For whom he did foreknow, he did predestinate and design a plan for us.

Surviving The Cyclone

Mark 4:38

And he was in the hinder part of the ship, asleep on a pillow: and they awake him, and say unto him, Master, carest thou not that we perish?

The storm was raging, sending water into the ship, but Jesus was in the hinder part of the ship asleep on a pillow. Notice how Jesus handles storms. When we're in a storm we may prance the floor or smoke nasty cigarettes; some try to drown their troubles in the liquor bottle; others sit and eat themselves to death and watch crazy movies on television; still others call and worry other folk half to death. Some people look for tranquilizers and nerve pills. But Jesus was sleeping during the storm. How can a person be that calm? Psalm 121, speaking of God the Father, says, He neither slumbers, nor does he sleep. When you have a good person watching over you; you don't have to stay awake since He's awake.

The disciples came to Jesus, and said, "Master do you care? I wonder if you have ever asked that question. Master, do you care if we perish? Lord do you know what I'm going through? I can hear the Lord say, I care enough for you to endure being whipped and gouged and have spikes driven through my feet and to die for your sins. And if he loves us enough to die for us, he loves us enough to give us all things to enjoy.

The Lord has already fixed it and prepared it for us. He says if you're going through something, I knew you were going to go through it, that's why I left my word behind. That's why you ought to always be familiar with the word of God. Sometimes you're going to need him and you can't catch up with pastor. Sometimes you're going to need him and your girlfriend won't be on the other end. Sometimes you're going to need him and you can't get in touch with a deacon. So you will need to have the word in your heart. Just a short walk through the word and you'll feel better.

Cool And Calm

Mark 4:40

And he said unto them, Why are ye so fearful? How is it that ye have no faith?

W*hy is it that you are so fearful? How is it that you have no faith?* Jesus says you are trying to put fear and faith in the same heart and it doesn't work. If you've got fear in your heart, faith steps back. But if you have faith, fear steps back. God did not give us the spirit of fear, but he gave us the power of faith. So if you've got faith, even if you're in the storm, you'll be able to say, "Weeping may endure for a night, but joy will come in the morning." If you have faith, it doesn't matter how dark the night, you can say, "But in the morning, the sun, it will shine."

Mark 4:37 says that a great storm of wind arose, but 4:39 says, "And He arose." Jesus arose with power. Whenever your storm shows up, the Lord will show up too. No matter where the storm finds you, the Lord is on the storm's trail. When that storm tries to come and devour you, the Lord will be right there. How easily the Lord handles the storm. He walked out to the edge of the ship and talked to the wind like I would talk to my dog. He said, "Peace." He didn't even have to holler. It seems like the disciples would have known he was the God of nature, that whatever He said, nature would have to obey him. If God says, "Sun stand still," the sun will have to stand still. If God says, "Jericho walls fall," they will all fall down.

The disciples had been with Jesus before, but when He calmed that storm somebody on board said, "What manner of man is this, that even the wind and sea obey him?" After Jesus spoke, there was a great calm. Storms can be raging in other places, but in your heart you have a peace of mind. You can sit cool and calm while others are running around with panic and fear. My Father has his eye on me so I don't have anything to worry about. If God can create heaven and earth, he's able to handle your little storm.

Conformed By The Storm

Psalm 107:29
He maketh the storm a calm, so that the waves thereof are still.

Many storms come along in our lives. Maybe you are having difficulty in saying goodbye to lost loved ones. One funeral happened not long ago, but now you are going through it all again. You know you love the Lord, but this is a situation that's hard to handle. There are others of you that have to wrestle with your own children. You've gone out of your way to try to give them the best you could possibly give them. But it looks like your best is not good enough. You may be in a marital situation and you really don't know what to do. You want to stay; you want to leave. You want to hold on and you want to walk away. You try to do the best you possibly can to love the people you love. But every time you try to love somebody, they mistreat you. Every time you get somebody in your arms or get somebody in your heart they break it; you're just tired of being hurt over and over and over again. You have been overlooked on your job. You've tried to work hard. You've tried to be an honest person because you love the Lord. You've done things that other people around there would not do. You've stood your ground. But everyone is getting promoted except you.

The Lord allows storms in our lives because he wants us to be conformed to the image of his Son. He wants us to favor Jesus. That's why He has to take us through a storm. When he gets through with us, we'll be just like his dear Son. Be prepared for a devilish storm but look for a deliverance from the Savior. Relief will come. Hang on a little longer; don't give up. If you're slipping, tie a knot in the end of the rope and hold on. Use the truths of God's word to understand what God is doing, even in your own personal lives. Storms will come, but they will pass over. He is the master of the storm.

Beyond Yesterday

Psalm 90:12
So teach us to number our days, that we may apply our hearts unto wisdom.

Whenever I think of yesterday, I have mixed emotions. I can remember I had some good days. But before I can shout too much over the good days I had, my mind focuses on some bad days. I had some yesterdays when I was laughing from morning until night. They were good days. But I also remember yesterday that I had some bad days. I can remember joy, happiness, and gladness, but before I shout too much, I remember some days I was wounded. I have scars on my heart that keep jumping up telling me about some stuff that happened yesterday. I made some good friends yesterday. But before I can shout too much, I can remember some enemies I made yesterday. I remember when I had a little extra money, but before I rejoice too much over the little money I had yesterday, I remember days when I was broke and couldn't even borrow anything from folk I knew that did have money. If I could think only of the good part, it would be all right. But I can remember some bad days yesterday.

I remember yesterday that I went to the hospital to see babies born. I watched my sisters and brothers being born. I watched my son being born yesterday, my grandson and my granddaughter. I remember the good days of birth yesterday. But before I can get too happy over the births of yesterday, I remember some funerals that I attended yesterday. I had to say goodbye to granddaddy, and grandmother, to my daddy and mother, to my brother, my cousins, and my best friends, Yesterday is a canceled check. Yesterday creates mixed emotions, so I'm trying to put yesterday behind me. God wants you to use the time wisely that you have now. Make every minute, every hour and every day count. Since Jesus paid the ransom price by dying for us, we ought to be willing to live for him.

Today's Agenda

John 9:4
I must work the works of him that sent me, while it is day.

Today is a little different from yesterday. Today, when today shows up, comes in running, as though it's in a hurry. Yesterday I was in my adolescent and tender teens and teachable twenties. But when today showed up in my tireless thirties and forceful forties and then my fevered fifties, today came in running. Today seems to say, "You'd better do what you can now because when you bat your eye, tomorrow will be here." And let me recommend that you try not to put off until tomorrow what you can do today. If you've mistreated somebody, don't wait until tomorrow to go and let the person know you're sorry. If you're going to do something for the Lord, don't keep moving the dates until tomorrow or next week or next month or next year. Do it today. There are those of you who are working on next year; however, you need to finish out this year. Next year is not promised to us. If you're going to praise him, do it now. If you're going to work for him, do it now. John 9:4 says Work while it is day because the night comes when no man can work.

I got tomorrow's phone number and tomorrow wouldn't answer their phone. Tomorrow wouldn't talk to me. Tomorrow is keeping me in the dark. If I only knew what to look forward to on tomorrow, how to deal with tomorrow, I would be all right. But I hear the Holy Spirit saying, "Handle today and let tomorrow take care of itself." Jesus said, "When you pray, ask God to give you this day your daily bread." Why couldn't I ask for tomorrow's supply? If you ask for it day by day, then you will have fresh bread everyday. You will have his presence everyday because he will have to show up tomorrow to give you another loaf. So stop worrying about tomorrow. Do what you can for God today. Another day may not be on your agenda.

Ruled By Riches

Luke 12:16

And he spake a parable unto them, saying, The ground of a certain rich man brought forth plentifully.

Parables are earthly stories with heavenly meanings. In this parable, Jesus spoke about how the ground of a certain rich man brought forth plentifully. The problem here is not that the man is rich. Richness does not affect you as long as you allow the money to be a servant and not a master. This means that you must control the money instead of letting the money control you. Apparently this man was a great entrepreneur because he made his money honestly. He was not a dope pusher; he was not a gambler. He was a farmer. And he was successful at farming. The grounds had been blessed, and everything he touched turned to gold.

If this rich man lived in our day and time, we would have him in almost every conference meeting possible. All of the prospective entrepreneurs would want to talk with him and ask him for advice. How did you become so successful just turning soil, raising fruits and vegetables? You have to give him credit – he was successful. He knew what he was doing. He knew the time to do what he did. A good farmer knows that there are certain types of soil you can plant in and other types of soil you cannot use for growing crops. You must also cultivate the soil correctly. You have to put the right amount of fertilizer in the soil and give it the right amount of water. The harvest must be gathered at the right time. After all this, the product must be marketed wisely to produce sales.

This man was so successful that he ran out of space. He ran out of barns. This man had made it and had made it well. He was known everywhere in the community. People knew him. However, this doesn't mean he was spiritual or that he knew God. Everybody that can manage money can't manage God's affairs. You have to have God, first, in order to manage affairs of the Kingdom.

Dialogue With Yourself

Luke 12:17

And he thought within himself, saying, What shall I do, because I have no room where to bestow my fruits?

And he said to himself. Now if you notice no one else heard him; he talked to himself. It may make you nervous to be around folk that talk to themselves. But sometimes it's good to talk to you. And if you get enough pressure on you, you will talk to you. Have you ever been sitting at a light and you see somebody talking and talking and talking, but there is nobody in the car but them? They just might be going through something and they need to talk it out before making a decision. Talk to yourself, because nobody knows you like you know yourself. Other folk will assume and think that they know you. But when you know you, you have to talk to yourself.

There was a man in the grocery store pushing a cart with a little boy in it. And the little boy was just crying and hollering. The man said, "Hang on in there, Albert. It will be all right Albert, just hang on." The little boy kept crying and he'd take the pacifier out of his mouth and throw it on the floor. The daddy would pick it up and wipe it off and put it back in the boy's mouth and say "Hold on Albert; hang on in there, Albert," with the little boy just screaming and hollering. "Albert, it's going to be all right." He got up to the counter to pay for his groceries and the cashier said to him, "Man you deserve to be commended. So much patience you have with little Albert. You constantly talked to him to try to get him calmed down." And the man said, "My name is Albert! His name is Mickey. I'm not trying to calm him down; I'm talking to myself." And every once in a while, you need to talk to yourself. Speak the truths of God's word to yourself. Apply the principles of the Word to the problem at hand. 1 Timothy 4:15 Meditate upon these things; give thyself wholly to them; that thy profiting may appear to all. Take time to think the problem through

What Stuff Controls Your Life?

Luke 12:18

And he said, This will I do: I will pull down my barns, and build greater; and there will I bestow all my fruits and my goods.

What shall I do? When you talk to yourself, be careful how you answer yourself. This man used too many I's and my's. Here is the way he would have recited Psalm 23: "I am my shepherd; I shall not want; I make in me to lie down in green pastures; I lead me beside still water; I restore my soul; I lead me in the path of my righteousness for my name's sake; yea, though I walk through the valley of the shadow of death; I will fear no evil because I'm with me. With my rod and my staff, I comfort me. I prepare a table before me in the presence of my enemies; I anoint my head with oil; my cup runneth over; surely, me, myself and I shall follow me all the days of my life and I shall dwell in my house forever. He was selfish and self-centered. The man counted on everything, but God. He said, "It's my barn, my grounds, my soul. Ha! He forgot to read Psalm 24 The earth is the Lord's, and the fulness thereof; the world, and they that dwell therein.

Here is a rich man who had it all. But he forgot that the ground really belongs to God. Even though it produced fruit, it was God's sunshine and God's rain, God's trees that made the lumber. He planned for his soul to take it easy. But there's nothing in the text to indicate that his soul can be at ease, because souls don't feast on corn. I know up north, you go to "Soul Food Restaurants". They've got ham hocks and collard greens, and turnip greens and fatback. They've got black-eyed peas, candied yams, crackling bread, blackberry cobbler, and peach cobbler. The sign says, "Soul Food." But how many of you know your soul can't eat that? Your soul will have to feast on the word of God. When you allow all the stuff to take control of your life, you're in serious trouble.

A Mistaken Scheme

Luke 12:19
And I will say to my soul, Soul, thou hast much goods laid up for many years; take thine ease, eat, drink, and be merry.

This man had it going for himself, but he made several mistakes. Listen to his conversation, "I have much goods laid up for many days." Who in here really can say I have many days? Because your time may be up today. It's never good to think we have a long time to live since God is the controller of our lives. I hope we're here for the next fifty years, but it's not a sure thing. I really think the man was a workaholic. Have you ever seen folk like that? They work so much that they miss life. They work twenty years, day and night, two or three jobs, and say, "One of these days, I'm going to be able to enjoy life." But you can work your whole life and never have the privilege of enjoying life. You work all your life stacking up, storing up, and somebody else will spend your money. Moreover they will forget you in the next two or three days. Sometimes you ought to stop and just have some fun for you. You ought to stop every once in a while and realize God has blessed you for you to enjoy what he has blessed you with. Enjoy yourself spiritually while you're able.

Just as sure as you have a day, night is coming, Logic tells you if there is a start then there is a finish. This man had made it good; he was rich. But the Lord called him a fool. Now it doesn't make a lot of difference if you call me a fool, because you might call a person anything. But when God says it, you can write it down because that's what you are. Psalm 53:1 The fool hath said in his heart, There is no God. When you forget God, you're a fool. You have everything else around you, but if you don't pen God into your life, you are nothing but a fool. What does it profit a man if he gained the whole world and then turns around and loses his own soul?

Be Rich Toward God

Luke 12:20-21

But God said unto him, Thou fool, this night thy soul shall be required of thee: then whose shall those things be, which thou hast provided? So is he that layeth up treasure for himself, and is not rich toward God.

One day, sooner or later, our souls will require another residence. This place is not equipped for our souls. This place is a good place for the body to be temporarily. But our souls will have to leave here and move to another place. You see what that man forgot about is that right now on planet earth the body and soul dwell on the same continent. Here is the problem. The soul doesn't die. Whether you're saved or lost, the soul moves to another place. If you're saved, your soul goes to live with the Lord. If you aren't saved, your soul goes to the bottomless hell. But what if you've been good around here? Be good all you want; if you don't have it right with God, your soul is going to the bottomless pit. Well, what if I speak to people? Speak all you want to. Except you have accepted Christ as your Savior and surrendered your life to the Lord, you will not have eternal life with Him.

I'm not taking any chances on the Lord delaying his coming. If he comes today, or if he should come to night, I'm not worried. I've made provisions. I made provision for him to return. As a matter of fact, I'll tell him to come on. If I never preach again, I thank God for the time he allowed me to be here. If I don't see you any more, I thank God for the little time he allowed me to hang around here. The God I serve has been real good to me. God said, "Thou fool, this night thy soul shall be required of thee." You might think God would have given him two or three weeks to get it ready, but the Lord said, this night. How many of us are praying to get through this night? 1 Thessalonians 5:2 tells us the Lord will come back like a thief in the night, Thy soul, yes sir, shall be required of you. Prepare eternally.

It's Only A Test

Genesis 22:1

And it came to pass after these things, that God did tempt Abraham, and said unto him, Abraham: and he said, Behold, here I am.

On a number of occasions, I've been watching my favorite TV program only to be interrupted with a clear screen, a round circle, and an unusual tune. After about sixty seconds, an announcement was made that it was only a test. If I had cut off my television the moment it went out, I would have missed the rest of the story. God takes us through tests. Many times when we experience tests, we give up the ship instead of being patient with God and seeing it through. Instead, we throw in the towel.

Abraham was a man who had experienced many tests. Here, the text says that God did tempt Abraham. We know that God tempts no man; God is not a tempter. The correct translation of this word is actually test; God did test Abraham. Now this was not the only test that Abraham had experienced. One of his first tests was his forsaking test. He had to forsake his home and his family and go to a land he knew not of. Later, he experienced a famine test during a drought. He had a falsehood test because he deliberately lied about his wife. He had a fellowship test because he had experienced a fellowship with his brother and his brother's son. He had to deal with a forgiveness test, because before he could be blessed, he had to get it right with God after lying about his spouse. He had a future test because God didn't tell him exactly where he was going. He had a faith test of believing God that he would father a child in his old age. He had the forbearance test when Hagar and Ishmael, his outside boy, had to leave home. He had a friendship test because he experienced a home visit with God and one of the angels. He had a farewell test because he had to say good-bye to Ishmael. He had a funeral test because he had to bury his wife Sarah. Tests, they are only tests.

A Painful Period Of Proving

Genesis 22:2

And he said, Take now thy son, thine only son Isaac, whom thou lovest, and get thee into the land of Moriah; and offer him there for a burnt offering upon one of the mountains which I will tell thee of.

Sometimes we panic after only one or two tests, but God will send test after test on top of test to get us where we ought to be. Now there's difference between being tempted and being tested. When I'm tempted, Satan is behind it. However, when I'm tested, God is behind it. Temptation may lead me into pleasure, but sometimes tests will lead me into pain. Temptation may help me have a good time, but testing will bring me into joy. Getting drunk may make you feel good for a while, but when you have joy it will last on and on and on and on.

Then God said to Abraham, "Take now thy son, thine only son Isaac, whom thou loveth…" Isaac is referred to as the lone son. Look at this verse closely, prayerfully and meditatively to consider what it is actually saying. The second time you see the word son, it is written in italic. Whenever you see anything in the Bible that's written in italic, it means that the translator added the word to help us understand the text. So it could read, instead of thine only son, thine only. That helps us a little bit because he was the lone son. How is that? It seems strange to call Isaac thine only son because Abraham had another boy. He had another son by his handmaiden, Hagar, whose name was Ishmael. But the text refers to Isaac as thine only son. God tells Abraham in verse twelve, "Lay not thine hand upon the lad neither do thou anything unto him, for now I know that thou fearest God seeing thou has not withheld thy son, thine only son." Genesis 22:16 By myself have I sworn, saith the Lord, for because thou hast done this thing, and hast not withheld thy son, thine only son. Son is an added word in both verses. God was referring specifically to Isaac.

Forfeiting Fully

Genesis 22:3

And Abraham rose up early in the morning, and saddled his ass, and took two of his young men with him, and Isaac his son, and clave the wood for the burnt offering, and rose up, and went unto the place of which God had told him.

Thine only son – these words reveal the magnitude of the sacrifice. Remember, if Abraham offered Isaac, he and Sarah wouldn't have any other children. If he offered up Isaac, his whole home would be empty. Isaac was the promised seed, the convenant that God had made with Abraham. And yet God said, "Take now thine only son." It's not hard to give up some things, but when you give up all you've got, that is a sacrifice. This is why Jesus was so impressed when the widow came and gave her two mites in the offering plate. It was because she gave all she had.

There was a sister who had another sister come in to visit a while from out of town. She said to the out of town sister, "Make yourself at home. Enjoy your stay while you're here. I must go to work everyday, but my house is yours." So the guest sister decided to go into the kitchen and fix herself some breakfast. But the kitchen door was locked. She thought, "Well, I guess my sister made a mistake and locked the door, so I'll go to the bathroom and take a nice hot bath." But the bathroom door was also locked. She said, "Well, there's a big screen television down in the den. I think I'll just go and watch television." She went down to the den to go in, but the door was locked. Even though she was in the house, she was restricted to certain areas.

Sometimes we treat the Lord the same way. We accept him as our personal savior, but we restrict him to certain areas of our lives. We lock him out from certain things. We keep part of our mind and use it for stuff that's not pleasing in the sight of the Lord. We want to give him our hand, yet hold on to our hearts. We must give all.

Fixed Faith

Genesis 22:6
And Abraham took the wood of the burnt offering, and laid it upon Isaac his son; and he took the fire in his hand, and a knife; and they went both of them together.

I saac was not only a very loved son, but he was also a law abiding son. He was not just a little boy when Abraham took him up the mountain. Sarah died four years after Isaac was offered as a sacrifice. And Sarah was one hundred twenty-seven years old when she died. Since Sarah was ninety when she gave birth to Isaac, then Isaac was thirty-three years old when he was offered as a sacrifice. Here is a young man, thirty-three years old, still following his elderly father around. Not once do you see Isaac rebelling against his father. Even when Abraham took the wood of the burnt offering and laid it upon Isaac with a knife and the fire in his hand, Isaac stayed next to him. Not once did he slow down even knowing that he was on his way to the sacrifice.

Then they came to the place of which God had told him, and Abraham built an altar there, and laid the wood in order, and bound Isaac his son, and laid him on the altar upon the wood. Have you ever asked why Isaac obeyed his father's wishes? One reason is that Isaac knew his father was moving by faith. The reason children rebel against their parents is because they don't see the faith in mama and in daddy. When they see you moving by faith, they will trust in you because faith really works. When your children see you have to light a cigarette every time you get nervous, then they will light up when they get nervous. They may light a marijuana stick. If you complain and worry about how you're going to make it, so will your children. The Bible says when you trust in Him, your way is already made. Our children often follow in our footsteps; that's why it is of the utmost importance that we do every thing based upon faith. You can't see faith, but it works.

When To Sacrifice

Genesis 22:2

And he said, Take now thy son, thine only son Isaac, whom thou lovest, and get thee into the land of Moriah; and offer him there for a burnt offering upon one of the mountains which I will tell thee of.

Take now thy son. When is the right time to sacrifice? Do it now. You see the delayed sacrifice in most cases is denied sacrifice. Have you ever talked yourself out of doing something for the Lord? You knew you needed to do it. You knew it was right to do it, but you kept reasoning with yourself. You kept talking to yourself until finally you convinced yourself to delay it over and over again. But did you know faith is a now movement? Hebrews 11:1 says "Now faith is." It seems like he could have said now or is. However, the words are: now faith is. If you missed the now you've got the is. So when should I make the sacrifice? He said do it now.

Well why should we do it now? There is a good answer. The reason you just do it now is because now is the only time you have. A whole lot of people would have good jobs if they had moved when the spirit told them. Many would be operating their own businesses. Instead, you kept on talking yourself out of it. A lot of you could have degrees right now, but you kept convincing yourself that you would do it the next semester, and next semester, and next semester. Before you knew it, gray hairs were all on your head, and then you were ashamed to go as an old person.

So when, you get ready to make a sacrifice do it now. Have you convinced yourself that you are going to get it together with God next year? Next year I'm going to get it right with God. But can I let you in on a little secret? Next year is not promised to you. I don't really know how long I'm going to live, so I'm doing all I can now. God wants us to make sacrifices for Him just as He did so for us. Now!

Expedient Obedience

Hebrews 11:17

By faith Abraham, when he was tried, offered up Isaac: and he that had received the promises offered up his only begotten son.

Abraham had to deal with giving up his son without an explanation. God did not explain to Abraham what he was doing. He just called him one night and told him to get up the next morning and take his son to a mountain and off him as a sacrifice. God didn't even tell Abraham which mountain until he was on his way. It is difficult to respond to God's request when He doesn't explain what He's doing. God doesn't always explain himself when he tells you to do something. Now eventually, if you stay with him, you'll understand Him. Even if you don't understand all the time when He tells you what to do, you will do well to do it if God said it. Abraham knew that Isaac was a promised child. If Isaac would die, then what would happen to the promise God had made to Abraham? You see God had said to Abraham, "I'm going to bless you and bless your seed." God made that promise to Abraham before a child was born. Then He said, "Not only will I bless your seed, I'm going to multiply your seed." Then He turns around and plans to take the only seed Abraham has. How could God multiply without having anything to start with?

Abraham had a serious problem to deal with. How could he go before the people around him and tell them that he had waited a hundred years for a son and when the son came up he took him and killed him. How could Abraham lift up his head if it got out he had killed his boy? Yet, Abraham rose up early in the morning and prepared to leave. He took everything he needed for a sacrifice. He carefully followed the proper procedures he knew for offering a sacrifice. Most of us think because we're under pressure, we can do it any kind of way. "Lord you know what I'm going through." But Abraham obeyed God.

Functioning By Faith

Genesis 22:4
Then on the third day Abraham lifted up his eyes, and saw the place afar off.

On the third day he lifted up his eyes and saw the place in the distance. If you continue trusting in the Lord, you will eventually see. There is a difference in faith and sight. Sight lets me look at the door. Faith will let me look beyond the door. Sight lets me see myself going to bed, but faith will let me see myself getting up the next morning. Sight lets me see myself filling out an application; faith will let me see myself retiring from my job. Sight lets me see myself getting a car on credit, but faith will let me see myself paying the last note. Sight lets me see myself paying my down payment on my house; faith will let me see the deed from paying my last note. Some people like sight, but I tell you it's best to depend upon faith.

You remember when God told Moses to take the Israelites and get out of Egypt. He told them to leave for a land flowing with milk and honey, but for some mysterious reasons there were some things on the journey God didn't mention. He didn't tell them that they were going to come to the bitter water or that there was a Red Sea before them. He didn't tell them they would run into a camp filled with snakes or that they were going to run out of food in the wilderness. He just told them to leave now.

I discovered that if God shows us the problems we're going to face, we never leave. If God shows us that we are going to run into an enemy, we will go in another direction. But that enemy just might be just a test. That enemy just might be a trapeze that God is using to help you leap over some stuff you otherwise wouldn't if you hadn't run into your enemy. If you knew you were going to get fired six months after you got your new house, you would never get one. But God allowed you to get the house, then lose your job to bring you to a new place in Him. He provides.

Outrageous Confidence

Genesis 22:5

And Abraham said unto his young men, Abide ye here with the ass; and I and the lad will go yonder and worship, and come again to you.

Here is an unusual promise. Abraham told his young men to stay with the ass while he and Isaac went up the mountain and then they would return. Now wait a minute, Abraham. Are you not going to offer your son? Didn't you hear God when he told you to go up and kill your boy? But you just said, "We're going up to worship and we're coming back." Abraham said he wasn't coming back by himself. What an incredible example of faith! Anytime a person can see God well enough to know that God is going to offer up his son and bring back the son he offered up, that is faith. And that's how God wants us to move is by faith.

Hebrews 11:17–19 By faith Abraham, when he was tried, offered up Isaac: and he that had received the promises offered up his only begotten son, of whom it was said, That in Isaac shall thy seed be called: accounting that God was able to raise him up, even from the dead… So Abraham said, "I'm going to give up my boy, but I know the power of God. God is able to raise him back up again." We may not see a door there, a way out, but God makes a door.

When we started building this church, I was convinced that we couldn't afford any more than the 2.5 million dollar structure. I talked to the contractor. However, he lied to me. (Although it took me a couple of years to get to this point, I'm now glad he did lie to me.) He said he could build the building for 3.8 million. If he had said then that it was going to cost 10.5 million, the church would still be at the previous address. We would have erased the idea of even making an attempt to come this far. But we had to trust God to go forward and He provided the rest!

Be Present At The Precise Place

Genesis 22:9

They came to the place which God had told him; Abraham built an altar there, laid the wood in order, and bound Isaac his son, and laid him on the altar upon the wood.

Abraham took Isaac to Mount Moriah. Moriah is mentioned one other time in the Bible in 2 Chronicles 3:1 where the Lord had appeared to David and David had worshipped Him there with a sacrifice. Moriah is right on the outside of Jerusalem just as Mount Calvary is right on the outside of Jerusalem. Isaac was thirty-three when he was offered up. Jesus was also thirty-three years old when he was offered. Isaac received his name from his father. Jesus received his name from his father. Because Abraham and Sarah were very old, Isaac was a miracle child. So also Jesus was a miracle child as Mary had not been touched by a man. Isaac was obeying the voice of his father. Jesus said, "I'm doing the will of my father." Isaac went up on the mountain with wood on his shoulder; Jesus went up on the mountain with wood on his shoulder. Isaac was laid on the wood on the mountain. Sin was laid on Jesus when he got to Mount Calvary. The only difference between the two is that Isaac came back down, but Jesus died on that hill called Mount Calvary.

God has a special place where he wants to bless you. But too many times we look for a blessing and we're out of place. In 1 Kings 17:4 God commanded the ravens to feed Elijah there by the brook; had he been anywhere else, he would have missed his meals. In 1 Kings 17:9 God told Elijah to move over to Zarephath of Zidon, where he had commanded a widow woman there to sustain him. God knows the right place for you to be so He can sustain you during the test. Some mountains are difficult to climb. But be willing to run all the way through pain and heartache, scorned by loved ones with maybe just a little sunshine ever now and then as Abraham did. I thank my Father for the privilege and for keeping and providing for His own.

Where Is The Lamb?

Genesis 22:7
And Isaac spake unto Abraham his father, and said, My father: and he said, Here am I, my son. And he said, Behold the fire and the wood: but where is the lamb for a burnt offering?

*I*saac asked, *"Where is the lamb for a burnt offering?"* Abraham had taught his son how to offer a sacrifice. Isaac knew the wood was ready; the fire was ready, and the knife was there. But there was a missing ingredient. You've got a missing lamb. I'm afraid we've grown up in a society now that we can worship in a whole worship service and never discover that the lamb is missing. The fire is there. The fire of excitement is in the place. We're jumping and shouting and speaking in tongues and running down the aisles. We've got the fire. The ritual of the wood is always present. In other words, let this house keep silent, the Lord is getting ready to speak. We've got the ritual down right, but where is the lamb? We have theological seminaries all over the country teaching about the fire and the wood, but they neglect to mention the lamb. You can stay in a whole worship service and the name of Jesus is never mentioned. But you cannot survive without knowing the lamb. Make sure you know the lamb.

Listen to Abraham's answer in verse eight. My son, God will provide himself a lamb. Abraham was saying, "First off, son, don't worry; this job is not mine. This job belongs to our heavenly Father. He is the one that will provide a lamb." And secondly he was saying that God himself is a lamb provider. And thirdly, what God and Abraham are really saying is that God is the lamb. God will provide himself because God needs the lamb to do what the lamb can do. Because the only way we can be saved is that the lamb has to die, and that's what Jesus is. Jesus is really God. Jesus is God, reincarnated. Abraham did not know exactly how, but he trusted God to provide the lamb.

In The Nick Of Time

Genesis 22:13

And Abraham lifted up his eyes, and looked, and behold behind him a ram caught in a thicket by his horns: and Abraham went and took the ram, and offered him up for a burnt offering in the stead of his son.

braham had built an altar and laid the wood in order. He hadn't done anything haphazardly, but everything was well planned and prepared. Everything you do for the Lord should be done in order. It is good to take the time needed to plan and prepare because God is a God of order. Abraham bound Isaac upon the altar and then he took the knife and stretched forth his hands. He got ready to come down and take his son's life. On his way down – he was on his way down, before he heard the voice of the Lord providing the answer.

Then Abraham heard a voice from heaven. It's always good to stay tuned in to heaven because you don't ever know when God is going to speak. He said, "Abraham, still your hand." What is God going to do now since He stopped Abraham from taking the child's life? "Abraham, go on with your sacrifice. I've got a lamb caught in the thicket." God had put a ram there and tied him up so the ram couldn't get away. Notice this about the ram. He was close, right behind Abraham. That means that when you need the Lord, he's close. You don't have to go looking for him. Not only was he close, he was also free. Abraham didn't have to pay a dime to get this ram. He just caught him and laid him on the altar. Furthermore, the lamb was ready to be offered up.

You know I get nervous sometimes because God is such a last minute God. I think, "Lord, If you don't hurry up and get me, it's going to be too late. It's 11:55 at night, I don't know if I can make it. My time runs out at midnight." Sometimes God will wait until 11:59. Just in the nick of time, God showed up. Don't panic; just pass the test!

Survive Suffering

1 Peter 2:19
For this is thankworthy, if a man for conscience toward God endure grief, suffering wrongfully.

I am convinced that many saved people are faced with situations that they really don't know how to handle. I see over and over again, believers filled with panic, crying, disturbed, baffled, walking the floor, losing sleep, losing appetites, all because you have been unjustly treated. You constantly ask yourself, why me? But if you would check the record, it has always happened. A saint in the Bible by the name of Abel was carried to the field by his brother, Cain, and was killed there although he had done nothing wrong. You remember Saul who set out to destroy David. You remember Naboth, an innocent bystander who was killed by Jezebel. You remember that Jezebel even ran the prophet Elijah out of town. John the Baptist was beheaded by not yielding to temptation. He only spoke and said to Herod, "It's wrong. It's wrong to have your brother's wife." You do remember the apostle Paul who by living a sanctified life was beheaded on a Nero's chopping block. We think of Stephen, the deacon, who was full of the Holy Ghost but stoned to death merely for telling the truth. You remember Jesus? He was born in a stable. They took him and had a kangaroo court set up against him. They crucified him on a hill called Calvary. So if other people were required to suffer, how about you, how about myself?

Suffering comes in many forms. Think it not strange when you are lied about. To be honest, you might think it strange if it doesn't happen because the Bible says in Matthew 5:11-12 Blessed are ye, when men shall revile you, and persecute you, and shall say all manner of evil against you falsely, for my sake. Instead you should Rejoice, and be exceeding glad: for great is your reward in heaven: for so persecuted they the prophets which were before you. The world will persecute God's servants.

Lust Turns Into Rage

Genesis 39:1

And Joseph was brought down to Egypt; and Potiphar, an officer of Pharaoh, captain of the guard, an Egyptian, bought him of the hands of the Ishmaelites, which had brought him down thither.

The scene opens with a man, a warden in a penitentiary named Potiphar, who had taken Joseph as a slave from the Ishmaelites. The Ishmaelites received Joseph from his own brothers who had sold him and told their father he had been killed by a wild beast. Now, it looks like Joseph should have endured enough and would be through with trouble. Here he is in the home of Potiphar, living a holy and sanctified life. However, we detect that there were some issues in the marriage. Potiphar's wife had a serious problem with young handsome men. She begged Joseph to come and lie with her, but he ran. When she saw that he had left his garment in her hands and she had evidence to try to convict him, her lust turned into a rage. She decided to make Joseph out to be the guilty one.

Notice how Mrs. Potiphar started stuff right away in the house. Instead of waiting until her husband came to discuss the matter, she called to the men of her house. She wanted to get the rumor started. She said of her husband, "He brought in a Hebrew." Instead of using a noun, she used a pronoun. All rumors start with he, she, or they. She is beginning to blame her husband for something he knew nothing about. He is at the prison making a living for his home while she is cutting up at the house. And she's blaming him for something she did herself. She is trying to throw in some prejudice by starting a racial issue, referring to the Hebrew; the Potiphars are Egyptian. She goes on to say the Hebrew is not only a threat to her, but to all the women and that her husband brought in the Hebrew to mock them. Whenever a person can not get you, they will try to destroy you. But God was looking out for Joseph.

Favored By The Almighty

Genesis 39:5

And it came to pass from the time that he had made him overseer in his house, and over all that he had, that the Lord blessed the Egyptian's house for Joseph's sake; and the blessing of the Lord was upon all that he had in the house, and in the field.

Potiphar's wife had repeatedly asked Joseph to lie with her, and he repeatedly refused. She was determined, so she asked him to just lie next to her. When he wouldn't lie with her or by her, she decided to lie on him. She deliberately made up this stuff to destroy a person who was living for the Lord. When Potiphar heard his wife's story, his wrath was kindled. He became angry. Not once did it say that he got angry with Joseph. His anger may have been more with his wife than it was with Joseph. Nevertheless, Joseph was the one who ended up in jail.

Potiphar was no fool. Genesis 39:3 says that Potiphar saw that the Lord was with Joseph and made all that he did to prosper in his hand. Potiphar was smart enough to observe Joseph's standing with the Lord. He had put Joseph in charge. If he watched Joseph, guess who else he watched. He watched his wife. This was not the first time this woman had done this. Some folk you fool, but sometimes you don't fool your own spouse. There are indications in the text that show Potiphar really didn't believe his wife's story, but he compromised.

So Joseph's master took him and put him into the prison, the same prison where the king's prisoners were bound. Genesis 39:21–22 tells us the Lord was with Joseph, and showed him mercy, and gave him favor in the sight of the keeper of the prison, who committed to Joseph's hand all the prisoners that were in the prison. It seems to say that regardless of what a person puts on you, if the Lord is with you the world can do you do harm.

Conserving Your Character

Genesis 39:23
... the Lord was with him, and that which he did, the Lord made it to prosper.

Joseph is a young man who stood firmly committed in spite of temptation. Unlike some other men, he did not yield to a woman. Admittedly he lost several things. Right away, he lost his reputation. Most of us get hung up on our reputation. I want to tell you that your reputation doesn't mean much. But if you lose character, you lose your reputation. If you lose your reputation, but you're in the favor of God, He will give you back your reputation, but if you lose your character, you're in a mess.

Joseph also lost his job because he was the right hand man in Potiphar's house. Some of you would rather lose your character than to lose your job. You're dealing with situations on your job that you know are wrong. But you stay there and live in sin and do all kinds of undercover stuff just to hold on to your job. When you take a stand for the Lord, then you've got the Lord's presence and power with you. God is more concerned with our character anyway than he is with our comfort. Joseph even lost his home because now he was living in jail.

Nevertheless, he was promoted while in jail. Instead of being bound in shackles, he was made a supervisor. God knew where he was carrying Joseph. You see one day Joseph would be the Prime Minister of Egypt. In order for Joseph to handle his part right, he needed to know how to survive at the lowest. He needed to understand what people were going through in their lives. If you've never been where I am, you don't know what I going through. If you've never been hungry you don't know how to deal with a person that has to go on without. So God took Joseph through the jailhouse. It looks as if Joseph is hemmed in, but it's only another test. In spite of what Joseph is going through, the Lord is with him in a major way.

Attitude Determines Your Altitude

Philippians 2:5
Let this mind be in you, which was also in Christ Jesus.

Joseph, a man destined for greatness, is in prison. A man that had committed no crime, yet in prison. What a sad place to be, especially when you've done nothing wrong. He was there as a result of being mistreated by his family. You expect some people to mistreat you, but not your family. However, notice Joseph's attitude while being in prison. He kept a positive attitude and remained true to his character. Joseph had a passion to serve. Some people look for a reason not to serve. Some people think up excuses. I've seen laborers around the church that will work harder trying to keep from working that they would if they would go on and do the job. But Joseph had a passion to serve.

Not only did he have a passion, but he also had patience. Some people mess up by being impatient. We must admit that some things don't happen over night. If you're going to accomplish goals in life, it takes a while to accomplish those objectives. It took Abraham a hundred years to get a son; it took Sarah ninety. They had to wait. It took Moses eighty years to be the Great Emancipator. He spent forty years in the school under Pharaoh and he spent forty years in the wilderness with his father-in-law Jethro.

It took John the Baptist thirty years before he could stand on Jordan and preach, "Repent for the Kingdom of Heaven is at hand." It took Paul fifteen years to move from the statement he made, "Every time I have a desire to do good, evil is always present," to the point where he said, "I can do all thing through Christ which strengthens me." Some things don't happen overnight. You will have to exercise patience. If you're going to arrive, you need to learn how to wait on God. Your attitude can determine your altitude. You can be free but have a bad attitude and it will send you down. Or you can be bound but with a good attitude, and you can make it through in flying colors.

Reliable In Small Matters

Luke 16:10
He that is faithful in that which is least is faithful also in much: and he that is unjust in the least is unjust also in much.

Even though Joseph was in one difficult predicament after another, he was faithful no matter where you found him. He was faithful as a son to his father Jacob. I often hear about people trying to get high positions who have not been faithful in low spots. Whenever Jacob said to Joseph, "Go to the fields," he went. Or, "Go feed your brothers," he went. When he became a slave, he continued to show faithfulness. Because he was so faithful in Potiphar's house, Potiphar promoted him. You see if you're faithful in low spots, God has a higher spot for you. Joseph was faithful to God when Potiphar's wife tried to seduce him. But he said, "If I have to make a choice between you and God, I've already decided to follow the Lord." So if you get caught in a predicament and nobody else is around, remember God is still looking. Be faithful to God.

As a sufferer, Joseph was faithful to patience. You see some of us can handle patience if nothing wrong is happening. Oh I'm patient as long as my icebox is full. As long as I have a check coming in every Friday, I'm patient; I can handle life. But as soon as it looks like it's getting a little dark, we're ready to throw up our hands and give it up. We need to have some patience, and the Lord takes us through things just to give us patience. Luke 21:19 In your patience possess ye your souls.

Observe the way God prepares to elevate Joseph. To us, it made no sense for Joseph's brothers to beat him up and put him in the pit or for the Ishmaelites to buy him as a slave. It made no sense for him to go to Potiphar's house and be mistreated again by his wife. It made no sense for Potiphar to respond to a lying woman and have this innocent boy placed in jail. Still, God's plan unfolds.

Dreams Of Doom And Delight

Genesis 40:2–3

And Pharaoh was wroth against two of his officers, against the chief of the butlers, and against the chief of the bakers. And he put them in ward in the house of the captain of the guard, into the prison, the place where Joseph was put.

While in prison, Joseph ran into a butler that had worked under King Pharaoh. He also ran into a baker that had served at the king's table. One night, the butler had a dream, a very unusual dream. He dreamed about a vine with three branches giving great clusters of grapes. The butler said that it troubled him because from the grapes he received juice and filled the cup of Pharaoh. He said, "I don't understand it." Then the baker said, "You know, I too had a dream. I was walking through the palace of Pharaoh with three baskets on my head. The top basket was full of meat and the birds ate the meat while I was trying to get to Pharaoh's table. So Joseph said, "Look let me interpret your dreams for you."

"You dreamed of a vine with three branches. God is letting you know that in three days Pharaoh will come and take you back to serve in his palace." Then Joseph said to the baker, "In three days Pharaoh is going to come and put a noose around your neck and hang you." Now the baker hadn't told his dream until he heard the interpretation of the butler's dream. Some people won't tell you what's happening in their life if they think it might bring doom. They always look for deliverance. But you've got to bear in mind that the same Bible that tells you what salvation will do will also tell you what sin will do. The same Bible that tells you about heaven will tell you about hell. The same Bible that tells you about the love of God will also tell you about the wrath of God. Most of us like to hear the love but don't want to hear about the wrath. And sure enough, in three days Pharaoh had a birthday celebration. He went and had the butler released, but he hung the baker.

Remember Me

Genesis 40:14, 23

But think on me when it shall be well with thee, and shew kindness, I pray thee, unto me, and make mention of me unto Pharaoh, and bring me out of this house: 23 Yet did not the chief butler remember Joseph, but forgot him.

Although Joseph had brought relief for the chief butler, he forgot him. He had made life pleasant for the butler, but he wouldn't have him in their speech. And on the other hand, when a person keeps you in their speech it is because they have you on their mind. I used to get real upset when I heard that people were talking about me. But when I discovered they don't talk about you if they're not thinking about you. So I detected that people were promoting me and I was fighting the promotion, because sometimes talk is the greatest publicity you can ever have. Don't get upset because people are talking about you. They can't talk about you if they're not thinking about you.

Now, the butler is out and the baker is dead. But Joseph is still in prison. Hardly ever does Joseph use the pronoun me. For once he decided to remember himself. Note what Joseph says in Genesis 40:14. But think on me, when it shall be well with thee and show kindness, I pray thee unto me and make mention of me unto Pharaoh and bring me out of this house. Joseph was a type of Christ, and that is exactly what Jesus says to us. That's why we have communion. Jesus says, "Do this in remembrance of me. As often as you do this, you show forth my death, burial and resurrection. Do this until I come again." That's why it's so important that every time we preach, we preach Christ. Not John but Christ. We need to hear is more about Jesus. If the world is going to be saved, Jesus will save it. There is no Co-Savior. We must focus totally on him. You wonder how you ended up in unusual spots. You think you accidentally came that way because of a detour. However, the things that we call a detour are often God's divine plan.

August

Pharaoh's Fitful Dreams

Genesis 41:8

In the morning his spirit was troubled; and he sent and called for all the magicians of Egypt, and all the wise men thereof: and Pharaoh told them his dream; but there was none that could interpret them unto Pharaoh.

Two years have passed since Joseph has seen the chief butler, who is back at the palace. Then Pharaoh has a dream. After the first dream, he woke up, thought about it, and went back to sleep. But he dreamed again. The second dream kept him up all night long. Pharaoh called in all the great men of his kingdom and told them to interpret his dream. However, none were able. They saw that Pharaoh was getting upset so the butler said, "You know my lord, I do remember when I was in prison some years ago, there was a Hebrew that interpreted my dream which came to pass exactly as he had said."

So Pharaoh sent for Joseph and told him the dreams. Recall that before Joseph left his father's home, he had two dreams. While in prison, the baker and butler both had dreams. So two and two is four. Now Pharaoh had two dreams. You see God gradually elevates you to higher heights. In the first dream, Pharaoh saw seven fat cows come up out of the Nile River followed by seven lean cows that ate the seven fat cows. In his second dream, Pharaoh saw seven full ears of corn followed by seven scrawny ears of corn that swallowed up the fat ears.

Joseph immediately told Pharaoh that God is the interpreter. He did not elevate himself. The first thing that came out of his mouth was praises about God. If you want to be successful in life, start your conversation off with praise. When you begin a new job, start your conversation with your fellow workers with praise for the Lord. When asked, "How you doing?" you should be able to say, "The Lord brought me." If somebody complements you say, "The Lord taught me; it is the Lord who has kept me."

From Pit To Palace

Genesis 41:39
And Pharaoh said unto Joseph, Forasmuch as God hath shewed thee all this, there is none so discreet and wise as thou art:

Joseph said, "Mr. King Pharaoh, let me tell you the interpretation of your dream. The fat cows and the full ears of corn mean that you have seven more good years, seven more years of prosperity. But the seven lean cows and the seven lean ears of corn mean that in seven years a famine is coming. If you don't prepare for rough times now, you are going to be in trouble. If you plan to survive the lean years, you need first of all to bring in a good administrator. You need somebody that knows something about agriculture. They also need to know how to handle people. You're a King and you don't know anything about raising cows or managing a farm. You have to bring in a Chief Executive."

Pharaoh thought, "Joseph, I've been watching you. You have a real good track record. You were faithful down at Potiphar's house. I pulled your birth record and you treated your daddy right. I have your prison record. I saw you didn't create any problems down in the dungeon. As a matter of fact, you did everything the warden asked you to do. So Pharaoh said, "Joseph, you shall be over my house, and according to your word shall all my people be ruled: only in the throne will I be greater than you.

Joseph started off down in a pit and even though he had to come up on the rough side of the road, God moved him from a pit all the way to a palace. Now if Joseph had stayed down with his daddy Jacob, he would have been a farmer the rest of his life. But God brought him on the rough side of the mountain. I used to complain about climbing up the rough side. But that's the best side of the mountain to climb on. The smooth side of the mountain has nothing to grip hold of, but when you have a rough side, every rock is a stepping stone, bringing you a little higher.

The Future Of The Faithful

Genesis 41:37
And the thing was good in the eyes of Pharaoh, and in the eyes of all his servants.

Prior to this verse I was a little disheartened about the things that my brother Joseph had to endure. It seemed so unfair for a young saved brother to be mistreated by his brothers, to be misunderstood by his own earthly father, to be treated like a criminal in his own house, to be sold to the Ismaelites as a slave, to be lied on by the master's spouse, to be placed in jail without committing a crime, and to be put in shackles and chains for no apparent reason. For thirteen years it appeared as though God was not listening. But when I read verse 37, it looks like a brighter day ahead.

One tragedy of the body of Christ is that we panic before our day comes. We believe God is fair with others, but not us. Others appear to have no problems. Everything seems to fit right in place in their lives. They come home understood. They never have problems with their parents; they get cars at the age of sixteen; at eighteen they're engaged to be married. College is no problem. They buy big houses and seem to be faring well. Yet your life is one problem after another. Every time you're getting ready to get a foothold, some thing else will occur in your life. You ask yourself, "Is God dealing with me fairly? If so, why must I go through these things?"

We must bear in mind that as saved people we're on a battlefield. We must go through extensive training so we will not crumble under pressure. The reason some people can endure so much is because they've already been in the fire. Through many dangers, toils, and snares I have already come. Joseph has gone through quite a bit, but he is still standing. However the sun is getting ready to shine. Joseph looked good in the eyes of Pharaoh and in the eyes of all his servants. Your future actually relies on faithful servants. The future of the faithful is always fruitful.

The Captive Becomes Commander

1 Corinthians 15:58
Therefore, my beloved brethren, be ye stedfast, unmovable, always abounding in the work of the Lord, forasmuch as ye know that your labour is not in vain in the Lord.

In order to be spiritually successful, you must be steadfast. Don't let winds or waves or doctrines move you to the side. Hold your hope, stand your ground, and be determined to go forward. You are who you think you are. If you think you can't make it, you're already whipped. But if you think you can make it, you can go through. Joseph moved from a slave to a prince in a palace. That's moving up, isn't it? His grief has been replaced with gladness.

Look at the mandate of Joseph's selections. Genesis 41:40 Thou shall be over my house. Now this is not the first time Joseph was placed over a house. Genesis 37:3 says Israel, (that's Jacob) loved Joseph more than all his children because he was the son of his old age and he made him a coat of many colors, meaning he had made Joseph superior over the whole house. Genesis 39:4 says Joseph found grace in the sight of Potiphar, who made Joseph overseer of his house and all that he had. Genesis 39:22 tells us that Joseph was given charge of all the prisoners.

Notice the way God elevates us. First of all, Joseph was moved up in his own house. Then in Potiphar's house he was elevated to be in charge of the slaves. When he went to jail, he was put over all the prisoners. And now he is in Pharaoh's house and has been elevated to the top man, but he had to begin by being faithful in his own house. You see too many of us want to be superior in other people's arenas and want to skip our own houses. If you want to be a great soul winner, start off saving the children at your house. Once you get them saved, then go down and save the ones on your job. You see God doesn't allow us to skip when it comes to promotions. We will have to do it from ground floor all the way up. Do it right at first.

Selected

Genesis 41:38
And Pharaoh said unto his servants, Can we find such a one as this is, a man in whom the Spirit of God is?

Joseph spent thirteen years in what I call the school of hard knocks, perhaps the best school one can go through. He was on his way to prominence but before he got there, God had to prepare him for what he was going to have the privilege of enjoying. So it took him thirteen years to get to this spot, but he finally made it at the age of thirty. Luke 3:27 says that is exactly how old Jesus was when he went out to preach the Gospel. And Jesus too had to go through some things before he made it to his thirteenth birthday. There is nothing wrong with going through some things if it will prepare you for what you will have to face in the future. I have discovered that it just doesn't happen over night. Isaiah 28:16 says He that believeth shall not make haste. When you believe the Lord, you don't have to get in a hurry because you know you will come out more than a winner. When you believe the Lord, He knows where you are and what you're dealing with even at the time you're dealing with it.

Observe Joseph, the man being selected. Genesis 41:39 And Pharaoh said unto Joseph, Forasmuch as God hath shewed thee all this, there is none so discreet and wise as thou art. The word discreet means one that knows how to keep a secret. That may be one of the reasons why God is not telling us much – because we can't keep it. When we find out anything we just have to tell somebody. And the Lord says some things in life you can't tell now because if you tell it, people won't believe it anyway. So Pharaoh is aware that Joseph has been in touch with wisdom. Consider what Pharaoh says about this Joseph's character. He is saying, "You've got something going for you." Pharaoh said unto his servant, "Can we find such a one as this, a man in whom the spirit of God is?

Sanctified, Then Sent

John 10:36
Say ye of him, whom the Father hath sanctified, and sent into the world,
Thou blasphemest; because I said, I am the Son of God?

This verse shows how sanctification is accomplished. Ye of him whom the father has sanctified and sent. Jesus was first sanctified, then sent. Now most people want to be sent first and then work on the sanctification part down the road. Too many people have been sent and are holding spots, but they have not been sanctified. It's hard to deal with sent people that don't have some sanctification. Now the Lord says you've got to first be sanctified. Only after sanctification are you required to be sent. How can I be sanctified? Do I need to have somebody lay hands on me? Do I need to go somewhere and tarry and wait on the sanctification to show?

John 17:17 says Sanctify them through thy truth: thy word is truth. We are sanctified through the Word. Be baptized with the Holy Ghost. Luke 3:16 says, Ye shall be baptized with the Holy Ghost. Acts 1:5 says Ye shall be baptized with the Holy Ghost shortly. Acts 11:16 says, Ye shall be baptized with the Holy Ghost. 1 Corinthians 12:13 says, For by one spirit ye are baptized with the Holy Ghost. If God promises you something, you can depend on it.

John 3:6 speaks of the first birth, that which is born of the flesh. This verse goes on to say, that which is born of the spirit is spirit. If I'm born again, the spirit had to usher in that new birth. Since I've been born again, I'm sanctified. That means I have been set apart for a holy use. Because the job is not mine, I don't have any business sanctifying myself. Since the job belong to God, He is the one who will do the sanctifying for me. I heard Jesus say in Luke 2:49, "Know ye not that I must be about my father's business?" You see the business is not mine; it belongs to the Lord. I should tell you, it is a big business.

The Path To Paradise

2 Corinthians 12:2

I knew a man in Christ above fourteen years ago, (whether in the body, I cannot tell; or whether out of the body, I cannot tell: God knoweth;) such an one caught up to the third heaven.

I think God cruises around and finds people that he can use as models. He showcases a person who can endure one crisis after another. Such a person was the Apostle Paul, who had set up churches all over Asia Minor. He was a person that loved God, believed in God, trusted God, and made sacrifices for God. Moreover, there were some privileges that Paul experienced that most of us never experience. The text says that he was caught up into the third heaven or paradise, the place where God is. Of course, to have a privilege like that it was very expensive. Never think that privileges come free of charge. For those of us who are saved, our privilege is that we have been born again. We have been washed in the blood of the lamb.

And because we have the privilege of sonship, of salvation, of security, we become a target for Satan, self, and sin. Sin is always moving around trying to degrade us, trying to make us believe we're not who we are. Self is constantly talking to us saying, "You ain't what you claim to be." Satan is setting traps to try to dethrone us. Satan doesn't bother his own and that's why some people are not tempted by the devil because they are still in the camp. You see, Satan will never fight Satan; he will never war against himself. But if you are attacked by Satan, that's good news. It's because you have moved from his camp to the will and the word of God. Have you ever asked yourself, "Why is it that since I have been saved, it looks like everything is happening to me." It means that you've moved from where you were to where you are. Satan doesn't take it lightly when you move out of his camp and start serving a true and a living God. However, exceptional things await us!

Impossible To Repeat

2 Corinthians 12:4

He was caught up into paradise, and heard unspeakable words, which it is not lawful for a man to utter.

What Paul saw was so exciting that he wanted to tell other folk. There may come a time in your life when things happen that you can't tell it yet. Too many of us like to tell about our experiences with God too quickly, but sometimes you need to hold it for a while. You must discern with whom you can share because when you share with some folk, you do more harm than good. They will not believe your story because it hasn't happened to them. When a person has not experienced a real move of God, it is difficult to get it over to them that God is real. You might be shocked to know how many folk laugh at you when you shout because they have never shouted themselves and they don't know the joy in shouting in the name of the Lord. They think it's a plaything when they see you running up and down the aisle. They don't know you're rejoicing because you've got legs to run with. They don't know that you were at the point of death or that God snatched you out of the jaws of hell and this is rejoicing time.

Also, not many folk have come back from heaven to tell you about it. Paul did have some fellows behind him that had experienced a lot of things, but they had never been caught up into the third heaven. Abraham left home with a promise for a land he knew not of but he wasn't caught up in the third heaven. Moses was a great emancipator who led 600,000 Israelites out of Egypt to the gates of the promised land, but he never experienced getting caught up into third heaven. Isaiah was a man of vision who could see 700 years ahead and said, "Unto us a child is born, and his name shall be called wonderful, counselor, mighty God, everlasting Father, the Prince of Peace, but he never got caught up into the third heaven. Paul had to hold his experience inside.

A Well Worn Thorn

2 Corinthians 12:7
And lest I should be exalted above measure through the abundance of the revelations, there was given to me a thorn in the flesh, the messenger of Satan to buffet me, lest I should be exalted above measure.

est I should be exalted above measure. Unless I get lifted in pride, unless I start thinking I'm more than others, unless I get to the point where I'll stop speaking to my sons, Timothy and Titus and these others. There was given to me a thorn in the flesh. When country folk think in terms of a thorn, you think in terms of a little splinter, something that got caught in your finger. That's not the thorn spoken about here. In the original languages, the word thorn means stick. It comes from the idea of one actually being placed on the cross. You may think this was just a temporary situation, but the text says that he had warred with this thing for fourteen years.

Now most of just cannot handle suffering fourteen days. If it is the right kind of suffering, fourteen hours is too long, and of course if it's serious enough, fourteen minutes. But here is a person that had experienced this matter for fourteen years. Although it was fourteen years ago, every time he would move he had to think about what he saw in the third heaven. Every time he would testify, he would get right up to this experience and have to cut it off. When he got ready to tell his next testimony, he had to cut himself short. When he got ready to preach a sermon, he said, "I want to tell you about... and he would have to stop. Sometime there are some things in your life you just want to tell, but can't. When you can't tell anybody else, you start telling yourself. It's hard to talk to yourself about the good things of God without getting lifted up. If you're not careful, there is a spiritual pride that gets you to a point where you'll start looking down at other folk and think you are more than they are. But the thorn kept him humble.

Purpose For The Pressure

2 Corinthians 12:7

And lest I should be exalted above measure through the abundance of the revelations, there was given to me a thorn in the flesh, the messenger of Satan to buffet me, lest I should be exalted above measure.

A messenger of Satan was given to Paul to buffet him. The word buffet means to hit with the fist. It means taking abusive treatment. He said, "Look, I really had a war in my private life. And I had a war for several reasons. First, I was under pressure." Pressure can create catastrophes. Lots of folk are over weight because they're under pressure. Some of you say that you smoke because of pressure. You can't sleep because of pressure. Paul had pressure.

In spite of the pressure, God had a purpose for the thorn. He wanted to keep Paul's feet on the ground. God knows all of his children. As a matter of fact, God knows us better than we know us. Most of us think we can handle being rich. You say, "If I can't handle it, I'd love to try." But God knows if we get a little too much too soon, our feet would leave the ground. And God would rather have us talk to him on a daily basis than to just hear from us at the end of the year.

I have been preaching for twenty-seven years. I have been studying the Bible for the last thirty-five years and I try to spend forty hours in preparing each sermon. I don't want to come on Sunday and you leave empty, because I've been in places where I've heard messages that meant nothing. If I could work forty hours a week on a job for myself, I can spend that much time studying the word for God's people. And even at that when I come to the pulpit, the Lord will do something over and over again to keep my feet on the ground. More than once I have studied forty hours for a sermon just to have the Lord take it as I walked to the pulpit He said, "You will have to rely on me."

243

If Only

Genesis 41:37
For this thing I besought the Lord thrice, that it might depart from me.

God didn't want Paul to get puffed up with pride. God said, "When you start thinking about how you can speak fourteen different languages, seven of them fluently, how you've established thirteen churches, how you wrote one third of the New Testament, that you have your doctorate of divinity, and that you have been caught up into the third heaven, people won't be able to touch you." So God had to keep Paul where he could use him. You see when God can't use you, then you're no good to the Lord. Actually, you become a danger to the body of Christ. But thank God, he always makes provisions. Never think that God does not watch us. He knows every trap we find ourselves in and He's always there to get us out of our dilemma.

Paul sought the Lord three times asking that the thorn might depart from him, but his prayer was unanswered. However, the Bible says if we ask for something, He will hear and answer our prayer. Paul was like some of us. He went to the Lord and said, "If only you would move this thorn." Lord I could serve you better if only I didn't have this low down boss on my job. I could do more for you, if only I didn't have this wayward child at my house. I could be more effective if I didn't have this drug addict husband. I could come to church more if I didn't have this sickness in my body. Lord, I could be more helpful in the body of Christ if only my finances were a little better. In other words, we're trying to run God's business. "I would do something for you Lord, but I've got this thorn in my flesh." God loved Paul but he didn't remove the thorn because it wasn't necessary. Paul was more effective with the thorn than most people in the New Testament. It's a shame when a one-legged man can cover more ground than a two-legged man.

Thankful For Your Handicaps

2 Corinthians 12:9

And he said unto me, My grace is sufficient for thee: for my strength is made perfect in weakness. Most gladly therefore will I rather glory in my infirmities, that the power of Christ may rest upon me.

If you've got God with you, it makes no difference about your thorns, your hindrances, and your handicaps. God can take any body and do what he wants to do. If you have some excuses today, this text is going to erase all those excuses. His grace—it is sufficient. What does that mean? It means my problem is not fatal. Whatever we have, it didn't take us out of here; I'm still here. No matter how difficult things are, I'm dealing with it; I'm standing on the ground and the ground is not standing on me. It's not final; it will not write the final chapter in my life. I've still got a tomorrow. But it is fruitful; it brings a person into fellowship with the Son. If you know you can't get rid of a problem, you can talk to God about. Prayer is required if you're going to make it through the tests of life.

My grace. The grace is personal. Jesus says, "My grace is sufficient for you." Whatever you're going through, the grace can handle it. Then he said, "For my strength is made perfect in weakness." The power is unlimited. Have you ever wondered how power becomes power? The way you get it is straight from God above. And when his power is released, it works best on weak folk. You see when you're strong you are trying to use your own strength. When you're wrestling and trying to survive on your own, God just stands back and allows you to go on and wrestle. But when you stop wrestling with yourself and say, "Lord here I am," hey, you are just right for God. "I can't make it by myself; I'll have to depend totally upon you." Then God moves in. Most gladly I will glory in my infirmity that the power of Christ might rest upon me. When God's power rests on you, then you can take pleasure in your infirmity.

Give Up The Nest

Deuteronomy 32:11
As an eagle stirreth up her nest, fluttereth over her young, spreadeth abroad her wings, taketh them, beareth them on her wings:

The mother eagle knows that the little eagles obtain strength only when they fly. If they refuse to fly, she puts them on her back and takes them out into the blue yonder. When they're sitting comfortably on mother's back, she dives out from under the little eaglets. Then she pulls up over them and watches them as they flap on their own wings. If one is unable to handle it alone, she dives back under him where he can rest a little on her back. She repeats the process it until they can make it on their own. She knows that eventually the eaglets will grow up, but she also knows they could be lazy and would like to sit around and do nothing. So the mother eagle prepares her nest a special way. She begins with clay and mud to which she adds thorns and thistles and allows them to stick up out of the clay. She uses straw to cover the thorns and then she sheds her feathers and covers the straw. When it is time for the eaglets to leave the nest, the mother eagle will stir it and move all the comfort out of the nest so the thorns and thistles will stick the bottoms of the little eaglets. The place of domicile becomes uncomfortable.

Sometimes God works with us like the mother eagle attends to the little eaglets. He may need to work with us the same way because we grow too comfortable in this life. When God sends us through test after test, what he is really trying to do is to carve out a testimony. But we cannot have a testimony without first having a test. What better person to give us a test than the person that died for us. We must remember that this is not our home. We're just pilgrims traveling an unfriendly land. And whatever God is doing to us and through us, he is preparing us for a better day. If you get the right character, the comfort will come.

Reaching The Other Side

Matthew 14:22
And straightway Jesus constrained his disciples to get into a ship, and to go before him unto the other side, while he sent the multitudes away.

Jesus had just finished working a miracle of feeding five thousand men plus the women and children. If you're not careful in the body of Christ, you will start thinking that the move of salvation is a meat and bread movement, that the reason you're serving God is so you can eat and sleep. Yet it's not about eating and sleeping; it's about soul winning. Even though you're saved, there is a multiplicity of people on their way to hell.

Straightway, Jesus constrained his disciples. In other words, he urged the disciples. He put something on them; he encouraged them to get in to a boat. Now Jesus has a number of ways to persuade us to do things, indeed things we said we would never do. Five years ago, some of you would have to be twisted or shot to make you come to church, especially on the Sunday after Thanksgiving. But here you are now and God knows what you've had to go through in order to get here. Sometimes he moved and took that which was near and dear. He might take your job or tamper with your health. Sometimes he does unusual or mystifying things and you say to the Lord, "That's enough. If you want, I'll serve you." He constrained his disciples to get into a ship and go before him to the other side. Jesus knew that before his disciples could teach others, they themselves needed to be taught.

Their destination was the other side. Where I'm going is to the other side. The old people used to sing songs about going to the other side. You hear them singing, "I'm on my journey and I can't turn around." They called it The Old Ship of Zion. I like this ship because it has already landed many thousands safely over. I like the security of the ship because Jesus is the Captain.

A Remarkable Weapon

Matthew 14:23

And when he had sent the multitudes away, he went up into a mountain apart to pray: and when the evening was come, he was there alone.

When he had sent the multitudes away. If you are going somewhere, there are some folk you have to leave behind, because if you try to hang around with certain crowds you won't go and neither will they. If you're going somewhere and a person doesn't want to go with you, let them stay. Invite them to come, but don't let them stop you from making it to the other side. There's a person over there I must see, an unusual person. With one arm he reached prayer from earth all the way to heaven. With the other arm he reached grace from heaven all the way down to man. With one leg he stands on time and the other on eternity. He can turn around and get so little until he can get in my heart and have me loving my enemies. I want to see the man that can take red blood and put it on a black heart and wash it whiter than snow. So I'm not going to let anything hinder me from going to the other side.

Jesus sent the disciples out on a ship and went up to the mountains to pray. If the Son of God prayed, then how about you? If God who has all power, knows everything, and is everywhere at the same time prayed, then we ought to pray. Prayer is an unusual weapon. Prayer is the greatest weapon any saint can have. When you cannot be victorious any other way, just pray, because prayer will change things. Prayer will change people, prayer will change conditions, and prayer will change the pray-er. If you pray you'll feel better. That's why you need to pray for your enemies. If a person mistreats you, it's hard to get on your knees and pray for him and still shoot him. Something will happen to you while you're on your knees. The average person that messes up is a person that didn't pray first. If you pray in the calm you can handle the storm.

Sudden Storms

Matthew 14:24
But the ship was now in the midst of the sea, tossed with waves: for the wind was contrary.

Storms can come odd times. This one came when the disciples were in the midst of the sea. Midst means somewhere in between. They started traveling in the evening just before sundown and somewhere around the midnight hour they were now in the midst. What does that mean? It means that you have gone too far to turn around because it's just as far going back as it is to go on to the other side. The Lord allows us to get in the midst of situations, and then he sends a storm. Now I better tell you that not all storms are sent by God. Some storms are sent by the devil. And some storms we bring on ourselves. In January, especially, many of you will be in storms you brought on yourselves from buying stuff you don't need with money you don't have trying to impress folk you don't even like. We would do better to spend more time sharing instead of shopping in order to avoid getting caught up in financial storms.

The storm came when Jesus wasn't there. Doesn't it look like trouble seems to come at the wrong time? Just when you thought you had it all together, suddenly a storm shows up without warning. There is no chance to prepare; the storm just showed up in the middle of nowhere. The ship was being tossed with the waves. It wasn't just sitting there. The storm was rocking their little ship. And storms will rock you. Storms will have you sitting at your table unable to eat. Storms will have you lying in your bed unable to sleep, rocking you. Storms will have you sitting at a red light that's green, rocking you. Storms will take you out of who you are. Don't make a mistake and ask a person in a storm how they are doing. They'll tell you about everything that's happening in their life. A storm will consume your life. We need Jesus in our storms.

The Storm Didn't Stop Jesus

Matthew 14:25
And in the fourth watch of the night Jesus went unto them, walking on the sea.

The fourth watch is about three or four o'clock in the morning. Can you imagine how hard they been toiling from evening to 3 o'clock. All of these disciples are drenched with water. Their eyes are red and their muscles are sore; fear and panic is all over them. Some say that the darkest hour is just before dawn. That's the time folk commit suicide, just an hour before daylight. It's just a few feet from the other side of the tunnel, and folk decide to give up before going through. It's a critical hour in the life of any person. When it come to getting out of situations, don't give up too soon. You've got to keep on fighting, keep on going forward. It was a trying time in the storm.

In contrast, I see the tranquillity in the storm. The Bible says that Jesus went unto them. I like that because any time a storm shows up in your life, Jesus will show up. It's kind of like some folk that seem to smell what you are cooking all the way from the other side of town. They show up at the same time you get the food done. Or a friend you haven't heard from in six months shows up the same time your check arrives in the mail. All of a sudden, there they are. Likewise that's the way Jesus does during our trouble. When storms come, Jesus will show up.

I like that about Jesus. He knows how much you can bear. He does just the opposite of what your friends do. When trouble comes your friends diminish to few. They watch their caller ID and see if it's you and then they don't answer. But not so with the Lord. When trouble showed up, Jesus came walking on the sea. Now that's the impossible; nobody can walk on water. But Jesus did. I think Jesus was saying, "I don't care where you are, I can get to you. You can be in the valley, or in your sick bed; but wherever you are, you are still in reach of me."

Drenched In Doubt

Matthew 14:26-27

And when the disciples saw him walking on the sea, they were troubled, saying, It is a spirit; and they cried out for fear. But straightway Jesus spake unto them, saying, Be of good cheer; it is I; be not afraid.

The disciples saw their good God in time of trouble. When they saw him walking on the water, they were troubled. They had some apprehension about his help. I have discovered in life that sometimes you can be so drenched in your trouble that you can't see your triumph. You can be so caught up in you circumstances that you can't see your savior. Your can be so bogged down with your doubt that you can't focus on your deliverance. If you put doubt in front of the deliverer, you'll walk around with your head down from now on. But you've got to know that all things work together for good to them that love God, to them who are the called according to his purpose.

Notice hat Jesus immediately responded, urging them to "Be of good cheer." I like that because he's always around to disperse cheer. Jesus knows how to cheer us up. You can be dying from cancer and Jesus will have you with a smile on your face. He can bring cheer to a person on their way to their death bed. Have you ever gone to see a person that was dying and when you left, they were happier than you were? They told you, "I'm all right; I got it fixed up with Jesus." Can't nobody do you like the Lord can. He says, "Be of good cheer; it is I; be not afraid."

I wondered, "Why did Jesus have to tell them who he was." But here again, you can get so caught up in your crisis until you forget who Jesus is. If you know who Jesus is, you'll stop crying at night over problems in your life. If you know who Jesus really is, you want panic because your bank account is low. If your name is scandalized, you'll count it all joy. When the doctor gives you bad news, you can say, I've got another doctor that's above all doctors.

Remain Focused

Matthew 14:29

And he said, Come. And when Peter was come down out of the ship, he walked on the water, to go to Jesus.

Peter said, "Master, if it's you, I want you to do something spectacular. Let me come to you on the water." Jesus said just one word, and that word was come. That word is mentioned 682 times in the Bible; it is a universal invitation. Then Peter did the unexpected; he walked out on the water. Some people would say that was foolish, but let me tell you, it took a lot of faith to step out of the boat. We often criticize folk for stepping out. Some of you have gone into business for yourself while other folk stand back and look at you with a critical eye. You didn't have enough money to do what you needed to do, but at least you had enough faith to try. You cannot fail unless you make an attempt to begin with. But let's assume that you failed; get on back up and try again. President Nixon ran two or three times before he became President of the United States. Every one of us are walking now because as babies we failed, but we got back up over and over. If you fall, don't drink tears of sorrow; get up and make another effort.

Can't you see Peter out walking on the water? One of the theologians said it would have been all right if a doubter hadn't been in the boat behind him warning Peter to look over toward the big wind coming. There is always somebody hanging around to discourage you, saying, "I wouldn't try that." When Peter saw the wind he started to sink because he took his eyes off the savior and put his eyes on the storm. If you are going to make it in life, keep your eyes focused on Jesus, not on your husband or on your wife, but on Jesus. Don't concentrate on your job, your boyfriend, or girlfriend, but on Jesus. Don't be engrossed in your money, but centralize your attention on Jesus the author and finisher of your faith. When Peter started to sink, he had enough sense to turn to Jesus and say, "Save me.

Faith Afoot

2 Corinthians 5:7
For we walk by faith, not by sight.

Enoch is an illustration of a faith that walks. Genesis 5:24 tells us that he walked with god. The Bible says that we walk by faith, not by sight. Walking is a posture. In other words it is a position that one must take in order to travel. You may be able to cause a dead man to stand up, but you can't make him walk. In order for a person to walk they must have life on the inside. Accordingly, if a person is going to walk with God, he must have life on the inside. Specifically, you must be spiritually alive and spiritually alert in order to be able to walk with God.

What does it mean to walk with God? First of all it means harmony. Amos 3:3 says How can two walk together accept they agre?. God doesn't want us to try and persuade Him to agree with us; we must agree with him. You see I haven't been here long enough to try to bend God over to think the way I think or to tell God, "I want you on my side." I need to agree with God. That's what confession really is, when you agree with God about your sins. We call sin weakness; God says it is wickedness. We call sin a defect; God calls it disease. Whatever God says about sin is exactly what sin is.

Furthermore, when you walk with God it means you are going places. You will never remain the same. You won't stay in the same old rut, do the same old things, or have the same old attitude and disposition all of the time. If you are walking with Him, you ought to be doing some progressing. You will be moving forward, stepping a little higher, and walking a little closer. Before following Him, you prayed a traditional prayer. But when you started following Jesus, your prayers changed. You began to stretch out on the Lord. And when you stretch out, you expect results from him. We no longer pray just to be praying; we expect to get an answer. A faith walk!

Transferred By Trust

Hebrews 11:5
By faith Enoch was translated that he should not see death; and was not found, because God had translated him.

By faith Enoch was translated and did not experience death. The word translated means transfer. In other words, Enoch actually received a transfer. It's like a person in the Armed Forces getting transferred from one country to the other. Others in the Bible were transferred by death, but Enoch was transferred by faith. Faith is the substance; faith is the conviction. It is the evidence or the assurance of things hoped for. In other words faith is not just an act of the mind. Faith is an actuality; it positively exists. It's not something you just scheme up and hope that it is going to happen. The Hebrew writer says, "It is the assurance." God will furnish you the faith for what you want."

Your faith cannot be in you. It cannot be in the stuff you've got because that's just simple faith. All of us have that kind of faith. When you lay down last night, you used simple faith. You just jumped in the bed without checking to see if the slats would hold you up. But we're speaking of extraordinary faith, faith that attains extraordinary things, faith that supersedes ordinary.

It is amazing how we can have it one moment and not the next. We have enough faith to take a 10 cent job and get a $30,000 car. We have 20 cent faith and get a hundred thousand dollar house. But as soon as sickness comes on us, we're ready to walk with our heads down and say, "I don't know if God can bring me through this." You have seen God work through faith all of your life and now suddenly here you are wondering if God can handle this little situation. But you got to have faith in him. Faith in you might fail because it's on the wrong object. Faith in your job might let you down; faith in your family might disappoint. Your faith should be focused on Jesus. The Lord receives joy from knowing that you trust him.

Time Spent Supremely

Genesis 5:22

And Enoch walked with God after he begat Methuselah three hundred years, and begat sons and daughter.

*E*noch walked with God for 300 years. If you analyze your life and add up the time you spent in church, you might be shocked to know how little time you've given to the Lord. Moreover, you have to erase the time you were not paying attention and the time you were not involved in worship service. The average person who lives to be 70 years of age will spend 20 of the 70 years sleeping. If you work on a job until you retire, you will spend 18 years working. You will spend 5 years in school, 5 years eating, and about 5 years in miscellaneous. (That's stuff you can't talk about.) If you start from the day you are born and live to be 70 years of age and spend 2 1/2 hours per Sunday for 70 years, it will equal to one year. Isn't that something? To think here I am, holy, sanctified, filled with the Holy Ghost and then I can't give God but one year out of 70. And then we have the audacity to talk about going up yonder to be with the Lord where every day is Sunday and Sabbath will have no end. You ain't ready to go honey. If you can't hang around church a little while, cancel heaven's reservations.

But here is a man that gave God 300 years of faithful service. We stop and then start. Can I let you in on a secret? Don't let nothing or nobody stop you from giving your best to the Lord. Unplug it, cut it off, take it out, whatever you can do with it, but get it out of the way. Do everything you can for the glory of our God. Serving the Lord brings rewards. When you walk with Him he preserves you. He keeps you young. He will put pep in your step and joy in your heart. Instead of frowning, you can smile through a storm. I told the Lord a long time ago, I'll walk for you even though some things I cannot see behind the wall, if you just see for me. I don't know what tomorrow brings, but I know the Lord can handle it. Keep walking!

Keeping Sheep

Psalms 23:3
He restoreth my soul: he leadeth me in the paths of righteousness for his name's sake.

D o you ever wonder what would happen to you if you turn down the wrong road? What if your foot slips? What if you make mistakes in life – bad mistakes that are difficult to recover from? Often people will not allow you to mess up but once. If you stumble or stomp your foot one time, your friends become few. Your family may warn you that they will forgive you once, but do it no more. You may lose a job or be put out of school by messing up just one time.

But it is good to know that we are serving a God that has already prepared a way to get us back into the fold. I'm serving the kind of God that will give me another chance even if I stumble. If you stumble and fall, God forgives you and wipes the slate clean. If you stumble again, He forgives again. So there is always a second chance.

This text was penned by a man who was not only a shepherd but he was also a sheep. David was a sheep of the greater shepherd. He knew all about sheep for he was a keeper of sheep. Psalm 100 says we are his people and the sheep of his pasture. If you are born again, you are a sheep. If not, whether you like it or not, you are a goat. If you are a sheep, this verse is for you.

A sheep is a helpless creature by himself. He cannot outrun any other animal in the field. If he gets in water over his head, he will drown. He doesn't have sharp teeth to fight off his enemies. If he eats too much and lies down, he can't get back up by himself. That's why a shepherd will leave the ninety-nine sheep in the fold to go look for the lost one. (Luke 15:4) He knows the sheep has a problem and will not make it back without help. If the sheep is sick, he applies oil to his wounds. If a sheep is stubborn, he uses his rod. If a sheep strays, the shepherd uses his staff to keep him in line. A good shepherd knows how to care for his sheep.

Obsess, Observe, Obey

John 12:26
If any man serve me, let him follow me; and where I am, there shall also my servant be: if any man serve me, him will my Father honour.

The Lord wants us to be obsessed with him. Have you ever seen anybody that was just obsessed with other folk? I've seen movies and read about women being so obsessed with a man that they trailed him. She watched him and followed him. The man was continually in her mind. Of course, we should not be obsessed with another person, but this is an illustration of how the Lord wants us to be preoccupied with him. He wants us to wake up calling his name. He wants us to go to bed thinking about Him. He doesn't want us to let any other god come before Him. He wants us to walk and talk in His name. Our God doesn't want a part-time lover. You can't just love Him on Sunday morning and forget Him on Monday morning. Lay down in His goodness and get up with His grace. When God sees that we are obsessed with Him, He knows we have been healed.

We must closely observe our Lord. It's difficult to follow somebody when you're far in the distance. You've got to get close enough to see where they are going. Don't get too far from your shepherd. Tune into his prayer. Find out where He's going. Ask Him to let you follow Him. We cannot learn His ways without getting close to Him. We must be instructed by Him and be continually reaching toward Him.

Also, as followers of the Lord, we must be careful to obey Him. Too many of us want to write our own script of what we want to do. We set up in our minds as to what. It is easy for us to go to a doctor we've never seen and do just what he says, taking the prescription he recommends. We put our faith and trust in the doctor although he may or may not be helping us. How much more should we obey God.

He Delivers Life Afresh

Psalms 23:3

He restoreth my soul: he leadeth me in the paths of righteousness for his name's sake.

When God gets ready to get something done, He will send somebody. For instance, when He got ready to start the human race, he got a man named Adam. When He was ready to bless the race, He used a man named Abraham. When he got ready to feed the race, He used a man named Joseph. When He got ready to lead the race, He used a man named Moses. When He got ready to march the race, He used a man named Joshua. When he wanted wisdom for the race, He used a man named Solomon. When He wanted strength for the race, He used a man named Samson. When He wanted a musician for the race, He used a man named David. When He wanted a weeper for the race, He used a man named Jeremiah. When He wanted patience for the race, He used a man named Job. When He got ready to baptize the race, He used a man named John the Baptist. When He wanted a preacher for the race, He used a man named Paul.

But when God wanted my soul restored, He didn't trust it in the hands of anyone else. The Bible says, He restores. In other words, "This is too serious to put in the hands of somebody else. I've got to do it myself." One of these days, this old body is going back to dust, so you can't put all your investment in your body. You shouldn't spend all your time trying to look and smell good. The taker will show up. But there's another part on the inside, the soul. When your body goes back to the dust, your soul will have to take wings and fly away somewhere to be at rest.

Not only does He restore my soul, but He also leads me in the path. There is a crooked path that we take on our own. You don't have to teach people how to be crooked; we pick that up on our own. But we must be taught how to do right, how to tell the truth, and how to live right.

Chilly Waters

Psalms 23:4
Yea, though I walk through the valley of the shadow of death...

We like to sing about death. I took the initiative to observe men while they were singing about chilly waters. They were all smiling and getting into it. We shout on those kinds of songs. I used to sing Save A Seat for Me quite often. Folk would just fall all out and run into each other. Songs of that nature seem to get our attention. I'm going to move upstairs. I'm toiling through the storm and rain. All of those songs have reference to death. We sing about it, but we don't like to discuss it. Most of the times when we hear of these kinds of messages, it is at a funeral. Our minds are never on the message. We are thinking of the person that passed. Some in the audience wish they could say something. There are others that say something then wonder if they messed up when they talked. Still others are angry. As a believer, we should not be shocked by death because we all know it is going to happen.

It doesn't make sense to me to know that you are going to move yet fail to make provision before that time comes. My family shouldn't have to fight over what I have. I already know their attitudes. If I don't write it down before I leave, it's up for grabs. It is so simple to take a moment with an attorney and write it out. Make out your own will down to the chair. Choose the color of your casket so they won't argue. I know some members who fell out over the color of a casket. Their momma is dead and they are arguing. Maybe you have an outside child somewhere and you love that child. Your family knows about the child. Don't just think your children will treat her right. No they ain't. That's going to be the first one they cut out. Sit down and write out what you want each one to have. And don't forget the church you love that has been such a blessing to you where you have gained your strength for twenty years.

Where Chilly Winds Won't Wail

Psalms 23:4
Yea, though I walk through the valley of the shadow of death, I will fear no evil: for thou art with me.

Now during the days of David, there was such a place as the valley of the shadow of death. It was away from Jerusalem, out close to Bethlehem. This valley started 27 feet above sea level, but at the other end, it was 1300 feet below sea level and surrounded by mountains. It is said that some sheep would walk to the edge of the cliff not paying any attention to where they were going and would fall to their death down in the valley. This person was walking through the valley indicating there was no fear of dying.

If a person is afraid, the last thing they are going to do is walk. Instead, they will stand and gaze or run. But when you walk it says that you are somewhat comfortable about this matter of death. If I am saved, I'm not afraid of dying. You can easily discern at home-going services when the family there doesn't know the Lord through their crying, weeping, and conversation. The people talk of the person as lost, which means they don't know where they are. But if you know where they are, they're not lost. 2 Corinthians 5:8 says Be absent from the body and be present with the Lord. Instead of saying I lost my mother, just say she moved where the chilly winds don't blow.

I am so glad that I am going where the chilly winds don't blow. I get so tired of getting caught up in winds of adversity, winds of disappointment, winds of heartache, and winds of midnight. However, one of these days the Lord is going to hide me behind the mountain. Which mountain? This mountain is kind of a moving mountain; it doesn't just stand in one place. This mountain is Jesus himself. Psalms 23:1, 2, and 3 refers to the Lord as being He. But in 23:4 David changes from He to Thou. That means that as I go through, He's going along with me. I know that I'm with the God that will be with me.

Suffering Stamped Out

Revelation 14:13

And I heard a voice from heaven saying unto me, Write, Blessed are the dead which die in the Lord from henceforth: Yea, saith the Spirit, that they may rest from their labours; and their works do follow them.

Philippians 1:21 says *For me to live is Christ, and to die is gain.* How is it a blessing or a gain when I die? It's a gain socially because I will no longer have to associate with liars, backbiters, peace breakers, and whoremongers; they won't be coming there. I'll be associating with other saints – saved people – so it's a gain socially. Intellectually, it is a gain because now we know in part, but then we will know as we are known. It is also a gain emotionally. Death will be a defeated foe. I shall rest from labor. Psalms 116:15 says, Precious in the sight of God is the death of His saints. When a saint dies, the Lord shouts and skips. He says, "Now I have one who is coming to live forever in my presence. They can rest from their labors."

Their works do follow. You might try to forget them, but the Lord said, "I have fixed this thing. If they have done something, it will be remembered." That's why he tacked on the back of Psalm 23:6, Surely goodness and mercy shall follow me. What is the purpose of goodness and mercy behind me? "God said, "First of all, you have done some good things and folk will try to forget it when you are dead and gone, so I have goodness coming along picking up the good stuff that you have done. When you are dead and gone, I'll highlight it. I'll spotlight it around your enemies in places folk don't want to know about it." Then God said, "I hate to tell you, but you have also made some mistakes and some blunders in your life. If I leave your mistakes scattered around, somebody will come along and stumble. So that's why I enlisted mercy. Mercy is back there picking up your blunders and putting them in the sea of forgetfulness where it won't rise against you anymore."

Search The Scriptures

Isaiah 34:16
Seek ye out of the book of the Lord, and read.

In my early years of life, I was very poor at reading, spelling, and pronouncing words. I've never wanted to be any less than the best that God had for me. So after the Lord called me to preach I knew I had to spend a lot of time in books to reach the level that God wanted for me. So I took it upon myself to read at least a book a week, usually a book pertaining to the word of God. I believe that if you are going to do God's will you should put forth every effort to make his plan come true. I promised God and myself that if He gave me strength to work forty hours a week for myself then I would work at least forty hours a week for him. I have taken this preaching business very seriously. I don't' have any play time or time to joke and to jest but I am to be serious about the work of the Kingdom.

One of the ways for me to encourage the congregation that God had placed in my hands was to be studious myself. A follower will never study if the leader doesn't take time to interpret the written word. Consequently every sermon that I have preached was above all to inspire the people to dig in to the Word. There are unique nuggets in the Bible designated only for you, the believers of Christ.

In my process of reading and studying, I ran across what are called the best sellers, books that have circled the world, but eventually the best seller disappears. You enjoy reading it once or twice but then it gets old. But this book that I want to share with you becomes newer and newer the more times you read it. It is the believer's manual. It's a manual that you don't have to look too far to find. It has been here and the writing has not changed. It is the same today as it was yesterday. Just as a car manual tells you everything you need to know about the automobile, the Word of God helps us to know how to survive and excel as a follower of Christ in this world.

The Best Book

Isaiah 34:16
Seek ye out of the book of the Lord, and read.

The book of the Lord is one that has been ambushes in many places including college desks and church pulpits. Snipers from foreign soils have tried to destroy this book. Archaeologists and physicists have tried to invalidate it. But this best seller has been around to eulogize the funerals of those that oppose this book. It is an unusual piece of art. It is so amazing that every time you apply it, lives are changed. There are 66 books wrapped up in one book, 39 books in the Old Testament, 5 books of law, 12 books of history, 5 poetical books, 5 major prophets, and 12 minor prophets. The New Testament consists of 27 books, 4 books of gospel, 1 book of history, 1 book of prophecy and 21 epistles.

This book is called the *Best Book*. Behind ten thousand events stands God. Compared to other books, this book is as far as a river is beyond a reel in reach, as far as an orchid is beyond a twig in fruit bearing. It is as far as the sun is above the flashlight in brilliance, as far as eagle wings are beyond sparrow wings in strength. This book is above other books because other books have no life within them. They are just the thoughts of somebody writing a piece of material – a piece of art. But this book is a *living book*. This book has done so much for so many. It is book stacked in books.

This book contains the mind of God, the state of man, the way of salvation, and the doom of sinners. But you have to read it to be wise. You must believe to be saved. You are obliged to practice it to be holy. It's a pilgrim's staff; it's a pilot's compass. It's a Christian's chariot and a soldier's sword. This book tells you the three stages of man – generation, de-generation, re-generation. You see the world formed us. Sin deformed us. Prison reformed us. Schools inform us, but only Christ can transform us.

Pages Filled With Purpose

Isaiah 34:16
Seek ye out of the book of the Lord, and read.

What is the purpose of the book? Its purpose is to introduce to us Jesus. Without the book you wouldn't know who Jesus really was. You wouldn't know the will of God, the way of God, or the work of God. And you would not know the worth of yourself. So this book was designed with the purpose that we might know Him. You want to know the kind of person who would leave the bosom of his father and come down to a sinful world. This Jesus left comfort and came to condemnation. He came from favor to fury. He came from majesty to misery. He came from praises to pain. And he came down for us. He came down so we could go up. He became poor for us to become rich. He suffered disgrace so we could have amazing grace.

You ought to want to know him. And when you read this book you get a chance to know something about the Father, the Son, and the Holy Ghost. You see God the Father is behind us; Jesus is ahead of us; the Holy Ghost is in us. Donated at Bethelehem. Demonstrated at Calvary, but illustrated at Pentecost. Bethelehem is God with us. Calvary is God for us. But Pentecost is God in us. Each time I read the Word I get to know Him a little better.

When I know him I discover my insufficiency. I discover how nothing I am. Without knowing him I would leave thinking I was somebody. But when I discover who He is and who I am, I am just blessed to know Him. We have all sinned and come short of the glory of God. The wages of sin is death, but the gift of God is eternal life. I deserve death. By getting to know him, I discovered what He did for me. The Lord stood in my stead. He gave me his righteousness and took my rags. Romans 3:25 Whom God has set forth to be a propitiation through faith in his blood, to declare his righteousness for the remission of sins that are past, through the forbearance of God. Know Him!

|||| |||| |||| |||| |||| |||| |||| ||||

|||| |||| |||| |||| |||| |||| |||| ||||

|||| |||| |||| |||| |||| |||| |||| ||||

||

September

Chosen And Cherished

1 Peter 2:9

But ye are a chosen generation, a royal priesthood, an holy nation, a peculiar people; that ye should show forth the praises of him who has called you out of darkness into his marvelous light.

Who are the people of the Bible? The people of the book are the chosen people. Many people think that the Bible runs references on every person on planet earth. Not so. I hear this question over and over again, "When Cain left Adam and Eve and went down to the land of Nod and knew his wife, where did she come from?" Don't be confused. God is keeping a record of the chosen race; that's what this book is about. It is not about every person. People living from the time of Abraham to the time of Christ are part of the chosen generation. From Christ on is the church. As believers, we are part of that royal priesthood. We are a peculiar people. You did not choose him; he chose you.

Ephesians 1:4 According as he has chosen us in him before the foundation of the world, that we should be holy and without blame before him in love: as he has chosen us. The word chosen is in aorist tense indicating that God acted by himself. He didn't go before a board of directors to make his selection; He chose us. To tell you the truth I wasn't worthy to be chosen. I should have been one left on the outside, because I was alone and idle. I was a sinner, too. But I heard the voice of Jesus saying there is work to do. He came looking for me. I didn't know the shape I was in until I met him. Do you know that you've been chosen by God? You don't have to walk anywhere with a hung down head thinking you are nothing and that nobody loves you There is one that loves you so much that he chose you. Your voice, your strength, your home, your job, and your knowledge are all gifts from Him. What you have, God gave you. What you know God taught you. Where you are God brought you. Thank God, I am chosen by Him

A Special Society

Genesis 18:18

Abraham shall surely become a great and mighty nation, and all the nations of the earth shall be blessed in him?

We are a special people. Let me call a witness. Three little men got in trouble. They didn't have to get into this dilemma. Their names where Hananiah, Meshael, and Azariah. We call them Shadrach, Meshach, and Abednego. Down in a little town called Babylon, they refused to bow to the golden image that king set up. They were warned, "If you don't bow, you will burn." They didn't bow. They made a vow that they would not worship any other god. The king summoned them to be placed in the fiery furnace, and he turned the dial up where it would be seven times hotter than it had ever been. I know fire was in there because the people on the outside got burned. But God conditioned these men to stand the fire. Some of you know that if you are going through some things, God doesn't always have to get you out; He can condition you to stand the fire. Some folk can stand a little more fire than others. It is not because of their strength; it's because God conditions them to stand the fire. Some people crack under any kind of pressure. But some folk can just go on through it.

Then God says, "They have been in this fire long enough." He sent his Son quickly and at once, sooner than right now. The only thing these men lost in the fire was what the enemy put on them. The enemy took rope and tied them up. But when the king looked in his report was that they were loosed and walking around in the furnace. Fire wasn't bothering them because Jesus conditioned them to stand. And the reason he did it is because they were chosen people. God will do great things for His special people. He parted the Red Sea and allowed Moses to lead Israel across on dry ground. As soon as the last chosen child got across, God withdrew his spirit, allowing the sea to come back and Pharaoh's army drowned. He takes of His special people!

A Publication Of Power

Isaiah 34:16
Seek ye out of the book of the Lord, and read...

There is power in the book. Matthew 28:18 And Jesus came and spake unto them, saying, All power is given unto me in heaven and in earth. The Greek word for power is exousia which means authority. God has given His authority to His saints. Now what kind of authority do we have? We have authority to do two things. (1) We can direct divine power; (2) We can destroy demonic power. Directing divine power is merely praying. You don't have to be at a person's door to pray and get deliverance. No, you can pray here and God can hear you in New York. If you've got a person up there in need of prayer, you don't have to travel there and lay your hands on him. You can pray where you are, "Lord my child up there needs you to deliver him." And don't you know God will hear. He will hear because you have the authority to direct divine power.

But you also have the authority to destroy demonic powers. You see the devil thinks he has power, but you've got power because God put power at your disposal. Acts 1:8 says Ye shall receive power. The church, the called out one, shall receive power The Greek word for power is dunamis, from which we get the word dynamite. One thing we know about dynamite is that it rearranges whatever it comes in contact with. So the Lord takes his authority, places it behind his "called-out church" and then equips the church with His dunamis or His power. Everywhere I go I have power to direct divine authority, but I also have power to destroy demonic authority. When the devil comes up on me I don't have to out run him. I can resist that old devil and I can rebuke him in the name of the Lord and the devil will do the running. You have power to destroy demons and demonic powers. Don't talk about how you can't get away from the devil. You can. Just stand on the word of God, because God's word has all power.

Promises Of The Book

Matthew 28:20

Teaching them to observe all things whatsoever I have commanded you: and, lo, I am with you always, even unto the end of the world. Amen.

There's one other thing I want to mention before I leave this best seller and that is the promise of the book. Yes, the Lord says, "Look, if you follow me, I have some promises that I will give you." We know that when Lord promises us something, He will never go back on his word. Other people have made promises that they did not keep. I have a card in my pocket that says, "Don't leave home without me." But I've gone to places where this card could not be used. In fact, it was about the only card that wasn't accepted. I've had family members to say, "Frank if you need me, just call me." But when I needed them, I got only their answering machine.

I've had church members say, "You know Reverend I'm with you as long as you're right." That's all right when I'm right, but what am I going to do when I get wrong? You see, you need more help when you're wrong than you need when you're right. When you are right, everybody is with you; folk you don't even know will stand by your side. But when you stumble, oh my, you need somebody to help you get back on your feet.

There are some promises from the Lord to those of us who are His people. Isaiah 40:31 They that wait upon the Lord shall renew their strength; they shall mount up with wings as eagles; they shall run, and not be weary; and they shall walk, and not faint. Hebrews 13:5 Let your conversation be without covetousness; and be content with such things as ye have: for he hath said, I will never leave thee, nor forsake thee. When I'm up, He's with me; when I'm down, He's with me. When I am weak, He is with me; when I'm strong, He will be with me. He is not going to leave me. How long will He be with me? Always!

Designer Dust

Hebrews 9:22
And almost all things are by the law purged with blood; and without shedding of blood is no remission.

Our Creator has always fascinated me, especially in the way He designed, shaped, and configured our human body. He went to great lengths to design us in such a unique fashion, to the extent that no two people are the same; each one of us is distinctively different. Even though, when God made man, He used some stuff we don't appreciate. He formed man from the dust of the ground – the stuff that we wipe off of our glasses and shine out of our shoes. We work hard to get it out of our clothes and keep it off our furniture. Regardless of how beautiful the person sitting next to you is, they are merely dust. Regardless of what they drove up here in, just dust. Regardless of what part of town you live in, you are nothing but dust. Job said we came from dust and we are going back to dust. It's always strange to me how one hunk of dust seems to be more important than another hunk of dust. You see dust rolling his eyes at other dust. You see one hunk of dust pointing at another hunk of dust. Just because one hunk smells better than the other, it's still nothing but dust.

God took that dust, formed it, shaped it, and stood it up with 263 bones, 600 muscles, 970 miles of blood vessels, 32 feet of intestines, a heart that beats 70 times a minute, and eyes that can take pictures like cameras. No wonder the Psalmist asked a question, "What is man that thou are mindful of him?" Nobody did it but God. It is he that has made us and not we ourselves. We ought to remind ourselves that I did not make me. Instead, sometimes we act as if we are self-made. We think we achieved all these things on our own. But there had to have been a creator. There can be no preacher without a creator. There can be no watch without a watchmaker. There can be no design without a designer. God is that master designer.

Importance Of The Blood

Hebrews 9:22
And almost all things are by the law purged with blood; and without shedding of blood is no remission.

In addition to God making man with all the fixed cells, He also placed within man's body mobile cells, which is the blood. Even when we prepare our diet, we should have our blood in mind. What you eat must be transferred into blood. So it's not your stomach you should be interested in; it's the rest of you. When you eat, that food is changed into blood to feed all the vital organs. Certain foods are much easier for the body to digest while other foods burden the body. A big steak dinner could take over 16 hours to digest in your system. But it takes apples, and oranges, and grapes about 20 minutes. Once you eat there is an instant energy that is transferred into your body through the bloodstream.

Our blood contains red cells and white cells. Both do a different job. The white cells serve as an emergency army. Whenever a problem occurs, it's the white cells that go and look for the recovery of your body. If I cut my finger, it will swell and get white pus around at the edge, which is really the death of the white cells that rushed over to help my finger recover. Once they complete their job, the red cells come and clean up the mess that the white cells left. You will see a scab indicating the red cells came by and did their job. In a few days healing has taken place.

If your blood has something wrong, you might have a fever. If so, your doctor will take a sample of your blood to look at under his microscope to see if there are too many white cells, indicating infection. If not, he will put some blue dye in your body so he can see all the way through until he finds the problem. Another function of blood is to take the waste – all the stuff that doesn't belong in there – and carry it to your human garbage can. Blood is the most important part of a person. The blood determines what happens to the rest of you. It's all in the blood.

Bad Blood

Hebrews 9:22
And almost all things are by the law purged with blood; and without shedding of blood is no remission.

Every one of us is related by blood. Regardless of what race, creed or color you came from, all of us are children of Adam. We came from Adam and Eve and then we came down through the lineage of Noah. That means that our daddy was a drunkard and a liar. You can't expect much out of us if we came from a family like that. It's in the blood. We came from a line of people of that nature. If you follow the line long enough you will discover that you are related to the person sitting next to you.

I grew up in the country. My mother and father were sharecroppers on a farm. The house where we lived had on one spot of ground apple trees, peach trees, pear trees, plum bushes, vines, wild onions, Bermuda grass, Johnson grass, four-leaf clovers, some poke salad all from the same ground. You can have one Adam or one ground. But you can have some red folk, some black folk, some brown folk, and some yellow folk coming from the same ground. We all came from the same family. Because of this, we are contaminated by our ancestors. Prior to the sin in the garden man was innocent. But after Adam sinned, his blood became contaminated. Sin got in the blood line of all his descendants. That's why his son Cain rose up and slew Abel – because of the stuff that was in his blood. Abraham lied because sin was in the blood.

You wonder why men go out drinking, acting like babies on bottles. Or people will go out to places where they have happy hour. Now what's so happy about losing your composure? When you go in, you know where you parked your car; when you come out, you don't know where it is. There's nothing happy about stuff like that. Folk get mad and lose their temper the same as Moses did years ago. It's in the blood. We need a transfusion!

Feed The Right Man

Hebrews 9:22
And almost all things are by the law purged with blood; and without shedding of blood is no remission.

Every one of us we was born in sin. Some of us think that since we are born again, the old nature is gone. However, the old nature is not far. And if you feed him, he will show up at your door. If you don't feed your spirit the word of God on a daily basis, that old nature will start rising up again. You will find yourself cursing when there is nothing to curse about or worrying when there is nothing to worry about. You will be complaining when you've got a roof over your head and you are blessed with good health and strength. You will think people don't like you. That's because you are not feeding the spiritual man. Just like you need to take your vitamins every day, you need to take the vitamin of the Word every day. When your spiritual man is fed, you will recognize the lies of the carnal man. You won't let him raise his head to you. He is no longer in control; you have a new master.

The carnal man or flesh man was in control in the days of Sodom and Gomorrah so God decided to destroy the whole place. He sent angels to bring out Lot and his family, but the homosexuals wanted the angels. The angels had to blind their eyes so they couldn't see them. Homosexuality is an abomination in the sight of God. It used to be hard working men and pretty women, but now you've got hard working women and pretty men. The reason they are still doing it is because it is in the blood. Where did that twisted wrist come from? How did you get in this family? It's in the blood. A woman can be a wonderful wife and mother; yet her husband goes out and gets him another woman. She wants to know what she did wrong. Nothing. It's in the blood. In Psalm 51:5 David said, "I was shapen in iniquity; and in sin did my mother conceive me." When I got here I was messed up. No holy children arrive here holy!

Branded With New Blood

Matthew 1:21
And she shall bring forth a son, and thou shalt call his name Jesus: for he shall save his people from their sins.

When I was young and still today I enjoy watching westerns. I watched them herding cows. They would catch a cow and take it to the person with a branding iron and put a brand on the cow. The cow may have been a stray before they got it. But after they put the brand on him, they would take the rope off and turn him loose in the herd. And I imagine the cows would start talking to each other, "Hey man what happen to you?" "Well a few minutes ago they caught me and branded me." "Say what does that mean?" "Well I don't know everything it means, but I do know this. It means I've got a new owner. And I have to abide by the rules of my new owner." When the Lord saved you, he took his blood and branded you and turned you loose where you used to be but you can't act like you use to act. If I go to a cafe now I'm not going to drink Bud Lite. Instead, I'm going to tell the bartender Jesus died one Friday and got up Sunday morning with all power in his hands.

Now since I'm messed up by blood, how can I rectify my problem? Aren't you glad God thought of that before he made the first man? He designed the woman to carry a fetus. The mother gives the baby all the minerals, vitamins, protein, the shape, and sometimes the color, but not the blood. The blood does not come from the woman; the blood is created through the fetus from the man. Why did God do that? Because he had a plan scheduled. He needed to bring forth a savior that would come and have the characteristics of a man, but would not have sinful blood in his veins. That's why in a little town called Bethelehem the Lord caught up with a girl named Mary who had never been intimate with a man. The Holy Spirit overshadowed Mary and she conceived and in nine months she gave birth to a son. And they called his name Jesus.

Willingly Given

Hebrews 9:22
And almost all things are by the law purged with blood; and without shedding of blood is no remission.

Notice again that blood is needed to get us out of the dilemma we are in. He said without the shedding of blood. Can I cry enough for the Lord to save me? No! No matter how much you cry, tears can't save you. It says without the shedding of blood. Notice he didn't say spilling, but shedding. There's a difference between spilled blood and shed blood. In reality Jesus was the only person that actually gave up his life. We say Martin Luther King gave his life. No he didn't. If Martin could, he would still be living. He didn't ask the sniper to shoot him down. He didn't want to die. He would still be dodging if he could. He just didn't know the bullet was coming. But Jesus knew. He knew the bullet was coming before he was born. I heard him say, "No man takes my life. I lay it down." If his life had been taken, it would have been spilled blood. But it was not taken; it was shed. It was in the plan; He had to die for your sin and mine in order for us to be saved.

I've heard it said that there was a search that went out for somebody to lay down his life. Abraham couldn't do it, because he had a lie on his record. Noah couldn't do it because he got drunk. Moses couldn't do it because he lost his temper. Job couldn't do it because he cursed the day he was born. Jeremiah couldn't do it because he backslid. John the Baptist couldn't do it because he doubted the existence of Jesus Christ. And the others cried unworthy. The sun and moon cried unworthy. The angels said, "We can't do it, because we know nothing about sin." But Jesus said, "I will come for the atonement." AT ONE MENT. That means that before Jesus came, we were at odds with God the Father. God had to turn his back on man. But at Calvary, Jesus fixed it so we would be AT ONE MENT with the Father. Now when the Father looks at me, He cannot see my sin

Just As If

Romans 5:9
Much more then, being now justified by his blood, we shall be saved from wrath through him.

Because of His blood I've been justified. What does that mean? Justification means just as if. If you take an eraser and erase something you wrote, you can still see the print of the writing. But the Lord says, "When I clean you up, I don't leave a print." Not only does His blood remove the stain, but it also removes the mark from the stain.

A man bought a Rolls Royce. After several months, he had some problems and took the car back to the dealership. The dealership contacted an ace mechanic at headquarters who said, "Just ship the car to us." So they shipped the car to headquarters where the car was fixed. The car was then brought back and returned to the owner. The owner waited weeks, but the bill didn't come. Months later, the bill still hadn't arrived. He came back to his dealership and said, "Look, you all fixed the car and did a good job. But I haven't received the bill. I don't want to wait for a huge bill later and I can't pay for it. Let me pay for it now." The office manager said, "Sir, we don't have any record of a bill." The man said, "Oh yeah, I brought the car here. You must have a bill." So they faxed headquarters requesting the bill for this man's repair work. In a few moments, the answer came back, "We don't have any record of anything ever happening to this car."

Well the same thing will happen in your life when you are saved. The devil is always trying to accuse the saints before God saying, "Look at Frank. Ain't you gonna wipe him off?" The Lord says, "Wait a minute, send a fax up to heaven's headquarters for the history of Frank E. Ray, Sr., Memphis, Tennessee. In a few minutes the record will come back. I'm sorry we don't have any record of anything he has ever done wrong. He's been covered by the blood. Justification. Just as if nothing has ever happened.

Completed By His Blood

Hebrews 9:13-14

For If the blood of bulls and of goats, and the ashes of an heifer sprinkling the unclean, sanctifieth to the purifying of the flesh: How much more shall the blood of Christ, who through the eternal Spirit offered himself without spot to God, purge your conscience from dead works to serve the living God?

His blood also brings sanctification. You see not only did he erase me, he also accepted me in the beloved. Sanctification means holy and without blame. It means set apart for a holy use. Now here I am, a wretch undone. I'm a vagabond; I'm nothing. When the Lord picked me up, I was like an automobile with the frame bent out of shape and an engine that had thrown its rod. The transmission was slipping; the universal joint had jumped out of its socket. My tires were flat, my battery was low, and my radiator was boiling over. My lights weren't working. But Jesus came along and restored me back into the family. And now I can say, "I have been sanctified."

1 John 1:7 But if we walk in the light, as he is in the light, we have fellowship one with another, and the blood of Jesus Christ his Son cleanses us from all sin. It is like a cleaning an oven. After the oven is sealed, the oven cleaner goes to work and cleans everything. So if you waste any grease, you don't have to go back and scrub; you can just wipe it off. Now if your oven cleaner will do that kind of stuff, can you imagine what the blood of Jesus will do? You see I've been covered with His blood. When a little stain of sin gets on me, the Lord just comes along and sends one of his angels to straighten it up.

I'm glad that the blood of Jesus brings atonement. It brings justification. It brings sanctification. And it brings redemption. I was on the auction block ready to be sold to the highest bidder. My sin debt had to be paid. But Jesus came to Calvary's cross and said, "I'll pay the price."

Serving From Love

Romans 1:1
Paul, a servant of Jesus Christ, called to be an apostle, separated unto the gospel of God.

Paul states his position as a servant. The Greek word for servant is doulos, which means slave. There are several kinds of slaves. One is just a natural slave, but then there is what you call a bond slave. A bond slave is different than a normal slave. A bond slave is a person that somehow fell in love with his master. The Jewish people had a custom that every seven years they would set slaves free. But if a slave had a good master and did not want to be set free, he would get an awl and put a hole in his ear. Then he put an earring in the ear indicating that he had been set free but chose to remain a slave. (Deuteronomy 15:17)

Paul was a preacher but his position toward the Lord was that of a servant slave. Jesus said, "I did not come to be served. I came to serve." One of the highest callings you can ever have is that of being a servant. Moses spent forty years thinking he was somebody; forty years discovering he was nobody; and forty years learning how God could take a nobody and make a somebody. When he died, God said, "Moses, my servant, is dead."

Called. In the Greek the word call means that God actually designated Paul for a specific purpose. To a certain extent, all of us are called because Romans 8:29 says whom the Lord did foreknow prognosis – knew before hand what he's going to do now, He did predestinate – progizo – marks off a boundary. For whom the Lord did foreknow them he also did justify to be conformed to the image or the likeness of his son. When He finds stuff in us that doesn't favor his Son, He prunes us. In other words, He cuts jagged edges off of us to fix us. He's working on us now to help us to shape ourselves to look like Jesus. Because God said, When He shall appear, we shall be like him for we shall see Him for ourselves.

The Unseen Power

Romans 1:1
Paul, a servant of Jesus Christ, called to be an apostle, separated unto the gospel of God.

Paul was called; he was given authority to do what he did. A police officer never says, "I say." He says, "The law says it." Because all he's really doing is wearing a uniform and a badge. He is under the authority of the person who sent him. If Sears comes by and fixes your washing machine and they don't fix it right, you don't get mad at the service person; you call the company. So when Jesus sends out somebody, don't get upset with the person He sent out. You need to talk it over with the one that did the sending.

Paul was called to be an apostle. There were thirteen original apostles. An apostle is an eyewitness of Jesus Christ. Paul said he was an apostle born out of due time. His calling came later. In other words he is saying he didn't deserve to be called. All of us can witness to that since none of us deserved to be called. Our righteousness is as filthy rags in the sight of God. Paul was called to be an apostle separated or set aside unto the gospel of God. The Greek word for gospel is euaggelion meaning good news. Paul said he was a good news carrier. We love to see people who have good things to say. Oh what a joy it would be in life if we could find a few good news carriers.

The gospel has power to affect every part of humanity. Not only does it deal with you spiritually, the gospel also has an effect upon you physically. I've seen the gospel get hold of people and change their whole expression. People come in mad but when the gospel gets through with them, they leave glad. A person with a hung down head will leave with their head up. I've seen people who did nothing but sit around; but once they heard the gospel they were eager to go and make a difference in their own personal lives. There is power in the person that sent you out to carry the gospel. The authority of Jesus produces the power in the gospel.

Talk About Promises Kept

Romans 1:2-3

(Which he had promised afore by his prophets in the holy scriptures,) Concerning his Son Jesus Christ our Lord, which was made of the seed of David according to the flesh.

According to the flesh. God lets us know about the humanity of Christ. Some say that Jesus was just the figment of a person's imagination, but Jesus was human. He had a natural birth and grew up as a natural child. Jesus lived like a natural person because he was human; he was of the seed of David. That which was far off became near. That which you could not see, you became able to see.

For the first time in a little town of Bethlehem you were able to look down and see heaven. Every other time, people looked up when they wanted to see heaven. You see we misunderstand heaven. Heaven is not just a place; it's a person. I mean, the devil was up there and lost his spot. Wherever Jesus is, that's heaven. My security is not in a place; it's in a person.

Prior to Jesus arriving, God had already promised that the gospel was coming. When God makes a promise, He keeps his promise. Now we might make promises with the intention of keeping them, but circumstances can change. Sometimes you can never get done the stuff you have all the intentions of doing. But when God says something, you can look forward to it He's able to bring it to pass.

We need to gossip the gospel. If you like to gossip, just gossip the gospel. If you need to find something to talk about, talk about the fact that Jesus was born in another man's stable, ate from another man's table, preached from another man's boat, rode another man's ass coat, suffered for another man's sin, died in another man's place, was buried in another man's grave, and rose on the third day for another man's sanctification. You can gossip, but make sure it's the gospel that you are gossiping.

Winners Are Workers

Romans 1:5
By whom we have received grace and apostleship, for obedience to the faith among all nations, for his name:

*B*y whom we have received grace or conversion and apostleship or vocation. The word apostle actually means sent one or sent out one. In the broad sense every child of God is an apostle because we have been graced through conversion. We have been saved by grace, which means we have been called but after conversion comes vocation. God didn't call us just because he wanted to do something; He called us to work. His fields are ready for harvesting, but there are not enough laborers.

Now I enjoy watching the NBA. You know some of the fellows that are dressed out never get to play; every game they're sitting on the bench. Even when their team is losing, some of them never get to play. It looks as though the coach is saying to them, "I'm going to let you just dress out and sit here." Well that might be the mentality that many of us have. I'm going to show up with my uniform on, but I'm never going to hit the floor. God is trying to find enough people that will get on the floor.

The NBA has its losing seasons but Christians don't ever lose As a matter of fact when you accept Christ as your Savior you're winning begins. It's the only team where you are a winner first and then you play on the field. If you're saved, you're no loser. You might not have a car but you're not a loser. You may not have a place to stay or anyone to call your own, but you're not a loser. You might not have a job to go to but you aren't a loser because Christ paid the sin debt for us.

For obedience. If you don't obey, it might be an indication that you haven't received grace. If you've been saved, your new nature is at work. If you don't work, you just might not be saved. But the characteristic of a saved person is an eagerness to go to work. Winners are workers.

Obedient To The Faith

Isaiah 40:31

But they that wait upon the Lord shall renew their strength; they shall mount up with wings as eagles; they shall run, and not be weary; and they shall walk, and not faint.

You start off flying, but then Isaiah says you shall run and not be weary. You move from a fly to a run and even to a walk. You start off flying, then slow down to running, and then even slower to a walk. When I was saved, I wanted everybody to know Jesus. Everywhere I went I was witnessing and passing out pamphlets. After a while when people started taking a little air out of me, I slowed down from a fly to a run. When people cut me to pieces, I moved from a run to a walk. But at least, stay on the floor and continue doing what God called you to do.

Some people give up hanging around the church because there are some things that aren't right. Have you ever noticed Noah's story? Noah went in the ark with two of every kind of beast; they closed the door and closed the window. I would imagine it was pretty stinky in that ark with lions, bears, elephants, hippopotamus, and skunks. But in spite of it getting nasty in there, Noah's family didn't come out. They hung on in there. Sometimes in church it gets kind of nasty when you get through with lies and backbiting and all that. It gets kind of rough, but you don't leave. You hang on in there because hear me when I tell you God keeps a detergent that can get the stain out.

We have received grace and apostleship for obedience to the faith. Not faith but the faith. There's a difference in saying the faith over and against saying faith. When you say the faith, you are talking about the substance of things hoped for, the evidence of things not seen. But when you say faith you are talking about the faith movement. If you take tackling and running out of football, it ceases to be football. If you take obedience out of Christianiaty, it is no longer Christian. Be obedient to the faith!

Problems Produce Perfection

Romans 8:30
Moreover whom he did predestinate, them he also called: and whom he called, them he also justified: and whom he justified, them he also glorified.

Whom he did predestinate, them he also called and then he justified.* Justification means just as if it never happened. So how am I justified? God looks at me in my sinful state; however, He is in his holy state. By rights, I'm not supposed to get in the presence of a holy god. To tell you the truth, I'm a candidate for death. Here's what the Lord does. He comes with his righteousness and because I have faith in him, He takes my faith for righteousness and He takes my sin and then gives me His righteousness. There's no need of me standing around bragging about how holy I am because I didn't deserve it. I can't go around and look at you under eyed because of how holy I am and how good I'm living. What I have on is borrowed from a holy God. So that means that what I need to do is thank him for letting me have what He has.

Whom the Lord justified, He also glorified. In other words when He justifies me, He still isn't through. He still has some more stuff to do in my life. He keeps on breaking me. He keeps carrying me through. He keeps on allowing stuff to happen to me. When trouble comes, I'll steal away somewhere and have a conversation with the Lord.

You can't get strong if you don't talk to him. If the Lord has to whip you to talk to you, He will do it. If He has to take your toys away to talk to you, He'll do it. If you are going through some hard times right now, it is because God isn't through with you. You aren't talking to Him right. All you're doing is begging God to get you out your trouble. What I have discovered is that you should not waste your troubles or your tribulations. If you're in tribulations and trials, thank God for it. God is using those things to bring you to a higher place.

Favor To The Saints

Romans 1:7
To all that be in Rome, beloved of God, called to be saints: Grace to you and peace from God our Father, and the Lord Jesus Christ.

Beloved of God, called to be Saints. The Greek word for saint is hagios. We are not Christians; we are saints. It was our enemies who labeled us with the term Christian. They were really trying to pick at us when they called us Christians. When they saw people following Christ they pointed, "There go those Christ-ians." It was at Antioch we were first called Christians. It's a nickname for the saints of God, but our real name is saints. It is disturbing when a believer says, "I'm not a saint." Then what are you? You're either a saint or you are an ain't. You're one or the other. The word saint comes from the word meaning holy. When you are a saint, you have characteristics that are holy. You still need some work done on you, but if you're a saint your heart's desire is to be holy.

Grace to you. Grace is God's unmerited favor. In other words, I'm getting something I don't deserve. There is a difference between mercy and grace. Mercy is when you don't get what you do deserve, but grace is when you get what you don't deserve. If a person shot a man and his sentence is thirty years behind bars, the judge can give him mercy and let him walk free. He deserved to go to prison but the judge let him go back to his family. But grace has to do with getting what you don't deserve. I am a sinner and the wages of sin is death. But grace switches it on you and instead of giving you death, grace gives you life. And not only that, but grace gives you life more abundantly.

Peace. Peace is freedom from constant restlessness. It is an inner peace down on the inside. It is not a substance you drink out of a bottle, money you get out of a bank, or something you find on a street. Peace is a person and His name is Jesus. It is only because of Him we are saints.

Tied Up In The Testaments

1 Corinthian 15:3
For I delivered unto you first of all that which I also received...

I've discovered that there are those who say they are preaching the gospel, but from all indications they don't know what the gospel is. A speaker in the pulpit may be able to keep your attention and entertain, but a person standing and talking is not necessarily preaching the gospel. Paul said you can stand on the gospel. Not only did you hear it and you're standing on the gospel, but it is also the gospel that saved you. We must keep in memory what is taught in the gospel; otherwise we have believed in vain.

Paul said, "I delivered unto you first that which I also had received." Too many of us are trying to preach and teach something we don't have. It's hard to lead in places where you haven't been yourself. It's hard to teach what you don't know. Before you can preach the gospel you must have the gospel. You need to be wrapped up in the gospel, tied up in and tangled up in the gospel.

I don't recommend that a person just decide to go to school to be a preacher; it's too rough. When you make up your mind to go on your own, people will send you back. You must be "a can't help it." You have to get to the point where you can't bring yourself to do anything else except preach. You can't eat; you can't sleep. It is the central focus of your whole life. Preaching is a lifestyle, not just a livelihood. How can a person start doing something God called you to do and then stop doing it? That's playing with God. When God calls you to do something, do it with the best you've got; do it with all you've got. Don't ever minor in God's program; major in that. If you teach, be the best you can. If God gave you a gift to sing, be the best you can. You may not lead but you can be a good follower. Do your very best to support God's work. When this life is over, hear the master say, "Well done, my faithful servant."

An Unlikely Friend

1 Corinthian 15:3-4

For I delivered unto you first of all that which I also received, how that Christ died for our sins according to the scriptures; And that he was buried, and that he rose again the third day according to the scriptures.

He died and He was buried. They wanted to put him in the grave. Why did Jesus have to be buried? 1 Corinthians 15:20 But now is Christ risen from the dead, and become the first fruits of them that slept. In other words, Jesus was not just serving as a sleep, he was also serving as a seed. When you get ready to plant something you sow a seed, but you don't sow a seed for the seed to stay there. You sow the seed because you have another purpose in mind for the seed. You expect a harvest one day. Someday we will die just as Jesus died. Your death is like a seed buried in the ground with dirt all over, but it isn't the end of you.

Some people think that when you're dead you're done. That may be for some people, but when you're saved death is merely sleep. Do you walk in the room where your baby is asleep and fall to pieces? When was the last time you saw your Momma taking a nap and you came apart? No, you don't do it because she's just asleep. When a person dies in the Lord, they are just asleep. Jesus was buried to let us know that the grave is not your enemy. The grave is a saved person's friend.

Jesus died without putting up a fight. He could have whipped anybody around. Since He had enough power to create heaven and earth, He could certainly handle a few little Roman soldiers. He could have easily taken care of Pilate and the other fellows. If it had been me they were nailing to the cross and spitting in my face and I knew I had all power in my hand, I would have come down off the cross and whipped them all up real good and showed them how bad I am. But when you know what you know and when you know Who you know, you don't have to prove anything to anybody. Death is the saved person's friend.

Christ Stood Again

1 Corinthian 15:4
And that he was buried, and that he rose again the third day according to the scriptures.

Jesus rose again the third day. Even at his death, Jesus was fulfilling the scripture. Too many of us are trying to do stuff that's not according to the scripture. People want to change things to fit today's lifestyles. You hear people say, "You know, this is the twenty-first century." Nevertheless, the scripture remains the same. Principles of God's word are the same as they were when our ancestors lived. His word continues to apply to our daily lives and situations.

Everything that Christianity is based upon is hanging on his death, burial, and resurrection. Nothing is anymore important than the fact that He died, He was buried, and He rose again on the third day. That's the gospel. If that's not the truth, if Christ be not risen, then your faith is in vain and you are still in your sin. (1 Corinthians 15:17) If Jesus didn't get up, nobody is saved. If Jesus didn't get up, then nobody has the Holy Ghost. If Jesus didn't get up, Moses and Joshua and all the old prophets were liars. But I am so glad HE DID GET UP!

Jesus was smart enough to know to let people see Him after He got up. Jesus wanted them to know He had risen from the dead. He was seen by many. Peter saw him before He died and he got a chance to see him again after He arose. Then all twelve got a chance to see him after his resurrection. After that, He was seen by about 500 brethren at one time. Then all the apostles saw Jesus. And last of all, He was seen by Paul.

I'm glad that I'm not ashamed of the fact that He died, He rose again and he was buried for your sins and for mine. Because he lives I can face tomorrow. Because he lives all my fears are gone. I know he holds my future and life is worth living just because he lives. I haven't seen him yet, but I know he lives. He walks and talks with me. I am His.

Remember Whose You Are

1 John 5:13

These things have I written unto you that believe on the name of the Son of God; that ye may know that ye have eternal life, and that ye may believe on the name of the Son of God.

John the beloved disciple was responsible for penning at least three books of the New Testament – the Gospel of John, the 1, 2, and 3 epistles of John and the book of Revelation. John met the Lord at the age of twenty-five. Now he is around ninety-five years of age. He has experience under his belt. He is an old man but he is equipped to get the story out.

The first epistle of John is a specific book just for folk that are born again. It's a book written for saved, sanctified, baptized, and filled with the Holy Ghost people. It is a book for the Saints. He wants his saints reassured concerning who they are and whose they are. The devil will try to convince you that you aren't saved. He wants you to believe that you don't have a thing. You need to have repeated reassurance of who you are and whose you are.

So there is a word used over thirty times in the epistles of John and that is the word know. That ye may know that ye have eternal life. You see if you can have Jesus and not know, then you just might lose him and not miss him. So I don't want to guess about my salvation; I don't want to hope I'm saved, or think I'm saved, or hope one day I will be saved. No, I need to know about that, because life is too precious for me to spend all that time wondering and not knowing until I get to the gate. Then it's too late.

I need to know I'm saved while I'm down here. There are too many fringe benefits for me to miss this while I'm here. I'm not saved just to go to Heaven; I've got some fringe benefits just by being saved. I have a closer walk with Him. So He places the key in the middle of the book to share with us the purpose of writing this book. He wrote the book for our assurance of eternal life through Jesus.

Sheltered From Sin

1 John 2:26
These things have I written unto you concerning them that seduce you.

Coconcerning them that seduce you. God wants to warn you and protect you from Satan and his devices. One of the ways Satan gets to us is by us not knowing his trickery and his devices. You see the devil is a shrewd operator; you might think he's coming one way today, but he shows up another way. If you think the devil just uses one trick, you're sadly mistaken. That devil has got a bag of tricks that he uses any which way he can to distract you and to keep you from focusing on the true and living God. So the second reason He wrote this book is for your protection.

The third reason He gave us this book is for your prevention. He says in1 John 2:1, My little children, these things I write unto you, that ye sin not. And if any man sin, we have an advocate with the Father, Jesus Christ the righteous. He wants you to be protected from sin. Sometimes folk commit sin simply because they are reminded that they are sinners. It is like continually telling a child how worthless they are. The child would do everything in their power to prove what you say. Well I may as will get into every thing because I have already been told, "I ain't nothing." If you tell your child, "You're dumb," he says, "Well ain't no need of me trying to study; they already told me I'm dumb."

If you go to an alcoholic and say, "Man, you're an alcoholic," they'll drink more because they have been reminded of what they are. But John said, "Look even though you are sinning, I want you to know that you have an advocate. Everywhere you go you have one with you. Christ is walking with you. If you mess up, He is your attorney. He goes in and pleads your case for you. Your past, present, and future sins are already taken care of. He already paid the price for you to be free of sin.

Person Of The Beginning

1 John 1:1

That which was from the beginning, which we have heard, which we have seen with our eyes, which we have looked upon, and our hands have handled, of the Word of life.

Man possesses five senses: sense of taste, sense of smell, sense of hearing, sense of sight, and sense of touch. Most of us will not believe in something if we can't see it, hear it, touch it, taste it, or smell it. If we, then we do not think it is real. However, there are some things that are real that you can't see at the moment; you can't just see yet. One of these days you will be able to see things spoken about in the Bible.

That which was from the beginning. This word beginning is also mentioned in Genesis 1:1, In the beginning God created the heavens and the earth. The word beginning denotes the commencement of a certain period of time in an eternal framework. At that time the whole Godhead joined together, because the word for God in Genesis 1:1 is Elohim, denoting a plurality of majesty.

This word beginning is found another time in Mark 1:1 The beginning of the gospel of Jesus Christ, the Son of God. Here again the Godhead is mentioned, but all in a single person. The text says, The beginning of the Gospel of Jesus – that's his person. Christ – that's his position. The Son of God – that's his power. Then again the word beginning is mentioned in John 1:1. In the beginning was the word (logos) and the word was with God (theous). In the Greek this text says, "That which was from the beginning". In other words, when the beginning first began its beginning. Ephesians 3:9 tell us, And to make all men see what is the fellowship of the mystery, which from the beginning of the world hath been hid in God, who created all things by Jesus Christ. Jesus was already present at creation. He is from the beginning. Revelation 14:7 "worship him that made heaven and earth."

An Unquestionable Reality

1 John 1:1
That which was from the beginning, which we have heard, which we have seen with our eyes, which we have looked upon, and our hands have handled, of the Word of life.

That which was from the beginning, which we heard. He heard. The tense of the verb here is suggesting that John didn't just hear him back then. But because of hearing him, John said his voice is still echoing in his spirit even now. Have you ever heard something and the person you heard it from is dead and gone but the voice is still ringing? My mother died November 8, 1985. She used to call me while she was living just as I was getting ready to travel to revival crusades where I was preaching. She would say, "Frank, Mama is praying for you." And Mama's been gone for fifteen years but her voice is still echoing in my spirit. John said that he heard him a long time ago, but his voice is still as fresh now as it was then. He said, "I heard."

John was not the only eyewitness. This word means that he didn't just glimpse him. He was able to sit down and look at him and to gaze upon him. Oh I wish I had been there that day to have a chance just to look at Jesus. What a sight it must have been to look at one man and see so much. When I read this Bible, Jesus comes alive right before my eyes. Paul said, "We shall see him. Job said, "That one day I will see him with my own flesh." But John says, "We have seen with our eyes which we have looked upon him." We didn't just pass by; we looked. We took us a good look. We saw the nail prints in his hands and the spear holes in his side. If Jesus had lived in our day, we could have a video of the real Jesus. We could record his voice. He really existed. Even though we can't see him, we have the joy of knowing that He's still living. And even though you can't touch him, He can touch you. Then John said, "Our hands have handled him." He felt the comfort of laying his head on Jesus' bosom. He experienced Jesus!

The Unseen Revealed

1 John 1:2

For the life was manifested, and we have seen it, and bear witness, and shew unto you that eternal life, which was with the Father, and was manifested unto us;

For the life was manifested. The word manifested is phaneroo, which means make it known that which was already here. In other words Jesus didn't just show up; he was already here. We just didn't know it. Jewish people had a belief that God spent his time in spots and places. They believed God was a local God; whenever God would show up, He was always in certain spots and particular places. When Daniel got on his knees and prayed, he raised the window in the direction of Jerusalem. Then he prayed to the God of Jerusalem hoping that the wind would blow his voice into Jerusalem and God would hear it and respond. When Moses got ready to talk to God, he went up on the mountain because Jewish people believed God spent his time in spots and places. Jacob had wrestled with an angel all night in a particular place, a little place called Bethel Then he had a dream that the angels were descending and ascending. When he woke up the next morning he said, "The Lord has been in this place." In other words it was a shock to him to discover that God would come to the valley.

There are some movements now that think that God only shows up at your little place of domicile. But you cannot hem God into one little place. God is too big for your building. Somebody tried to make a bed for God and wanted him to lie down at his house, but he discovered the bed was too narrow and the cover was too short, because God is from everlasting all the way to everlasting. He isn't someone you can turn on and off when you get ready.

Then He was manifested. He was made visible so that we could see him. Jesus was not a counterfeit made up by man, but He was God manifest in the flesh.

The Correct Crowd

1 John 1:3
That which we have seen and heard declare we unto you, that ye also may have fellowship with us: and truly our fellowship is with the Father, and with his Son Jesus Christ.

*O*ur fellowship. Fellowship is the Greek word koinonia which means the fellowship of the believers. Notice this fellowship is horizontal, because he said you have fellowship with us. However most of us try to have our relationship vertical. We spend a lot of our time trying to have to a vertical relationship with God. We try to eliminate having a horizontal fellowship with our brother. Now you may socialize with unbelievers, but you really cannot have fellowship with unbelievers. You might be in their company, but you're on a different level than they are. 2 Corinthians 6:14 says, Be ye not unequally yoked together with unbelievers: for what fellowship hath righteousness with unrighteousness? and what communion hath light with darkness? Don't let saved marry unsaved.

But the Lord says, "Look, you've got to get it right with your brother." You heard Jesus when He prayed in Matthew 6, "And after this manner pray ye our father." Your prayer has to be horizontal. Before it goes up it has to go out to your brother. You have to have your brother in mind when you get down on your knees. He said pray our – horizontal. Father – vertical. You cannot be vertically right and horizontally wrong. If you're going to have it right with God, you've got to have it right with your brother.

Truly our fellowship is with the father. When you get in with the God family, your fellowship goes out, but it also goes up. When you are in fellowship, you don't run from God you run to God. When you step out of his will, you stop fellowship with God. It doesn't matter what isn't going right in the Church of the Living God, when you're in fellowship with God you want to be with God's people.

Delightfully High Spirited

1 John 1:4
And these things write we unto you, that your joy may be full.

John says, "I am writing for your promotion. I am promoting your joy." If you don't read the book for any other reason, you ought to read it for the fact that you finally found somebody that's promoting joy, especially in light of the fact that most folk like to come around and demote you. Have you ever had any joy snatchers that won't let you be happy? You do your best to try all you can to be happy and they can't wait to steal away your joy. They will call you on the phone and make you miserable. They find somebody that you love and talk them down. They talk about your children; they talk about your daddy and your mother – anybody they can talk about to steal your joy. And if they can't get it that way they just hang around you and look sad.

That your joy may be full. You see sometimes you get just a little touch of joy, but before you know it, it's gone. Psalm 100 tells us that when you're saved, not only do you have joy, but you also go around making joy. We are to worship the Lord with joyful singing and bless His name for His goodness and His mercy. Enter in with thanksgiving and go into his court with praise. Make a joyful noise unto the Lord. James 1:2 tells me to count it joy when I'm down and when I'm broke. When I've got enemies all around me, count it joy. When it doesn't look good in my life count it joy. Count it all joy when trials and temptation are all around. Why? The reason you can have joy is because you know something. When you're laughing and being joyful, other folk frowning won't be able to take away your joy. Your laughter is more powerful than their grumpiness. The world didn't give me this joy that I have and the world can't take it away. You don't know like I know what the Lord has done for me.

Count All The Problems

James 1:2
My brethren, count it all joy when ye fall into divers temptations.

The book of James is a book of behavior. In contrast, the gospels of Matthew, Mark, Luke and John are all books that teach us the plan of salvation. James says, "My brethren." He wants us to know we are in the same family. We are related. We have been purchased by the same blood. The book is written to saved folk. It is written to people that love the Lord and have been born again, blood washed saints. And saved folk need encouragement. Many times we pretend that we are strong, but when a crisis shows up, weaknesses surface in our lives. But James says to count it all joy when problems arise.

The word count in the Greek text comes from the idea of having a spreadsheet. When you are ready to declare your assets and liabilities, you lay out a spreadsheet and list your assets on one side and your liabilities on the other side. It is the same way with life. You put your assets on one side and your liabilities on the other and see which one balances out the scales. For instance, the accident you had last week was a liability. The raise you got last month was an asset. Suppose you had a child you didn't plan or want. However, think of what the child will do for you. The child is going to teach you discipline with your money, time, and sleep. The child will teach you selflessness. You cannot spend every dime on you now; you must share it.

But James said, "Don't do that." He says to count it all. When these things happen in your life, liken it to having a casette recorder. When you're not where you want to be, you press fast forward. If you are going through trouble now, don't sit back and grumble and complain and have pity parties; hit the fast forward button. Life won't always be the way it is now. When God allows the stuff to happen, He has a bigger picture in mind. Problems are assets.

꧄ ꧄ ꧄ ꧄ ꧄ ꧄ ꧄ ꧄

꧄ ꧄ ꧄ ꧄ ꧄ ꧄ ꧄ ꧄

꧄ ꧄ ||

October

The Be's Of Life

John 3:3
Jesus answered and said unto him, Verily, verily, I say unto thee, Except a man be born again, he cannot see the kingdom of God.

We hear all the time about various things that we should be or what we should do or what we should have. This is a get age. We tell our children to go to school to get a good education and get a good job. It is always about getting. I want to focus on what we should be before we focus on the getting. Let's go to the first Be. John 3:7 Marvel not that I said unto thee, Ye must be born again. Jesus didn't say you should or ought to be or can be; he said, "You must be born again." Eventually we will leave here with there are only two places to go, heaven or hell. I don't wish hell upon anybody because that's not a good place to go. Hell is a prepared place for an unprepared people. Heaven is a prepared place for a prepared people. There is no in between. And there's only one way you can get to heaven and that is by being born again.

According to John 8:44 when you are unsaved, you're in the devil's family. But when you're born again, you have a new father. In addition, you have a new family. I thank God for my earthly family, but my spiritual family is greater. My earthly family will die, but my spiritual family will never leave me; they unite with us. No one ever has to say, "I lost my mother or father." When they are saved, you know where they are. You also have a new future. You receive eternal life the moment you are born again. John 5:24 says that whoever believes on him as the scripture has said has eternal life; I've got it now. I'm just as saved now as when I stand before God in heaven. And I have a new finance because I no longer have to worry about making ends meet. The only way to have these blessings is to be born again. A person who runs from being born again is running from the best blessing they could ever have.

Be Made New

John 3:7
Marvel not that I said unto thee, Ye must be born again.

Stop worrying about what you can get and focus on what you should be and that is being born again. This is our highest priority in life. What does a person need to do to be born again? The answer is – nothing! You don't have to walk hell on a spider web to be born again. You don't have to sit and wait and tarry for the presence of the Holy Ghost to be born again. Just believe. Believe that Jesus is the Son of God and that he died for your sins and that His father raised Him from the dead. When I was in school, most of the questions I missed were the easy ones even though the answer was right under my nose. The difficult questions were the ones I was able to pass. Sometimes that's why we miss salvation; we think we have to do something spectacular to be saved. God said the work is already done. He accomplished the goal at Calvary. You must only believe that the work is done and accept Jesus your savior. You must be converted; you must be regenerated. You receive a new spiritual life through Jesus.

An elderly lady was in the hospital on her death bed. She was born again. The saints went over to the hospital where she was and tried to pray her back. She said, "No! Look, don't pray for me no more." The saints said, "What do you mean. Are you insulted that we've come?" She said, "No that's not what I mean. I was getting ready to go home a year ago and I let ya'll come in here and crowd my hospital ward and prayed me back and I have been suffering in pain for the last year. You're not going to stop me this time. Thank ya'll but I've got a new home." There is nothing wrong with moving when you've got somewhere to move to that is better than where you're moving from. An unsaved person always has to look back to rejoice. But a saved person has something to look forward to; their best days are always ahead.

Be Transformed

Romans 12:2
And be not conformed to this world: but be ye transformed by the renewing of your mind, that ye may prove what is that good, and acceptable, and perfect, will of God.

*B*e not conformed to this world. Don't be fooled by the dictates of this world, because this world will have you thinking you can't make it. You'll think that you will have to work on a five dollar an hour job the rest of your life. But God wants to help you change your mind. Your mind can help you out of a lot of ruts. Somebody is singing the blues today because the mind says it's blue's time. Sometimes God has to break in and take something from us to help us see the bigger picture of success.

Be ye transformed. Our minds need to be transformed. A person can be in a rut so long that they will automatically think of themselves in that way. All their actions will be based upon that way of thinking. Many African Americans still believe they have to come up on the tail end of the ship. Even after thirty years, if we're not careful we'll still go to the back of the bus although we're able now to buy buses. Because that's the way we think. We think the whole world is against us; and if you think that way, that's the way it will be. If you think you have to be defeated because of the color of your skin, you'll be defeated because of your mind set. We think we can not make it. It is false thinking. The God I serve is color blind.

Likewise we believe because sin is so dangerous and so powerful that we must live as slaves to sin. We think we cannot live without committing acts of sin and our excuse is that everybody is doing it. However, when you have help you can do a lot of things. It just so happens we do have help. God the Father is behind me taking goodness and mercy. Jesus is ahead of me, the Holy Spirit is within me, and angels are on both sides of me. I have the whole heavenly host with me. We are not slaves to sin.

Be Settled

1 Corinthians 15:58
Therefore, my beloved brethren, be ye stedfast, unmovable, always abounding in the work of the Lord, forasmuch as ye know that your labor is not in vain in the Lord.

Be steadfast. Don't let the contrary winds of adversity get you off track. Don't allow little insignificant things to take you out of sync. Some people become so upset over changes that they let it take them out of sync and they literally retire on God. I've seen people getting upset because of a person and they allow that person to keep them from serving God. God didn't do anything to us, but He did do something for us; He saved us and blesses us.

Be unmovable, always abounding in the work of the Lord. Talk shouldn't move you; criticism shouldn't move you; having a headache shouldn't move you. It doesn't say that only on Sunday abounding in the work of the Lord. I notice He didn't say worship; he said work. You see God called us to a field of labor. He wants us to work. What does he want me to do? He says in Acts 1:8 And ye shall receive power after the Holy Ghost is come upon you and ye shall be witnesses unto me. Where? In Jerusalem, that's at home. In Judea, that's down the street. In Samaria, that's the crossbreed country. Be a witness.

You can't be a good witness if you're not willing to testify. You can't testify if you don't have a testimony. You've gone through things in your life but you're afraid you would be laughed at you if you told it. That just might be your testimony. Maybe the person living next door to you is on their way to hell and God put you there so you can tell them of the reality in serving a true and living God. Your labor is not going unnoticed. The Lord sees you and has an unusual way of putting you at the right spot at the right time, giving you favor with people you don't even know and others you thought would never pay you any attention. Settle in with God and abound in His work!

Be Ready

Matthew 24:44
Therefore be ye also ready: for in such an hour as ye think not the Son of man cometh.

*B*e *ye also ready.* This is not our home; we can leave here at any moment. If you wake up every other person in the grave that didn't get saved before they died, they will tell you, "I was aiming to get it together, but I put if off too long." If the Lord would come in the next thirty minutes – and he can, would you be ready? Or would the Lord catch you out of place? Do you have somebody to whom you need to apologize? Are there secret sins that you have been intending to get rid, of but you decided to wait? Do you have grudges on somebody?

Be strong. You can not make it if you're not strong. A brother owns a gym called The Body Center. The gym has all the stuff you need to build your body. But when the Lord gets ready to make you strong, he doesn't have you pumping iron; instead he lets you go through adversities in life. He enrolls you in the school of hard knocks. You see, you make sissies out of children when you don't let them have a few hard knocks. A child has to be able to stumble and fall and even get a bruise or need a bandage once in a while. If he doesn't fall now, he won't know how to handle it when he falls later.

Falling is good for you. Doors closed in your face really helps you out. Needing something and having nobody there to respond is good for us. We do more harm to people than good when we help them every time they need aid. They'll stop trying to rely on God and start knocking your door down. If you're going to be strong, you have to go through some things in life. In basic training, you train in both hot and cold weather. Then they have you train in rainy weather. You just might be in war in the rain. And if you didn't train in the rain you might back up if you have to fight in the rain. Be prepared and ready!

Be Full Of Fruit

Galatians 5:22
But the fruit of the Spirit is love, joy, peace, longsuffering, gentleness, goodness, faith.

If you are a child of God, the Bible says you really ought to produce fruit. The thing about fruit is that the fruit will come without any effort on the tree's part. I've been around fruit trees and I've never had a one grunting, trying to disperse fruit, because if it is a fruit tree, it will produce fruit. So if you are a child of God, then when the world sees you, there should be no questions about your salvation. When I am in the Florida area where those orange trees are, I never have to ask the driver the kind of trees. They are filled with oranges. If you are a child of the King, the world ought to see you and know who you are. The world should know whom you belong to. The first thing they will detect about you is your love. The thing about love is that you can not hide it. If love is there, love will lift its head every time.

There was woman called Mary who couldn't contain her love. She showed it by taking a box of expensive ointment and pouring it on the feet of Jesus. Then she took her hair and wiped His feet. That was love. When love is present, you'll know it because when you love somebody you will be talking about the person all the time. How can we say we love Jesus and never bring up His name? But when a person is really in love, they don't care where they are. They talk about you in the beauty shop; they talk about you in the barber shop; they'll bring up your name on the job. And that's the way it ought to be if you are in love with Jesus. Bring up His name wherever you are. You don't have to gossip in garbage. No, no, there's enough about Jesus to keep you busy all day long.

Your fruit will also be joy and peace. You can be on hard times and still have joy. When you've got joy, it will fall off on somebody else. People around you can't stay sad. You have the peace of knowing God will make a way.

A Psalm Of Perfect Praise

Psalms 103
Bless the Lord, O my soul: and all that is within me, bless his holy name.

If you were taking a course in Hebrew, this would be called an "Envelope Psalm." An envelope is known for the stuff that's on the inside. An envelope Psalm begins and ends the same. The first verse says bless the Lord and verse twenty-two says bless the Lord. It contains twenty-two verses, the same number of the Hebrew alphabet. In the twenty-two verses of the text you will find the word Lord mentioned eleven times. That's exactly half of the number of the verses. In each of these verses you will find exactly two lines. He seemed to even out the number of the verses.

Most of the verses in the Bible that we seek out are passages that have us in mind. We look for one that's going to be a blessing for me. But this passage opens with, "Bless the Lord." How often do we say to someone, "Look you've been such a blessing; what can I do for you?" The Psalmist says every now and then the Lord seeks and searches for somebody that will bless Him. But how do you bless a person that has everything? Well you look for something that will give him glory. You look for something that will give him honor. Living a holy life brings honor to God. If you want to grieve God's heart, give him a child that is contrary. If you want to make God feel bad let him find a child that's going opposite of his will. But if you want to make him happy and bless him, let him run into a child that's striving to live for him, one who is striving to walk up right for him. Find a child that is striving to please him. Instead of taking all the credit yourself, give it all to him.

Oh my soul and all that is within me. This speaks of the inside of a person. It's not the outside God is so concerned about. He's more concerned about what's on the inside. Man looks at the outward appearance, but God looks in the heart. Bless His Holy Name!

Picture Of A Saint

Psalms 1:1
Blessed is the man that walketh not in the counsel of the ungodly, nor standeth in the way of sinners, nor sitteth in the seat of the scornful.

This is a fascinating passage. At first, it appeared that the saint of the writer was sleeping on the job. In most cases whenever you run into any blessings, the blessings come at the end but never at the beginning. Before a diploma, you must first finish school. Before retirement, you must first work. The blessings normally come at the end. But this Psalmist was so excited that he issued out blessings at the beginning. Saints are like that. We actually get our blessings on the front end. When we accepted Christ, He gave us the package deal up front. Most of us just don't know it. We think we have to wait and wait and wait to be blessed. But I'm already blessed. When I accepted Christ as my personal savior, He gave me right then everything I needed. He just knows how to issue it out at a given time. Picture a saint as a blessed person.

I like it because God himself uses math differently from the way we use it. God counts differently from the way we count. Man says one plus one plus one equals three. God says one plus one plus one equals one – the Father, the Son, and the Holy Ghost. We say two multiplied by five equals ten. The Lord says two multiplied by five equals 5,000. Two fish multiplied by five loaves of bread fed 5000 men plus women and children.

We say in order to get you must add. The Lord says, "No, in order to get you must divide." The rich young ruler asked, "What must I do to inherit eternal life?" The Lord told him to go and sell all he had and divide it among the poor. We say in order to get up you've got to go up. The Lord says, "No the way up is down. The way to become rich is to become poor." Jesus came down for us to go up. He became disgraced for us to have amazing grace.

Path Of A Saint

Psalms 1:1
Blessed is the man that walketh not in the counsel of the ungodly, nor standeth in the way of sinners, nor sitteth in the seat of the scornful.

Here we are shown the path of the saint. A saint does not walk in the counsel of the ungodly, which means a saint doesn't listen to sinners. Don't get advice from the ungodly. Most of us have a very small perception or a short vision of ungodly people because we put the ungodly in one little basket. We say ungodly people are pimps, prostitutes, gamblers, dope addicts, whoremongers, and a few liars. They are ungodly, but they are not the only ungodly. You might sit next to an ungodly person in church and never know. You just might be living with an ungodly person. An ungodly person is a person that isn't walking in the will and in the way of the Lord.

Don't stand in the way of the sinners. Not only should we not listen to the ungodly, but we shouldn't linger with the ungodly. Don't hang around with sinful folk. You have other things to do when you are around them. Try to win them to the Lord. But don't be buddy buddy with ungodly people. We don't want to laugh at their mess. Don't laugh when you see a drunkard or a person strung out on drugs because without the grace of God, it would be you or me. Be separated from the world.

A saint should be satisfied with the word. Psalm 1:2 But his delight is in the law of the Lord; and in his law doth he meditate day and night. A saint is satisfied with the word. It fills him up. When sinners spend time together, they come home empty. A saint can be home alone, yet still be satisfied because the sincere milk of the word is comfort when you are lonely. It lifts your burdens when your load is heavy. It can be food for you when you're hungry. It can be a battle ax in the time of war. That's why the writer said, "I hide his word in my heart that I might not sin against God."

Portrait Of A Saint

Psalms 1:3
And he shall be like a tree planted by the rivers of water, that bringeth forth his fruit in his season; his leaf also shall not wither; and whatsoever he doeth shall prosper.

The saint should be like a tree. Why a tree? After all God used the wind, water, and fire to accomplish many wonderful things. Can't I be like water? No, because water likes to take the image of everything it gets next to. If you put water in something flat, it will lay flat. Put water in something crooked, it will be crooked. Heat it up, it will evaporate. Freeze it, it will turn to ice. So saints should not be like water. Neither should a saint be like the wind that is constantly changing. It comes from the south this minute, the north the next, then the east or the west. A saint must be solid. And a saint can't be like fire, because God is saving His fire for the last days. All liars shall have their part in the lake that burns with fire. The same fire that warms now will burn later.

God says, "I want my saint to be like a tree." Let's examine a tree. Although other things lie down when they die, a tree dies standing. It becomes a hazard to those around. A dead tree limb can hit you in the head and kill you on the spot. Have you known people that killed your spirit through only a look? Just looking at them changed your whole attitude from happy to grumpy. These people are a hazard while standing up.

Most living things shed their heavy garments in the summer and put on more in the winter. A tree is just the opposite. A tree takes off its clothes in the winter and puts on its clothes in the summer. If I'm a saint then that means I ought not to act like the world. The world doesn't need to look at me and think I'm one of them, because I'm different. I look different; I act different. I live in a completely different way because I'm not following the world. The world needs to follow me.

Preparation Of A Saint

Psalms 1:3

And he shall be like a tree planted by the rivers of water, that bringeth forth his fruit in his season; his leaf also shall not wither; and whatsoever he doeth shall prosper.

Most things grow up, but a tree grows down before it grows up so the roots can grip themselves underneath the soil in order to feed the tree. A tree is not seasonal as some flowers and plants that die when the weather changes. A tree is being fed from under the surface. So when other stuff dies, the tree keeps on living. Likewise, when saints have a firm foundation, they can handle the changes. When the world commits suicide because of surface stuff, saints keep on living. Saints have a reservoir underneath the soil that keeps feeding and supplying during the hard times. Folk who stand strong during the storm have taken the time and effort to lay a firm foundation in their Christian life. Then when your storm comes, you will be able to handle it. Take time to grow some good roots.

It is just as easy to spot a tree with shallow roots. As a storm hits the tree, it falls over and the roots lay bare. When the storm comes to the tree with long roots, the tree will bend and then bounce back. I've seen folk who were in a storm ten years ago and hadn't made it back yet. They're still leaning and bending. They say, "Momma died and that shook me." Other mothers have died. "I lost my job." Folk lose jobs everyday. It's not so much your problem that messes you up; it's how you handle the problem. Your attitude affects your altitude. If you have a good attitude in the midst of your storm, God will lift you high above it.

The tree grows down to grow up and gains endurance each year. Last year a little wind would blow it over, but this year it takes a stronger wind. Before long, a hurricane won't even bring it down. The stuff that used to get you down doesn't even shake you now. You've got to have bouncing back endurance.

Prosperity Of A Saint

Psalms 1:3
And he shall be like a tree planted by the rivers of water, that bringeth forth his fruit in his season; his leaf also shall not wither; and whatsoever he doeth shall prosper.

He brings forth fruit in his season. A saint's prosperity is that he brings forth fruit. If momma and daddy know how to handle a crisis, when storms come they will sit down and say, "This too will pass." When your child sees you calm and handling the storm, they will sit down and do the same when they have a storm. They won't worry. They will be able to sleep and get rest. However, if momma walks the floor when trouble comes and says, "I don't know how I'm going to make it," the little boy will be right behind her walking the floor when his trouble comes.

A saint's prosperity is that he shall bring forth fruit in his season. He's planted. He's not there just because a wind blew him and sent him out. He's not there just by chance. A saint says, "The reason I'm where I am is because God planted me here." When the Lord plants you, can't nobody but the Lord move you. You see, sometimes we let other folk make us nervous about our position and about what we have and we start thinking they will take it from us. But if God plants you, can't nobody get what you've got, because what you have is tailor made to fit you. My blessing won't fit you and your blessings won't fit me. A well planted tree brings forth fruit, weathers the storm, and prospers.

Whatsoever he doeth shall prosper. Whatsoever. You have heard it said of a person, "Looks like everything he touches turns to gold. Whatsoever he does. In other words, he prospers in his work life. He prospers in his wedded life. He prospers in his war life. He prospers in his word life. It seems as if God has put his hands on everything that person has set out to do. I'm glad that I don't have to worry because (1) I've been planted here (2) I'm walking in the right path and (3) My pleasure is in the word of God.

Picked Out To Be Picked On

Matthew 10:16
Behold, I send you forth as sheep in the midst of wolves: be ye therefore wise as serpents, and harmless as doves.

Isn't it amazing some of the things that God sends his servants through? Whenever you are born again, you've been picked out by God. The Lord went through things to get you. He set out to select you. He brought you out of darkness into the marvelous light. You didn't just happen to be a Christian, you were chosen by him and now he calls you a chosen generation, royal priesthood. You think that if God would go out of his way to select a person or people to work for him that he would safeguard them from all crises, all trials, and all tribulations. It seems strange that he would call me and then send me on the battlefield. And then once he sends me there, he allows me to be picked on. I know he knew it when he called me based upon what he said.

God says some will come and literally kill you and think that they are doing right. But he says don't worry about it, Paul himself lost his head on Nero's chopping block. John the Baptist was beheaded for telling the truth. Mark was boiled in a kettle of oil; Peter was crucified with his head down and heels up; John was banished to the Isle of Patmos for the testimony of God's word and as a witness to Jesus Christ merely for taking a stand for the Lord.

I send you forth as sheep in the midst of wolves. What a strange comparison because sheep don't fight, but wolves do. Wolves select sheep for their prey. Wolves take sheep and tear them apart. He sends us as sheep in the midst of wolves and then tells us how to act. Be wise as a serpent, but be as harmless as a dove, meaning know that my enemies are coming, but don't fight back. Put on the whole armor of God that you might be able to stand against the wiles of the devil. He says, "I know you thought you were going to a party, but it is actually a wrestling match." God never said it would be easy, but that he will be with us.

Count On Criticism

Matthew 5:11
Blessed are ye, when men shall revile you, and persecute you, and shall say all manner of evil against you falsely, for my sake.

Many people get in the race and get out because they are shocked when they run into opposition on the Christian battlefield. Have you ever heard anybody say, "I'm quitting because people don't like me? I'm giving up because somebody lied on me; I'm throwing in the towel because they are talking about me." That's the same as a football player going to the field to play and quits the game because he was tackled. If you're going to get on the battlefield or on the ball diamond, expect to be tackled. If you're going to get in this Christian journey expect to be criticized. You are in good company; these things will happen to you.

You're also going to spend some time suffering. Some suffering we bring on ourselves; some God brings upon us, and Satan causes the rest. When you come to Christ, it's because you left somebody – Satan himself. And the devil doesn't like you leaving him; so whatever he can do to hinder your progress, he's going to do it. Never expect Satan to applaud and congratulate you because you're coming to the Lord. You notice how he is often busier on Sunday than any other time because he's trying to keep you from coming to the worship celebration. He will create any problem he can to disturb or depress you.

The Lord says, "You don't need to worry about being picked on because you must bear in mind that whenever they challenge you, I will get them." The fire burned the same folk that put Shadrach, Meshach and Abednego in the fiery furnace. The same lions ate the folk that put Daniel in the lion's den. Old folks had a way of saying, be careful how you dig ditches because the one you dig for me just might be for you. God has a way of allowing things to come back around. God will never leave you alone.

Recognize The Rival

Acts 16:18

This did she many days. But Paul, being grieved, turned and said to the spirit, I command thee in the name of Jesus Christ to come out of her. And he came out the same hour.

Two men, Paul and Silas, were doing missionary work for the Lord when a notorious young fortune teller got caught up in the crossfire. She started bragging on Paul and Silas saying, "These are the men of the most high God. These men are doing a great work." There was nothing wrong with what she was saying. It was who was doing the saying. Sometimes you can be promoted by the wrong folk. When you're promoted by the wrong folk, it can demote you instead. If all you have is drunkards telling everybody how good you are, it might discredit you. If a fool talks well of you, you have to look at where it's coming from.

Paul and Silas perceived that the woman's real need was to know the Lord. So they turned around and witnessed to her and she accepted Christ as her personal Savior. It looked like everyone should have rejoiced that this one girl was delivered. She had gone around the community with a python snake wrapped around her neck. The snake would serve as a ventriloquist and speak through the little girl and she made much money for her master. But when she got saved, she could no longer participate in that evil.

When you get saved there are some things that you can't do any more and there are some businesses you have to get out of. There is some company you can't keep and environments you can't be around any more. Once you get saved, you can't keep acting like a sinner. Now there are a lot of people who don't want folk to be saved. Businesses would have to close; a lot of jobs would be suspended. That's why you see all of the stuff that hinders you from coming to the Lord. Low-down talk shows criticize the church and men of God, causing people to lose respect. The devil is busy trying to keep folk from coming to Jesus.

Grumblers And Gripers

Acts 16:19
And when her masters saw that the hope of their gains was gone, they caught Paul and Silas, and drew them into the marketplace unto the rulers.

When the girl's masters discovered she had accepted Christ, they fell out with Paul and Silas, and right away they turned the crowds against them. It's amazing how crowds like to turn against the preacher. The preacher is the butt of jokes. He's criticized in barbershops and beauty salons. Whatever he does, it's not right. If he's broke, he ought to have some money. If he's got some money, he doesn't need any. If he's got a little sense, he's too top heavy. If he doesn't have any, he's too ignorant. If he's got a family, he's spending too much time with his family. If he doesn't have one, he needs a family. If he has children, he doesn't need all of those crumb snatchers. If he doesn't have any, he needs some children. If he goes somewhere, he needs to stay at home. He can never satisfy folk. But be careful how you talk down the man of God.

The church is not man made; God built the church. He says, "Upon this rock I will build my church." When anybody says anything negative about the church of God, they are actually saying something negative about God himself, because God planned for the church. I thank God for the church being in the community. Even though only 20 to 30 percent of the population attend church, I thank God for that. The Bible says, we are the salt of the earth. We are light in the community. I believe the 30 percent controls the 70 percent of the city. The church is full of people who used to be gamblers, prostitutes, murderers, dope pushers, and dope addicts who are now good citizens in the community. It is disturbing to hear of anybody rising up and saying negative things about the church. Romans 10:15 How beautiful are the feet of them that preach the gospel of peace, and bring glad tidings of good things!

Serious About Soul Winning

Acts 16:23
And when they had laid many stripes upon them, they cast them into prison, charging the jailer to keep them safely.

The rulers took Paul and Silas and put them in the dungeon saying these were the men bringing trouble to their city and teaching things they did not want to hear. It was not enough to lock them up; they had also torn off their clothes. They could have told Paul and Silas to undress, but they wanted to embarrass them more by tearing off their clothes. Then they took whips platted with pieces of metal and dried bone and whipped their backs until blood gushed from Paul and Silas.

Paul and Silas stood in jail for preaching the gospel. However, this was not enough so the accusers decided to put them in the inner dungeon, what is called now a lock down. It was a place with no light, no food, no nothing. They said, "Well, even this is not enough." They had already stripped them and beat their backs, but now they put shackles on their hands and shackles on their feet.

Why are they there? There are there because they love the Lord and trusted in Him. When the Lord sends you, he did not promise you wouldn't have any trouble. As a matter of fact, he said, you will have it. John 16:33 These things I have spoken unto you, that in me ye might have peace. In the world ye shall have tribulation: but be of good cheer; I have overcome the world. Since I'm going to have trouble, how does God want me to handle it?

God says, "Be of good cheer." That's something. With their backs whipped, they're in chains in the inner jail and the Lord says, "Be of good cheer." It's rough enough to go through something, but it's even rougher to go through and try to have a good attitude. Yet neither Paul nor Silas said a mumbling word. It is amazing! They're going through all of this for winning a soul. And we will give up just because it looks like it's going to rain!

A Tough Ordeal

Acts 16:25
And at midnight Paul and Silas prayed, and sang praises unto God: and the prisoners heard them.

Paul and Silas decided even while they were in pain to do some praising. One of the greatest medicines for pain is praise. When it looks like everything is going wrong, just start praising. You don't need pianos or organs; just start singing a melody in your heart – Jesus I love you, Jesus you mean so much to me; Jesus you brought me from a long way. Shut out everything else. Cut off your cell phone. Spend a little time just praising the Lord.

While they were in pain, they started praising. Paul could say, "I've been in shipwrecks where I've had to pray through. I've been in prison before; I've been bitten by a snake. I've had churches to not want me; I've had to pray through that. Paul and Silas are praying and singing; that's a good combination. They were a duet. What messes too many of us up is we try to handle life solo. I can handle this by myself. Find you a prayer partner, somebody you know who can get a prayer through. Lay down your liquor bottle and walk away from your dance partner and find yourself somebody that knows how to talk to God. The day will come when all that other stuff won't mean anything. When you find somebody that can talk to God with you, if your prayer doesn't get there, theirs will help boost yours on. The prayer of the righteous availeth much.

I really don't know what they sang and what they prayed. But can I tell you what I would have prayed. I would have bowed and said, "Now Lord, you know me; you're the one that picked me out. You're the one that sent me on this mission; you knew when you called me that I didn't know what I was doing or where I was going. It was you that told me that you would be with me. I don't want you to destroy my enemies. Now if it be your will, give me strength to make it through this ordeal.

The Other Side Of Midnight

Acts 16:29-30

He called for a light, and sprang in, and came trembling, and fell down before Paul and Silas, And brought them out, and said, Sirs, what must I do to be saved?

It was the midnight hour, a difficult time. Paul and Silas moved from pain to praise and God sent an earthquake to set them free. But after praises there was a panic in the jail. The jailor had a sword ready to take his own life. If you pray right your enemies will panic. They don't know how to handle the power of prayer. When you love the Lord, and when you've been picked out, you don't have to run from your enemies. You don't have to beat the devil running. Stand still and the devil will flee from you.

There was pain, there was praise, there was a panic, and then there was a plea from the man who was to keep them jailed. Won't the Lord take your enemies and make them a footstool? He said, "Sirs, what must I do?" That's a good question, one that all of us ask occasionally. When you're flat broke and bills keep coming in, you say, "What must I do? When your son or daughter has gone astray, you want to know, "What must I do?" When your spirit is low, and you can't feel His presence, you ask yourself, "What must I do? Watch the answer. Paul said, "Believe on the Lord Jesus Christ." Your answer is trusting in the Lord.

When it's dark in your room, when your bank account is closed, and when problems keep stacking up, trust in the Lord. He may not answer the way you think He will, but he will show up just in the nick of time. Looks like He's not going to come, but He's on the way. The more you trust, the stronger you get and the better you'll feel. How many times have you been in situations and had just enough strength to make it through? If it had happened yesterday, you would have taken your own life, but God gave you enough strength to make it. Turmoil and disappointment will give way to joy. Make it to the other side of midnight!

Orderly Prayer Appointments

Daniel 6:11

Then these men assembled, and found Daniel praying and making supplication before his God.

Praying time. One of the great weapons that every believer has is that of prayer. It is very easy to pray and to communicate with our Heavenly Father. I don't know where I would be if it were not for prayer, if I didn't know how to talk to God and listen for him to talk back to me. All of us need to know that prayer is in order. Prayer is like a boat throwing its anchor to the land. Someone takes hold of the anchor and reels the ship in to the land. You never find anybody reeling the land out to the ship. Prayer is like that. When you pray, it's like taking the anchor of faith and throwing it up to God. When you start reeling, you don't reel God down to you. You actually reel yourself up to God. When you get through praying, things look a little clearer for you. Your burdens get a little lighter. Your pathway becomes brighter after talking to the Lord.

Daniel was a fellow that was familiar with prayer. He was a good example that all of us could pattern our lives after, especially when we are going through a crisis. Daniel was an upright and straightforward man. The name Daniel means God will judge. Dan means judge and el stands for God. Regardless of what people may say, judgment day is coming. On earth if you get in trouble, you get a good attorney. Your attorney can get you off in spite of your being guilty, because the attorney goes by what he thinks and what you say. But God is not like that. God knows your thoughts before you think them. He not only sees what you are doing, He also knows what you are thinking. He doesn't judge us based only upon what we do; he also judges us based upon how we think. So be careful not to use reckless thoughts. Philippians 2:5 Let this mind be in you which was also in Christ Jesus. Jesus went to a mountain to pray, and continued all night in prayer to God. (Luke 6:12)

An Excellent Spirit

Daniel 6:5
We shall not find any occasion against this Daniel, except we find it against him concerning the law of his God.

Daniel superseded most people because he's about the only one in the Bible other than Jesus the Christ with whom you can't find anything wrong. Daniel was the character in whom they could find no fault. Daniel had an excellent spirit. Sometimes we take this too lightly, but it is very important to have an excellent spirit. You can have a Ph.D. and degrees all over your wall, but if you have the wrong spirit you won't go very far. You can be attractive, overflowing with beauty and charm, but if you've got a nasty spirit then you are really ugly. It's hard to be around cantankerous folk and people with nasty spirits and nasty attitudes. If you've got a nasty spirit you ought to erase it.

I've seen it over the country. I know pastors that you can't touch. They preach good, but you can't touch them. They've got nasty spirits, nasty attitudes. So whoever you are, watch yourself, because if you ever get down, the folk you thought were with you will go the other way. You can lose your fancy possessions over night along with your so-called friends. However, a pleasing attitude and a nice disposition will draw folk. You know where you are now, but you don't know where you are going. A good spirit will make folk want to hang around you. So if you have a nasty spirit, straighten it up while you can.

I shake hands with everybody. If they don't come to shake, I go them. The person I might not want to touch might be the one that gives me a helping hand. And if they can't say anything else about me, they can say, "Well he was nice. He did have a good spirit. He did have a good attitude." A good spirit will carry you a long ways. I know pastors that can't preach a tap. And you can't get in the church because there's so many folk. He has a good spirit. He's a good man. He's always trying to do something kind.

Elevated By God

Daniel 6:2
And over these three presidents; of whom Daniel was first: that the princes might give accounts unto them.

Daniel had been selected to be in charge of the presidents. Daniel was a little fellow from a foreign land who had now moved to be Prime Minister. Now brothers and sisters when you get elevated you create more enemies. If you are the top boss on the job, you've got a lot of folk that don't like you. It isn't because you did anything wrong, but just because the spot you got. When I was young and coming up, I enjoyed shooting things in the trees. And sometimes the tree would be full of birds. It could be big birds on the limb or it could be a little one on the top limb. And the one on the top was the one I would aim at. And the devil is like that. The devil likes to get the top bird. He likes to get the one that's holding the top spot.

Have you ever been elevated somewhere and you thought everybody wished you well? You thought they were waiting congratulate you and give you a pat on the back. But they acted like you hadn't done a thing. They don't like you. They have problems with you when you've been elevated. That's what happened with Daniel. Three presidents got together with their committees and said, "Look, we don't need to let Daniel stay in this spot. Let's see if we can do something to destroy him. Let's cut him down. He can't be that good. Ain't nobody that good."

So they followed him and watched his every step. They put a tap on his phone and trailed his chariot to find out where he was parking it. They investigated his past. After several weeks they had their committee meeting saying, "We can find no fault in Daniel. Let's create a fault. If the devil can't get you one way, he'll fix something in order to pull you down. But they were plotting against the wrong man. It would all come back on them. God had elevated Daniel and man would not take him down.

Bow Down

Daniel 6:10

He kneeled upon his knees three times a day, and prayed, and gave thanks before his God.

When a farmer needed to carry stuff from one part of the desert to the other, he used a camel. The camel was so tall that he had to bow down whenever his master would get ready to put a load on him. The master put a load on and the camel would carry that load half of the day. Around noon the camel would begin wobbling and perspiring. The load would start to shift. And the master would get in front of him and tell him to bow down. He would get next to him and straighten up the load. That night the camel couldn't rest with a heavy load so the master would get in front of him and make him bow down so he could take off the load. And the camel would rest well all night long.

Our master has a load for us to carry. He warns us before we leave home in the morning to bow down. You say I don't know why God has put so much on me. It's just a load. When the Lord puts it on you, He's walking right under you helping you carry your load. The old folks said, He won't put no more on you than what you can bear." When you are going through the day, you've got to dodge lies and being falsely accused. You've got to dodge doors being closed in your face. Your load can start to shift on you. Around noon you ought to bow down and let the Master straighten up your load. And you get up and go the rest of the day carrying your load.

But at night you can't sleep with a heavy load. You are wondering where your children are. That's a heavy load. Wondering what's going on with your spouse. Wondering what's going to happen on your job tomorrow. Wondering what the doctor will say. That is a heavy load. But instead of trying to sleep with it, bow down, because your Master will take that load off and you can rest without worrying about a thing because God will lift your heavy load.

Instruct The Newborn

Galatians 6:1
Brethren, if a man be overtaken in a fault, ye which are spiritual, restore such an one in the spirit of meekness; considering thyself, lest thou also be tempted.

Brethren. The writer of this epistle is talking to saved folk. There is a difference between the gospels and the epistles. The gospels teach us how to be saved, but the epistles teach us how to behave. Many saved people have not yet learned how to behave. A saved person with bad behavior will make others think they aren't saved. They will give the church and God a bad name because they have been saved but they haven't been taught how to behave.

When a person comes down the aisle and gives the preacher their hand and gives God their heart, it is similar to the birth of a newborn baby. There is still a little after birth left on them. They have to be cleaned and bathed. The baby is still connected to the mother through the umbilical cord, which must be cut. In other words, a new believer has still got a few lies in them; a little envy, a little malice, and a little strife is still on the inside. The other thing is they are still connected to somebody in the world. When they came down, they spend only two hours at church. They will go back home and spend 166 hours that next week with some liars, backbiters, and cheaters. They will work beside gamblers, whoremongers, and peace breakers. They will be exposed to all of the things of the world.

We are sadly mistaken when we assume the work is complete the moment a person accepts Christ. God sent them to us for us to be nurses and surrogate mothers so that we can aid and assist our brothers and our sisters and bring them to a higher level. How do you think it would look if you gave birth to a child and once the baby was born you left it at the hospital with your business card saying, "If you need us call us"? When we do people that way who come to Christ, we are doing the same thing.

Defeating Faults

Galatians 6:1

Brethren, if a man be overtaken in a fault, ye which are spiritual, restore such an one in the spirit of meekness; considering thyself, lest thou also be tempted.

If a man be overtaken in a fault. The text didn't say sin; it says a fault. The text is actually talking about sin. Now a sin is a fault but a fault doesn't have to be a sin. Notice also that the sin is not named. He just called it a fault. He didn't even name what it was because what could be a fault to you may not be a fault to somebody else. If the sin was named, then those people not involved in that particular sin would think that they got by.

Ye which are spiritual. You've got to be able to stand. When you walk in the light, he is in the light. You have fellowship one with the other. Beginning in Galatians 5:17, the Bible tells us that we ought to be able to stand. For the flesh lusteth against the Spirit, and the Spirit against the flesh: and these are contrary the one to the other: so that ye cannot do the things that ye would. If you have stood, then you can fall. You cannot fall if you are already down.

This is a huge family that we're in. One tragedy about this family is that many times we lose the war in our own barracks. We find ourselves fighting each other. Many times we fight other denominations. We fight other races and other colors. We even fight each other in the same fellowship. We find ourselves shooting fiery darts at each other, cutting each other down and criticizing within the same fellowship. We're in the same family, listening to the same message, on our way to the same heaven. But we find ourselves talking each other down. What a tragedy! The writer here seems to say that we should not air out dirty laundry among the unsaved. These are things that need to take place among family members. Every once in a while you need to call the family together and just talk to the family. Regardless of being saved, we still are human.

The Journey Of A Soul

Galatians 6:1
Brethren, if a man be overtaken in a fault, ye which are spiritual, restore such an one in the spirit of meekness; considering thyself, lest thou also be tempted.

You cannot board in heaven while living on earth. You are going to be confronted with some things while you are down here. Salvation is a process involving three stages – penalty, power, and presence. Now you may be up at the second, you may think that you're at the third, and you might be going through just the first stage. The penalty from sin means that I have accepted Christ as my savior. If I die tonight, I will go home to be with the Lord. I know I'm saved, but the tragedy is that I'm still struggling with sin. I'm still struggling with weaknesses and shortcomings. What's happening to me? Why is it that I can't do what you can do and can't be as strong as you are or stand like you can? It's not as easy as we say. We need power over sin.

There are some folk that ought to know better than to do the stuff they are doing. Sometimes when a person brags about how strong they are, they are just indicating to us how weak they really are. If you really think that you have passed the second stage, let somebody walk up and slap you real hard. You will discover you're still being saved. If you say you don't ever get mad, then I need to talk to you because there are some things that will get on your nerves. There are some things that will get under your skin.

Sometimes things will get next to you, but you have to look at the fact that there are three steps to salvation. I am being saved. Paul said, every time I have a desire to do good, evil is always present. Then you hear him make another statement, "I can do all things through Christ which strengthens me." Before he could get to that statement, he had to experience a shipwreck; he had to be beaten; he had to experience jail. Salvation is a process of progressive growth. The Lord knows the best procedure for each of us.

The Big Squeeze

Galatians 6:1

Brethren, if a man be overtaken in a fault, ye which are spiritual, restore such an one in the spirit of meekness; considering thyself, lest thou also be tempted.

If a man be overtaken. Notice he did not say if a man undertake. If you undertake something, you have planned it. It was your decision. You set out to do it. You marked the date on the calendar. You made provisions. That was a set up you planned. But the text means something different. The text is talking about when you're trying to live right, when you're trying to follow the Lord, and when you're trying to do the best you can do. When you're trying to go that extra mile for the Master. Then in spite of your trying to do the best you can, you have been overtaken.

The Bible talks about going through tribulation. The word tribulation in the Greek text means pressure. Have you ever noticed what happens when you mash an orange and what comes out of it? Well, whatever is in there. Whenever you apply pressure, two things can happen. Either the pressure brings out the best or, quite often, it brings out the worst. All of us have got some stuff in us and sometimes it has to be pressured out. I hear people saying when they curse, "Oh no, it slipped out." But that was some stuff in you. It couldn't have come out if it had not already been in there. All of us have some rubbish in us.

No one can get the rubbish out any better than the Lord. You see if I would try to pry it out, you would stay angry with me, but God can get it out and you will love him. You'll go back and say, "Lord I thank you so much for bringing me through." After all the things David experienced, He went back to the Lord and said, "It was good for me that I was afflicted. Job lost all of his children and after that the Holy Spirit left him. He said, "Though God slay me, yet will I trust Him." You see, pressure will bring out the worst, but it will also bring out the best.

Overtaken

Galatians 6:1
Brethren, if a man be overtaken in a fault, ye which are spiritual, restore such an one in the spirit of meekness; considering thyself, lest thou also be tempted.

Satan sits back and watches the stuff that can get you. He checks you out. He checks your pulse to see what it is that makes your heart beat faster. He watches the books you read and observes the movies you watch. He searches out your weak spot. You think nobody knows except you, but Satan knows where your weak spots are and he begins setting up traps. Beware of the wiles of the devil because he's a tricky scoundrel. So he starts baiting your hook with stuff you like and keeps throwing it right at you. It doesn't take much to get some people.

But the devil has patience. He doesn't give up like people do. We may try once or twice to do something, and if we fail, we sit down, but the devil keeps going. Maybe he didn't get you this week, this month, or last year, but he keeps trying. A good fighter keeps going back hitting at the same spot. When the opponent knows he's getting you, you start flinching. He got you there and he keeps going back.

He watches you when you get lazy and feel like hanging around the house one Sunday. The devil says, "Uh hmm." He marks it down. He jots it down when you miss a couple of days reading your Bible. He writes it down when you jump up in the bed without first praying. Folk used to disappoint you and you went right on, but now he sees you sitting a little depressed because you were let down. He makes himself a note. Then he brings pressure on top of pressure in your life and he sees you weakening down. Instead of reading the Lord's word, you look for a book or a movie. Then the devil throws the bait at you again and you nibble at his hook. Finally, you take the bait. That's why as a saved person you must stay strong in the Lord and in the power of his might because the devil keeps going.

Influenced By The Spirit

Galatians 6:1

Brethren, if a man be overtaken in a fault, ye which are spiritual, restore such an one in the spirit of meekness; considering thyself, lest thou also be tempted.

Ye which are spiritual. He says, " I want to talk to people who are spiritual." Here is a description of spiritual folk. Galatians 5:22 But the fruit of the Spirit is love, joy, peace, longsuffering, gentleness, goodness, faith. You are more like Christ when you have love then you are at any other time. Love brings joy. And before you can bring peace to somebody else, you've got to have peace yourself. If you're messed up, you can't help somebody else get it together. Have longsuffering, gentleness, and goodness and live by faith. It is the spiritual who are to do the work of restoring. The text didn't say, ye which are preachers, deacons, mothers or tri-guild members. Preachers and deacons ought to be spiritual, but not all of them are. So it is the spiritual person who can achieve spiritual results.

Galatians 5:24, They that are Christ's have crucified the flesh with the affections and lusts. God doesn't want a person who is still living in the flesh out trying to restore somebody. If you have shortcomings coming behind you, don't try to get somebody else together. If we live in the spirit, let us also walk in the spirit. He doesn't want any super spiritual folk, ones who talk in spiritual tones all the time, "Thank you Jesus, Hallelujah, thank you Jesus, praise the Lord, how you doing?" Let your life style and your life make a difference. It is not what comes out of your mouth, but the things that come from the heart that are important.

Let us not be desirous of vain glory. The Lord doesn't want anybody working for Him to get name recognition. "I brought him. I brought her. It was my prayer that did it." You don't deserve any glory. You are only His mouthpiece. When people go around looking for glory for themselves, they aren't about Christ. Be influenced by the Holy Spirit!

Mend With Meekness

Galatians 6:1

Brethren, if a man be overtaken in a fault, ye which are spiritual, restore such an one in the spirit of meekness; considering thyself, lest thou also be tempted.

*R*estore. The word restore means to mend. In the Greek, it could be compared to a man with a broken arm. The arm is mended rather than being cut off because it can be used again. It is the same as a person who has fallen. Have you ever made a mistake while trying to live for the Lord? Have you behaved in a way you knew was not of God? If so, you need to be restored.

Restoration does not come through criticism. The word does not say, ye which are spiritual go criticize them and tell their business all over town. We should not do all we can to bury him. When a brother has fallen, he's already down. His conscious is whipping him. He can't get a prayer through. The spirit is whipping him. Know that God will take just so much. But it is up to God to decide the time.

When God gets tired, He will chasten you or warn you. If you don't listen, then he will rebuke you. He'll get his stick out. If you continue in sin, God will literally take you out. Somebody will wake up one morning looking for you and you won't be there. You weren't sick. God says, "Look you are damaging to my ministry so I'll just take you out privately. No one will know what happened. It is better for me if I get you off planet earth. You cannot play with God.

Restore such a one in the spirit of meekness. Be gentle to the fallen brother. Show kindness. Give him some tender loving care. Don't stop shaking his hand or speaking to him. When you're strong in the Lord, you realize the brother or sister sinned against God, not you. If you know Whose you are, you won't let anybody take away your spirit or stop you from doing what you're supposed to do for Him. God reaches way, way, way down to pick us up and bring us to a better place. Be a restorer!

Consider Carefully Your Conduct

Galatians 6:1

Brethren, if a man be overtaken in a fault, ye which are spiritual, restore such an one in the spirit of meekness; considering thyself, lest thou also be tempted.

Consider yourself. That's a hard text. What does it mean to consider myself? What I need to do is go to him and say, "Brother, you've fallen, but I want to help you back up." I need to look at him and think if I was where he is, how would I want him to treat me? Consider if it were me. No one is exempt from falling. You may be fifty or sixty, but you aren't dead yet. In a weak moment, you could get caught up in some kind of business scheme and lose every dime you have. Your spouse could rub you the wrong way and you could go off and do something you ought not to do. You may never fall; thank God if you don't.

Let's say I'm looking down at Miller. Miller has fallen whether he tried to or not and he's out of fellowship. But remember, he's still in the family. Just assume his name is Miller Ray. Even though he's a rascal, he's still a Ray. If I've known him for forty years and he just did this after his fortieth birthday, then I need to back track and look at his record. I see he was a good guy up until forty. If he made such a drastic change, what happened to bring him to that point, because for forty years he stood. He was teaching Bible class and singing in the choir. He was paying his tithes. I need to at least give him credit for standing for forty years. But all of a sudden he has fallen. Maybe he got a little mental block or maybe he's disturbed over something or maybe he's being lead by somebody.

Lest thou also be tempted. If you don't handle things correctly, God will snatch the cover off your sin and make it worse than the sin of the brother you are trying to expose. If you rejoice because your brother or your sister has fallen, God will expose you and let somebody take a real good look at you, because you are a candidate for the same sin.

𝍤𝍤 𝍤𝍤 𝍤𝍤 𝍤𝍤 𝍤𝍤 𝍤𝍤 𝍤𝍤 𝍤𝍤

𝍤𝍤 𝍤𝍤 𝍤𝍤 𝍤𝍤 |

November

Focusing On Calvary

Luke 24:7
Saying, The Son of man must be delivered into the hands of sinful men, and be crucified, and the third day rise again.

Go with me to this hill called Calvary, an unusual spot of ground. If you take a close look, you still see the stain of blood that ran down Calvary's hill. It was at Calvary where my sin debt was paid. It was at Calvary where the bitter waters of life were made sweet. The serpent's head was bruised. My eternal check was signed and my ransom price was paid. A young man showed up by the name of Jesus that knew no sin, but for us became sin.

Unlike many of us, Jesus knew before he left heaven what was going to happen on planet earth. We don't know what's going to happen from day to day. We can be healthy and robust today and tomorrow we can fall into a dilemma that will change our lives forever. We wait until crisis shows up and then try to find a solution. God prepares the solution before the crisis. It's good to walk with him.

Jesus came to suffer and to die for the sins of the whole world. Jesus is hanging on the middle cross with nails in his hands, spikes in his feet, and thorns on his head. On a cross at each side hangs a thief. Jesus' enemies thought they could humiliate him by allowing Him to die in the midst of criminals. People are still trying to embarrass Jesus. When you listen to comedy hours and things of that nature, you hear jokes about Jesus. As a matter of fact, they like to crack jokes about people that follow Jesus. But be careful how you laugh at jokes about Jesus because Jesus is no joking matter. Jesus is real. He is serious. And he paid an awesome price for my sins.

While He's hanging on the cross, Jesus is lifted about eighteen inches from the ground. God uses his enemies to do mission work for him and then sends them on to hell. They failed to realize that in John 12:32 God said, And I, if I be lifted up from the earth, will draw all men unto me.

Our Excellent Example

Isaiah 53:5

But he was wounded for our transgressions, he was bruised for our iniquities: the chastisement of our peace was upon him; and with his stripes we are healed.

While Jesus was hanging on the cross, there were those around who rejoiced because they thought it was over for Jesus. Many people hope that you fail in life. They don't think you'll last. But when you are in the God movement, you can literally be on the cross and God will raise you up. Jesus said, "I'll come and die for the sins of mankind." He hung on the cross bleeding from his hands, his forehead, his feet, and his back If he was willing to suffer and die for me, the least I can do is live for him.

Oh he died for me I tell you. And every time I get a little slow and a little lazy about doing what God wants me to do, my mind goes straight back to Calvary. Every time I want to throw in the towel and give up, that spirit shouts back, "But you know he died for you." When I'm ready to curse out somebody that mistreated me, my mind goes back to Calvary first. If you think about what He did for you at Calvary, you will straighten up your act.

The Bible says, And when they brought him to the place. To the place of shame. To the pace of criticism. To the place of anguish. To the place of heartache and heart break. There they crucified my Lord on the cross. Usually during a crucifixion, the person who was dying would die cursing. He would die arguing and fussing. Sometimes he would even spit on his accusers. We don't see Jesus doing any of these things while He was hanging on the cross. He wasn't blaming others or complaining about his hurts and aches. No, no, He's praying. Calvary wasn't designed for a prayer place, but Jesus told us that you can pray anywhere. How does his prayer begin? Father. That's not strange for him because he kept his father's name on his lips. His thoughts never left the Father. What an example for us!

Only God Can Forgive

Luke 23:34
Then said Jesus, Father, forgive them; for they know not what they do. And they parted his raiment, and cast lots.

In this text, Jesus is actually putting his son ship on the line. He said, "I know that I'm sin now." He that knew no sin became sin so that we who are sinners would be forgiven of our sins. And so he said I'm putting my son ship on the line. In this text, he didn't say my God, he said, "Father." You know who I am; I am your son.

Father forgive them. Jesus Himself had forgiven sin during His time on earth. Mark Chapter 2 talks about men who tore up a roof in order to get a paralyzed man to Jesus. And Jesus looked at him and said, "Son because of their faith, your sins are forgiven." The scribes became angry saying, "No man can forgive sin, but God. Jesus said that ought to tell you something. I forgave sin and the man is walking. So evidently I must be God.

But now at Calvary, Jesus is not forgiving sin. Instead he said, "Father you forgive them." Even though He forgave sin before he made it to Calvary, at Calvary He became sin. And sin cannot forgive sin. So he said, "It's out of my hands now. Father you forgive."

Them. Instead of saying them, why didn't Jesus name some people? Why didn't he say, "Father forgive Pilot, because Pilot had a good opportunity to let me go." Or "Father forgive Herod," because he sent Jesus to the cross. Herod had tracked him down from a baby to age two up until Calvary. He could have said, "Father forgive the Roman soldiers," because they were the ones that actually nailed his hands. Or, "Father forgive the Roman centurion," who cried out, "Surely this must be the Son of God." The reason he didn't get into name calling is because it would have taken too long to name everybody. It was not only those around the cross who needed forgiveness. Everyone from Adam and Eve to David needed forgiveness. He said them.

Chariot Of Mercy

Luke 23:34

Then said Jesus, Father, forgive them; for they know not what they do. And they parted his raiment, and cast lots.

Forgive them. Them is really a chariot of mercy. Every one of us had to fit in the chariot. Jesus prayed for you on Calvary's cross. Isn't that something, Jesus is dying yet He's concerned about the folks that are killing him? One of the greatest blessings a person can have is that of being forgiven. When you know you've been forgiven, it's like a weight lifted off you. You can handle life better when you know you've been forgiven. You may think you haven't sinned in a long time. We like to stop at just five little old sins, but there are 113 recorded sins in the Bible and you can add to that list. There is the sin of co-mission. There is sin of omission. There is sin of being ungrateful. There's a sin of having a proud look. If you got up this morning, you have committed sin. There are too many for you to miss.

But thank God at Calvary, Jesus prayed for our sin. He said, "Father forgive them for they know not what they are doing." It sounds like an excuse for the sin. But Jesus, "I saw them put thorns on your head. They knew what they were doing. Jesus, I saw them nail your hands and feet. They had to know the pain that caused. They knew you would die." Jesus said, "Well that's not really what I'm saying. They didn't know whose head it was. They knew that they were nailing hands, but they did not know it was the hand that touched blinded eyes so they could see and healed sick bodies. They did not know it was the hand that could turn lunch baskets into banquets.

They were sinning out of ignorance. There are some things that we do, and we ought to know what we are doing. But when you really know what you are doing, sin starts to stink in your nostrils. Because every time you sin, it is against God. Whenever you commit the tiniest sin, it is against the person that died for you. Receive His mercy.

Out Of Sight For A Time

Luke 23:46
And when Jesus had cried with a loud voice, he said, Father, into thy hands I commend my spirit: and having said thus, he gave up the ghost.

Jesus was on the cross for your sin and for mine. He fulfilled John 3:16 where it says For God so loved the world that he gave his only begotten Son and whosoever believeth in him shall not perish but have everlasting life. His life fulfilled Matthew 16:21 From that time forth began Jesus to show unto his disciples, how that he must go unto Jerusalem, and suffer many things of the elders and chief priests and scribes, and be killed, and be raised again the third day.

You see Jesus knew all along what he was doing. He knew all along that his death on the cross meant life for me. His death on the cross meant eternal life for me. His short life meant that I'll live forever. Jesus died at the age of thirty-three. I have discovered that it doesn't make any difference how long you live, but it's what you do while you're living. You can live to be a hundred years old, yet if you've done nothing beneficial while you are here, then your living is in vain. However, if you live only ten days, but in those ten days you were with the Lord, you've lived a successful life, because only what you do for Christ will last.

He died while he was there on the cross. On Friday he died. On Friday they took him down and put him in the grave. On Friday He died for your sin and for mine. He stayed there all night Friday night and all day and night Saturday. Everybody thought it was all over. The demons were dancing saying, "We got Him." The enemy said, "He won't get up." However, out of sight certainly doesn't mean out of mind. Out of sight doesn't mean it's all over. Sunday morning that old grave started reeling and rocking. Sunday morning the stone rolled away. Sunday morning He got up out of a dusty grave with all power!

Cookies And Cream

Matthew 7:7
Ask, and it shall be given you; seek, and ye shall find; knock, and it shall be opened unto you.

Many of us live beneath our privileges. We think we've gone as far we can in life. However, your heavenly Father is rich in houses and in land. Romans 8:32 says that if he spared not his own son but offered him up for us, how much more will he freely give us all things. 1 Timothy 6:17 says he will give us richly all things to enjoy. Earthly parents often struggle to supply the needs of their children. But when they move from a struggle to middle class living, they go beyond the needs and give the child some of the things that the child wants. God allows the cup to run over so that you will have more than enough. Psalms 24:1 says the earth is the Lord's and the fullness thereof, the world and they that dwell there in. So sometimes we just might be living beneath our privileges because we did not ask our heavenly Father for what we want or need.

Often God will put us on a waiting list if He sees that we are not ready to handle the blessings. God has to keep some of us where He can keep his hand on us. It does not diminish the power of God or the ability of God to supply those needs. But sometimes God can handle us better walking than riding, because we might ride right on by the house of God. When we have our own place of luxury, we will think that's our little heaven when God has something much bigger for us. God wants us to have the foundation in place before He goes up with the super structure. Before going home, you have to touch first base. First base to us is being born again. Before we look for cars, cash, clothes, creature comforts, and a cottage in the country, He wants us to be born again. You can have religion and still be lost. God wants you to have a personal relationship with Him. When you are born again and have a personal relationship with Jesus, everything else become cookies and cream.

Jesus Passed Through

Mark 10:46

And as he went out of Jericho with his disciples and a great number of people, blind Bartimaeus, the son of Timaeus, sat by the highway side begging.

Here, Jesus is between Judea and Jerusalem in a little place called Jericho. Jericho was the place where Joshua and his army marched around until the seventh day when God made all the walls come tumbling down. Jericho is the place where Zaccheus climbed up a sycamore tree in order to see Jesus. Jericho had a wonderfully sweet fragrance from the beautiful flowers grown there. Honey was in abundance. Jericho was in a setting surrounded by beauty and water. It was a great rich place to be. Jesus decides now to go through Jericho on his way to Calvary.

Thank God Jesus came through. I'm glad Jesus came through Memphis. If he had not been through this area, I don't know where I would be. But thank God, He came through town. Whichever town He stops in or goes through, He makes a difference. Are you glad he came through your town? Whenever He shows up, He changes things in the town. We must invite Him often.

Jesus was yearning to perform another miracle. I think Jesus is cruising around the church today yearning to perform another miracle. He majors in working miracles. Some think that the miracles are over, not so. As long as Jesus lives, there will be miracles. He is a miracle worker. Jesus is still healing sick bodies. He is still baffling the minds of doctors that say you can not be cured but you are. Somebody tried to describe a miracle. I heard a country preacher give me the best definition I've ever had. He said a miracle is something that can not happen, but it did. That's good enough for me. It wasn't supposed to happen, but it happened. Some of you have experienced a miracle. You have been in a situation when others had thumbs down for you, but thank God Jesus had thumbs up.

A Righteous Rumor

Mark 10:47

When he heard that it was Jesus of Nazareth, he began to cry out, Jesus, thou Son of David, have mercy on me.

There was a massive crowd following Jesus. A man there had heard rumors about Jesus. Now there is a difference in hearing of a person over and against actually knowing the person. When you hear of a person and don't know him, you are merely a spectator. The reason many people are not as close with Christ as they ought to be is because they are merely spectators. You need to have a personal encounter with Jesus. You need to know when you met him. You might meet your neighbor and forget it, but when you meet Jesus it ought to be an experience that you will never forget, because he changed your life. He turned you around. He performed spiritual surgery on you. He took that old stony heart out and put a brand new heart on the inside. When somebody starts talking about Jesus, you ought to have something moving on the inside if you know Him and have had a spiritual experience with Him.

This man had heard about him. When you're sick, you search for solutions. This man was blind, but something inside was telling him he didn't have to stay in the shape he was in. You must have an inward experience to move from the shape you are in. If there is an inner desire saying I can get up from here and go forward, you are ready to be successful in life. This man was not only blind but he was also poor. What a difficult predicament to be in. There was no Social Security or welfare. His only survival was to beg for what he could get. He had done nobody wrong. He had not committed any crime, yet he was living beneath other folk. He is a laughing stock, blind and poor with his privileges cut off. He couldn't see the sunrise. He could smell the flowers but couldn't see them. He could touch his family but didn't know how they looked. Everyone else is going about their business, while He is begging for mercy.

Watchful Bartimaeus

Mark 10:48
And many charged him that he should hold his peace: but he cried the more a great deal, Thou Son of David, have mercy on me.

What a perplexing state to be in. Bartimaeus was a blind beggar. People then had a belief that if you were blind it was because you had committed some kind of sin. People often tag others when they are going through something difficult. They imply that you must have done something wrong. If your house burns down or you have an auto accident, people rush over to discover what it is that you have done wrong. But you don't have to commit sin for trouble to come; it will show up. If trouble has not made it to your door, just keep living. Sooner or later it will come by and you may as well get ready for it.

You are better prepared to handle a personal crisis if you treat others well during their time of trouble. Don't look at folk with an eye of disgust because they going through it. You ought to lend them a helping hand, because when you get down somebody will come by and give you comfort and support. Treat everybody the best you can while you can because one of these days you might have to reach out and say, "Hey brother/sister, I need you to help me through this dilemma."

Bartimaeus positioned himself by the side of the road. Just sitting there he couldn't see anybody but he could hear folk as they were passing by. You know when you sit in public places you hear everything. He heard all the rumors and gossip. But finally he heard a crowd that had a good story. The Christ following crowd ought to have a different noise, one that will attract folk instead of running people away. A noise that makes a blind person desire to see you. Evidently somebody in the Jesus crowd said the right thing. Jesus came to the neighborhood. Bartimaeus called loudly, "Jesus thou Son of David have mercy on me."

And Jesus Stood Still

Mark 10:49
And Jesus stood still, and commanded him to be called. And they call the blind man, saying unto him, Be of good comfort, rise; he calleth thee.

Bartimaeus knew who to go to for help. The disciples were there, but he didn't ask the disciples for sight. Notice he did not ask the multitude for sight although they were there. He asked the right person. If you want something, you've got to ask the right person. Otherwise, you are wasting your time. You can't tell everybody about your crisis because some folk like to see you down anyway. Sometimes folk are just waiting to hear you are behind in your rent or about to lose your car. But thank God there is one you can tell your troubles to. He said, "Thou Son of David." It is obvious he had been listening to Gospel because he didn't just say Jesus. He knew to refer to him as the Son of David.

Thou Son of David. In other words, "You're the one we have been waiting on. And I heard in the Old Testament that when you come, you would open blinded eyes. I know who you are. I know you have the capability of doing something special in my life." In essence he said, "I'm not looking for justice because I've made some mistakes. I'm not looking for what I deserve, because I deserve death, hell, and the grave. But I want you to have compassion on me. I want to get into your innermost being. I want you to look at me and see that I need pity and compassion."

When was the last time you prayed a prayer serious enough to stop Jesus in his tracks? Now you know he had other things he had to do. He was on his way to Calvary to die for our sins, but here is a blind man that caused Jesus to stand still. Jesus said, Now man, tell me what you want. Bartimaeus went right to the point. He didn't hand Jesus a long list of all the folk he wanted Him to bless. When you stop God, know what you want and ask Him for it.

Ignore The Obstacles

Mark 10:51
And Jesus answered and said unto him, What wilt thou that I should do unto thee? The blind man said unto him, Lord, that I might receive my sight.

Jesus called for Bartimaeus. You are where you are because the Lord called for you. We did not choose him, He chose us. Ephesians 1:4 says According as He has chosen us. God acted alone. The word He is in the middle voice indicating God acted not only by Himself but also for himself. God chooses us by himself and also for himself. That's why God doesn't want you to be down and out all the time; you have been chosen for him. You should spotlight the Lord wherever you go. When others observe your ways and attitudes, they ought to be able say, "There goes a child of the King." They should desire the same close walk you have with the Lord. Even though you may not know what the future holds, you know who holds the future. But it's hard for folk to see you with the Lord if you are always grumbling and complaining. It makes no difference how dark things are, God never panics. He can take a crooked stick and hit a straight lick.

Now whenever you come to the Lord for a blessing, there will always be some obstacles. There will be some hindrance to keep you from getting to the Lord. Here, the crowd charged him to shut up and stop the noise. And these were not outsiders; they were Christ-following folk, people that were following Jesus everywhere he went. Have you ever sat beside someone in church who rolled their eyes at you because you were making too much noise?

Jesus asked, "What do you want man? He quickly answered, "Lord, that I might receive my sight." He didn't just come to Jesus; he came to Him with faith. He had faith to believe that Jesus could make a difference in his life. Do you have f faith in the Lord today to believe that He can make a difference in your life?

Cast Off The Old Junk

Mark 10:50-51

And he, casting away his garment, rose, and came to Jesus. And Jesus said unto him, Go thy way; thy faith hath made thee whole. And immediately he received his sight, and followed Jesus in the way.

And he cast away his garments. Bartimaeus was a beggar and he carried an old quilt to wrap around himself while sitting on the side of the road. But when he heard Jesus calling him, he got up and said, "I don't need this thing any more." When you meet Jesus there are some things you don't need any more. You have been trying to shield yourself, but now you have new freedom in life. I know of people who keep bodyguards with them every where they go. Go on if you want to, but when you are saved, there are some things you don't need anymore because God gives his angels charge to keep watch over you so you can sing all day and all night.

The Bible says this man was made whole. Now there is a difference in being healed over and against being made whole. Being healed and having wholeness are not the same. A whole lot of folk today have been healed, but they aren't whole. When you are healed, that means your body doesn't hurt. But when you are made whole, that means your heart doesn't hurt. When you are healed of blindness, you can see physically, but when you are whole, then you can see spiritually. When you are healed, you can walk, but when you are whole, you can walk in wisdom.

Thank God he's able to make you whole immediately. I'm so glad He doesn't stop at healing, but He goes on to make a person whole. He gives us more than what we ask for. Bartimaeus asked Jesus only to give him his sight. Yet, this was going to be a two-part miracle. Jesus went on to make him whole. Certainly, if you make one step toward the Lord, He will make two. Bartimaeus was able to cast aside the old things and walk in newness.

The Valid Viewpoint

John 17:1

These words spake Jesus, and lifted up his eyes to heaven, and said, Father, the hour is come; glorify thy Son, that thy Son also may glorify thee.

These words spake Jesus. There are times when you hear people talking. They say one thing before you, yet they say something just the opposite when you are not around. Jesus however, was truthful before our faces and behind our backs. In John 17 He literally allowed the Holy Spirit to take a picture of his heart to share with the universe how much he truly loved us. Whenever Jesus says something, it is profound, it is sufficient.

Jesus lifted up his eyes. When most of us are headed for crisis or crosses, we look at the cross of crisis. Jesus would do just the opposite; He would look up. Most of us focus on our situation. But you have to look above the stuff you are dealing with and look at the Person who can do something about it. There is no need to spend restless nights over stuff you can not change.

He lifted up his eyes towards heaven. Whenever you lift up your eyes, there's a refreshing Spirit that rests in your bosom. Something about looking up encourages you to go forward in the body of Christ. Jesus lifted up his eyes toward heaven and said, "Father." You also ought to be on talking terms with your Heavenly Father.

Don't try to live this life without being on talking terms with God. If your relationship is not right with God, get it right. It doesn't matter who you have against you if God is for you. So make sure that you are on talking terms with Him. After I've had a conversation with the Lord, I feel better regardless of the situation. Sometimes God doesn't change the situation; He just equips you to handle whatever it is that's coming. He makes you tough enough to be able to walk through situations. God may not move the Red Sea but He will give you strength to go through the other side.

Smile Despite Suffering

John 17:1

These words spake Jesus, and lifted up his eyes to heaven, and said, Father, the hour is come; glorify thy Son, that thy Son also may glorify thee:

Father, the hour is come. Jesus mentioned the hour at least eight times in the gospels. Anytime the Holy Spirit repeats something, it's good for us to take notice. Jesus was really talking about his hour of suffering. You see, Jesus is the only person who knew before He got here how much He had to suffer while He was here. Most of our suffering usually slips up on us, but Jesus knew before he arrived how much he had to suffer. In Luke 2:49 Jesus said He must be about His Father's business. His father's business was for him to be the sacrificial lamb and die on a hill called Calvary, be buried, and rise again on the third day. He knew he had to suffer.

My hour has come The tragedy of his suffering is that He didn't suffer for himself. He suffered for you; He suffered for me. You ought to love a person some if they are willing to suffer for you. Nobody wants to suffer for a person that's trying to destroy you. Jesus suffered for his enemies. He suffered for folk that meant him no good. All of us have been enemies of Christ. We were born in sin and shaped in iniquity. Namely, everything we did was against God. And yet he suffered enough to die in our place.

Glorify me so that I can glorify you. Jesus was saying to his father, "Look, I'm on the way to Calvary. While I'm going, don't allow me to look bad. When my hands are nailed, fix it so I can stand the nails. When they put a crown on my head, fix it so I won't curse them out. When they hang me on the cross, allow me to hang there and dispense blessings instead of cursing. When I arrive at Calvary and get on the cross, make me look good in spite of all I have to encounter. Help me through this. God will do the same thing for you and help you smile through tears.

A Never Ending Gift

John 17:2
As thou hast given him power over all flesh, that he should give eternal life to as many as thou hast given him.

Thou has given him power over all flesh. The Greek word for power is authority. Now if I had had the power, the prestige, and the position at the age that Jesus had it, perhaps I wouldn't have given God credit for that. But Jesus always gave the credit to his Father. We often hate to give credit to other folk. We want people to think that it was our idea. But God is the mind regulator, so don't take credit for whatever little idea you have. The government passes out budgets, the school system passes out books, but God passes out brains. If it took thinking to get it, you've got to give God the credit for it. Even if you decide not to do something you knew was wrong, you've got to give the Holy Spirit credit for convicting you.

That he should give eternal life. Some teach that you must earn eternal life. One movement believes that baptism saves you, but if you're not saved before you get baptized you're not saved after you get baptized. If you go in the water a sinner, you come out a sinner. If water could save you, we wouldn't need Jesus. His salvation is a gift. He gave us eternal life. If it is a gift; I didn't earn it. If I earned it, it's not a gift. It's a gift, but once you are saved, you ought to work. I'm not working to get saved; I'm working because I am saved.

Eternal life is not just duration of time, but it's also a quality of life. You move to another level. You move from earth's brutality to heaven's blessings. From earth's fury to heaven's favor. From earth's killings to heaven's kindness. From earth's liars to heaven's lovers. From earth's miseries to heaven's majesty. From earth's pains to heaven's praises. You move from earth's wounds and weariness to heaven's worshipping. Aren't you glad that when you leave here you've got another place to go?

We Are Gifts

John 17:2
As thou hast given him power over all flesh, that he should give eternal life to as many as thou hast given him.

To as many as thou has given him. In other words, I am a gift to Jesus. You are a gift. You are a gift that God gave his son. God cruises around and picks whom he pleases and gives them to his son. Take this one and that one. Ephesians 1:4 says, "According as he has chosen us in him before the foundation of the world." We have been chosen by God. If you're saved, you have been chosen by God. It's a privilege to be chosen by God. When God selects you for any reason that's a blessing. Through the years, I have watched how God works. When God gets ready to do some great work with somebody, He knows how to work on that person.

Maybe you've made up your mind you're not going to be saved, but you're going to be a devil the rest of your life. Then the Lord will let a saint move next door and you'll be peeping out your window while they are getting ready to go to church. You'll start being curious why they get up every Sunday morning and go to church. What's so important? Every time you talk to them, nothing but words of joy and love flow from their lips and you will begin saying to yourself, "If I could just be like that person." God has a way of getting next to you and before you know it, you will be sitting up in church without aiming to be there. God knows how to deposit eternal life down in your own soul.

Eternal life is knowing the father. Paul said in Philippians 3:10 Oh that I might know him. Saints you need to get to know Him. You will never know everything there is about Him. God will give you only nuggets because if we knew everything about Him, our little puny minds could not comprehend it. But everyday of our lives, we must try to get to know him. I want to know the One who can put one foot on time and put the other foot on eternity.

Practices, Power And Principles

John 17:4

I have glorified thee on the earth: I have finished the work which thou gavest me to do.

I have glorified thee on earth. Jesus glorified the Father with his Person. At his baptismal service at River Jordan, the Holy Spirit in the form of a dove descended and lit right over Jesus. God the Father stuck his head out of heaven's window and looked down and said, "This is my beloved Son in who I am well pleased." Merely looking at the person of his son made the Father glorified.

Jesus also glorified the Father with his practice of performing miracles. He went to Jairus' house to take care of a little dead girl. A woman that had an issue of blood for twelve years pressed her way through the crowd to touch only the hem of Jesus' garment. Jesus looked at the woman and said, "Your faith has made you whole. When Lazarus had died, Jesus wanted to glorify his father. He walked to the grave and looked up and said Father it's not for me, but it's for these folk standing around. And Lazarus got up.

Jesus also made his father glorified by using power. When the disciples were afraid during a storm, Jesus walked out and simply spoke to the wind and the waves and said, "Peace be still." And there was a great calm. He manifest the power given to Him by the Father.

Jesus kept with principles which glorified the father. When Jesus set out to do something, he always used the principles in the Word. When Jesus had an encounter with Satan in the wilderness, He didn't have to use the Word. He had enough power to just blow on the devil and send him off to kingdom come. Instead, Jesus said, "It is written." In other words, He used the same thing that Ray can use when the devil comes after him. You can't cut the devil, you can't shoot the devil, and you can't step on him. He's got more power than that, but you can use God's Word to defeat the devil. It is good to glorify the Father.

Moral Madness

Malachi 3:7
*Even from the days of your fathers ye are gone away from mine ordinances,
and have not kept them.*

Have you ever noticed how bad our moral life is? There was a
time that we would hide when we would do wrong. We do
it openly now. There was a time when you would make a
mistake and you would try to make sure no one knew about it. Now
you tell it yourself. We have bad morals. We do anything that we are
big enough to do and do it proudly without any shame at all. In the
past, even men that didn't have any training knew how to respect
ladies and knew how to treat people; but it's no more.

There was a time that a man thought it not robbery to take care
of his house. He wouldn't send his woman out hustling, begging, and
borrowing. He would make sure bread was in the house and that the
utilities were paid. He had means to make ends meet. But now he will
lie up in the house and wait on her welfare check to show up. And she's
comfortable with that kind of living. Morals are so low that you have
to take men to court to make them pay for their own children. That's
really honest to goodness low.

There was a time that we had respect for the house of God. When
a person came near to God's house, they were careful in the way
they would conduct themselves. But now you might catch some little
hoodlums gambling on the doorstep of the church because they are
imitating the adults in their lives. It's a shame our morals are so low
that at times we don't even possess good dog sense.

The other day I watched a dog trotting down the street when he
saw a dog house with no door, but the stray dog wouldn't go in. Even
though it was open, he knew the house did not belong to him. But here
we are with college degrees and with all kind of sense and education
and we have to put wrought iron on windows to keep other smart
alecks from coming in. It is moral madness.

Creatures Of Habit

Malachi 3:7
Even from the days of your fathers ye are gone away from mine ordinances, and have not kept them.

Even from the days of your father He said that one of the reasons you have done this is that you inherited this custom from your parents. We are creatures of habit. We do what we saw others do. I knew of a sister who cut the four edges off a pot roast every time she cooked one. One day her neighbor came to eat pot roast with her and commented on how delicious the roast was. She noticed that the four edges had been cut off the pot roast and asked why. The sister said it was what her mother did. She thought it made the pot roast taste better. Next time she saw her momma, she asked her about the why she cut the corners of the roast. Mother said, "Well baby, to tell you the truth, I don't really know why. I think it has something to do with the flavor, but I got it from my momma. Every time she would cook she would cut the corners off the pot roast. I think it makes the pot roast tender. I'm not sure, but when I go out in the country, I'll ask your grandmother about it. And she did. Grandmother said, "Well baby, when you was at home, I had a pan that was too small to hold the pot roast. And for it to fit in the pot, I had to cut the corners off the roast for it to fit down in the pan properly." They had gone through three generations and nobody ever asked anybody why the corners were cut.

In our churches today, we have $2 members who put $2 in church because your momma put $2 in church. And the reason your momma put $2 dollars in church is because her mother put $2 in church. But if you ask momma she would tell you that what she made every day was $2. But you don't make no $2. None of us make only $2 a day. You give $2 out of habit because we are creatures of habit. But God said, "You have gone away from mine ordinance."

Send Back God's Part

Malachi 3:7

...Return unto me, and I will return unto you, saith the Lord of hosts. But ye said, Wherein shall we return?

*R*eturn. The word return means repent. You see, unless you repent to God about the wrong you've done, you'll keep on doing it. You might listen to a sermon today and say, "Well I'm convinced today and I think I'll start right now." No, you need to do more than just start today; you need to repent for mistreating God. Every time you fail to tithe, you are mistreating and robbing God. God didn't save you for you to turn around and be his enemy. When you fail to tithe, the Bible says you are a thief.

I don't want to be called a thief in any kind of a way, especially robbing the One that wakes me every morning. I don't have a bill anywhere in my house as big as what I pay God. If my house note is $1000 I'm going to give God at least $1100 because I've got no income as great as God's. When all of this other stuff is gone I will have to depend on Him. At the age of twenty when I started paying my tithes, I took some members to eat. There was a 10% gratuity on the bill. I said, "I'm not going to put a waiter on the same level with God." All the waiter did was bring my food and give me a little extra tea. Now they deserve everything they get because their salaries are very small; they need tips. My point is I couldn't keep God where I had the waiter.

And so I moved up God to 15%. It wasn't very long before they start having 15% gratuity so I moved God up to 20%. Now I'm hanging around 25% and I don't miss it, because when you move God up like that God shovels blessings right back to you on every hand. Isn't it amazing how some people trust the slot machine? You would stand a better chance of being struck by lighting twice than to win one time big with a slot machine. But with God you're always a winner; you never lose. He gives me everything I need. How dare me back up on that kind of God.

God Robbers

Malachi 3:8
Will a man rob God? Yet ye have robbed me. But ye say, Wherein have we robbed thee? In tithes and offerings.

How are you treating God? Maybe you make it a point to treat your momma and daddy right. Possibly you even treat your husband or wife in a respectful way. However, how careful are you in the way you treat your Lord and Savior? After treating others special, do you turn right around and rob the God that wakes you every morning? Hebrews 7:9 tells us that Levi, a priest, who received tithes, turned around and payed tithes to Abraham.

When you fail to tithe, you are spiritually and morally low, because God does more for you than anybody. As a matter fact, you can't think of anything you have that God didn't give to you. Where you are God brought you. What you have God gave you. What you know God taught you. And so it's hard for you to look under eyed at your child mistreating you and you treat God that way every week.

You get on your knees and say, "Lord I need a good job. Lord I need you to bless me with finances. Lord I need you to keep a roof over my head. Lord my health is bad; I need you to keep me in good health and give me strength. Lord my enemies are around; I need you to protect me from my enemies." And then every Sunday you march around and tip God instead of paying Him tithes.

The writer asked a question, "Will a man rob God?" Will a finite rob infinite? Will dust rob divinity? When you fail to pay your tithes you're getting in trouble with your God. You're getting in trouble with the God that woke you up this morning. The God that clothed you in your right mind. The God that gave you a reasonable portion of health and strength. Say what you will or may, but the text says you are a God robber when you fail to return to Him his portion. And you can get by much easier robbing a national bank than you can by robbing God.

Stop At The Storehouse

Malachi 3:9

Ye are cursed with a curse: for ye have robbed me, even this whole nation. Bring ye all the tithes into the storehouse.

God allows you to rob Him because He could stop you, you know. Don't ever think you're getting away with any thing concerning God. And when you rob God, He charges you interest. If you fail to pay some bills, you are charged interest compounded daily. One hundred dollars becomes $500. God charges you compound interest when you fail to pay him on the due date. God will collect. Stuff happens that you don't understand. Why did my car transmission go out? That's your tithe money. My refrigerator broke. That's your tithe money. My roof starts leaking. That's tithe money. You can't get away from God. I'd rather pay God and be blessed than to rob God and then be cursed.

Ye are cursed with a curse. That means the curse that cursed you is cursed. Consequently, if you come to me for help and God has cursed you and I try to help a cursed person, God will whip me for trying to help you. When God starts whipping folk that won't tithe, ain't no need of you trying to bail them out. Ain't no need of you trying to pay their mortgage for them or pay their utility bill. If you keep fooling around, God will whip you. You want to help these folk but there's nothing you can do about it because God will do what he said he's going do.

But then He said, "Bring." In other words, he wants you to put forth an effort. He said, "Now don't send in your tithe". Some folk get so important they just send it. But God says, "Bring ye all the tithes." Where? Into the storehouse, God's house. There are some things that your money won't buy for you. Your money might buy a good time, but your money can't buy you happiness. Your money might buy you a mattress but it can't buy you sleep. Your money might buy you a great big house, but it won't buy you a home. You need the Lord to bring the blessing.

Blessed Or Cursed

Malachi 3:10

Bring ye all the tithes into the storehouse, that there may be meat in mine house, and prove me now herewith, saith the Lord of hosts, if I will not open you the windows of heaven, and pour you out a blessing, that there shall not be room enough to receive it.

I'll pour. You get more from a pour than you do from a measure. Something measured is limited, but when you pour, it falls everywhere. That means your blessing will fall on your children. Your blessing will fall on your dog. Your blessing will fall on your mother and your grandmother. God says He will pour you out blessings that you don't have room enough to receive. This is a wonderful verse. Every child of God is living in one or the other verses. You're living in verse nine which says you are cursed for robbing God or you are living in the blessing of verse eleven. Which verse do you want to camp in?

Verse nine says you are cursed with a curse and verse eleven shows you how to have problems blocked from you. You've got some enemies that try to get next to you, but God will shield you from your enemies. You've got some sickness that is trying to invade your body, but God will shield you from your sicknesses. You've got a mind that wants to go bad, but God will regulate your mind. He said, "I will rebuke the devourer for your sake and your fruit will not fall before its season." Namely, my blessing wont' go by me when it gets to me; it will camp right at my door.

I'm blessed and I know I am. I'm glad I'm blessed. I'm glad God keeps on opening doors. I'm glad he continues making ways for me. I might spend my house note; I might spend my car note; I might spend my clothes bill; or I might spend my grocery bill. But there's one check I'm not going to bother and that's the one I owe God. I don't care who you are, you aren't getting that one. It belongs to the Lord. I owe the Lord too much to hold back on Him.

Confess And Be Blessed

Malachi 3:11

And I will rebuke the devourer for your sakes, and he shall not destroy the fruits of your ground; neither shall your vine cast her fruit before the time in the field, saith the Lord of hosts.

If you know that you have been robbing God and you have intentions of stopping, I recommend that you do it now. Make a confession to God and say, "I repent of the times that I have robbed you because I owe you so much. I've taken advantage of you. I have a job because you gave it to me. I've got health because you will me to have it. I've got a family that doesn't give me any trouble at all that you blessed me to have. I've got transportation while other folk are trying to get a vehicle. And it's all because you've been good to me. Lord, I know I have not treated you right. I have not paid my tithes as I ought to and I should. And I know better and I need to repent of it right now and make it right with you, O Lord." Commit to tithing.

Do it now. The only way you can get it right with God is by telling Him that you know you are wrong and ask the Lord to make it right this very moment. You must to do that. And saints you can't let nothing or nobody stop you from treating God right, because God has never done any thing wrong to you. The devil's plans are for you to struggle. He wants to see you living from can to can't.

When you fail to tithe, it's against the Lord. It's not against the church. Don't lie about your tithe. When you get a raise, change the amount you have been tithing. You have to face God on this one. When you fail to tithe, you tie God's hands. He can't bless you because you are not trusting in Him. I would be afraid to death to drive an automobile and be out of fellowship with God. No matter how angry you are about something; whatever it is, never take it out on God, because in your own private chamber you'll have to depend on him – on nobody but God. Trust!

A Time Of Anguish

Psalm 86:1
Bow down thine ear, O Lord, hear me: for I am poor and needy.

It is obvious that the writer of this psalm was going through some kind of calamity. The person was dealing with some kinds of problems, pressures, and situations that led him to have a personal conversation with God. This psalm is believed by some to have been written by David when he was running from Saul. Saul was a king that fell out with David. You don't have to do anything for folk to dislike you. You can be minding your own business. You don't have to say anything negative about them or to them. You can create enemies by just being you.

If you are saved you do have enemies. Some people may not like you because they don't know you. If you would get to know people, the folk you can't stand you may find yourself embracing. And then often we don't like certain people because they remind us of us. We see so much of ourselves in them that since we can't get mad at us, we just get mad at the person that reminds us of us.

However, other commentaries say David was distressed because of his son, Absalom, David's prized possession. He was the apple of David's eye. David wanted Absolom to have everything. But the problem was that David's own son rose up against him. When your enemies move in your house, it's a horse of a different color. You can handle your enemies when they are down the road or even next door, but it is difficult when your enemies move right in your house. Your enemy is part of your own family.

Absalom disliked David so much until he coveted the position that David had. Absalom devised a plan to turn the people's hearts toward himself and set out to make himself king. It was Absalom that led David to write Psalm 55:6. Oh that I had wings like a dove for then would I fly away and be at rest. He called on God in his distress.

When Trouble Comes

Psalm 86:1
Bow down thine ear, O Lord, hear me: for I am poor and needy.

ow down thine ear, O Lord. Obviously, this writer wanted God's attention. There comes a time in your life when you want the attention of God. Now you may not want it all the time, but when you are in trouble you want to get the ear of God. There are some situations that you can find yourself in where nobody can help you but God. Some things you can talk your way out of, some things you can pay your way out of, and some things you can play your way out of. But some things you'll have to pray your way out of. When you learn how to talk to God, He will bring you through any and every situation.

Hear me. The writer was not praying for a congregation. He was not praying for his household. He said, "Look, I'm in this situation and I need you to hear me. I've got a problem I need you to solve. I've got a situation that can't nobody get me out but you. I know you can do it so God I'm calling on you." One of the greatest privileges any person can have being able to talk to our Heavenly Father.

I'm humbled by being able to pick up the phone and call the mayor of the city and have a conversation with him. I'm humbled by that. To be able to call the governor of the state means much to me. How special to be invited to a dinner given by the President. That's great, but nothing compares to being able to have a conversation with God. Everyone else is limited. There are things they can do and there are some things they can't do. A mayor is only mayor in one city. When he is in another area, he's a visitor. The governor is the head of one state. Even neighboring states are not part of his territory. The power of the President is largely limited to the United States. And you know we've got some trouble on the other side of the water. We need to have somebody that can handle stuff across the river.

No Other Help Will Do

Psalm 86:1
Bow down thine ear, O Lord, hear me: for I am poor and needy.

I am poor and needy. If you're poor, you are not by yourself, because Jesus says the poor you will have with you always. Even though many of us look like we've got a few dollars, we are just about two weeks from welfare if we happened to miss only two paychecks. Our lights would start blinking and we would be almost out of gas. We may have good credit, but it won't last long. So we can't walk around with our chest stuck out like I'm Mr. or Mrs. It. We know the truth. And we've got friends who work at the bank and the loan companies where we borrowed money.

We all need something from somebody. That's why we ought to embrace each other. That's why we ought to lean on each other. If you are down today, there's no need of me laughing at you, because the tray could turn. You are on one side of the seesaw, and I'm on the other, but a seesaw goes up and down. Next time I'm going to be down and you'll be up. It is important to learn how to support one another and unite together.

However, the text is speaking of something more than physical poverty. The psalmist was really saying, "I'm empty." Have you ever been to the point when you felt empty? You can have all the finer things in life and still feel empty. You can have filet mignon on your table and alligator shoes in your closet, but you feel depleted. If you don't have the fullness of Christ down on the inside, all this other stuff won't amount to anything. You can still be suffering the same as the writer of this text. Fine food and fine clothes didn't take away his suffering. Unless God reached down and touched him, he wouldn't make it through his trial. He was afflicted in such a way that only with God's intervention could he overcome and have victory. He felt destitute and was begging God for help.

Shelter My Soul

Psalm 86:2

Preserve my soul; for I am holy: O thou my God, save thy servant that trusteth in thee.

Lord I need you to preserve my soul. Saints, you see that soul is the real you. Every time Satan comes after you, he comes for the purpose of damning your soul. All the stuff you see on television and read in the newspaper and hear on the telephone is intended to damn your soul. Here is this woman with some rag tied around her head talking about reading your future. And here she with is with the Internal Revenue after her. If a person is that smart, they ought not to be in trouble with the IRS. I don't need anybody to tell me about my future when I'm living with the one that holds my future. There is no need of telling me about something that you can't do anything about it.

The God I'm serving is preserving my soul. I heard Him talking one day to His Father. He said, "Father, all you gave me I have kept." In order for the devil to get to me, he has to go through the Father, the Son, and the Holy Ghost. By the time he goes through the Godhead, that devil will be saved himself. You see the devil can't get to us, but he's like a roaring lion seeking whom he can devour. In other words, the devil will make you hurt yourself.

Once I was conducting a revival and I decided to go out and do a little jogging around the hotel where I was staying. While jogging I came upon a huge yard with a huge German Shepherd dog. The dog jumped and started leaping after me and I said like Sanford, "This is the big one. I can't out run him." I didn't know how I could handle a dog that size. But right before the dog made it to the street where I was, a chain came up out of the ground and pulled that big dog back. That's exactly the way the Lord has the devil. The Lord has a chain on him and the only way the devil can get to me is by me going down in the devil's yard. But if I stay out of his yard, God will preserve my soul.

Consecrated Trust

Psalm 86:2
Preserve my soul; for I am holy: O thou my God, save thy servant that trusteth in thee.

The psalmist says, "Preserve my soul because I am holy and I trust in you." He is saying, "Watch over me because I am living in a godly manner and I am trusting in you." Now that's a good combination. The reason he is holy is because he is trusting in the Lord. And the reason he can trust in the Lord is because he is holy. If you're going to be a Christian, your job is to please God. You can try again and again to please other folk and they will never be satisfied no matter how hard you try. You can crawl on the ground and they will tell you to walk. You walk and they tell you to crawl on the ground. If you laugh, they tell you that you ought to frown. If you frown they tell you that you ought to laugh. If you're jolly, they complain that you are too happy. If you're not jolly, you are criticized for looking mean all the time.

Since I know that I cannot satisfy folk, I have made up in my mind who I'm going to satisfy and that's God himself. Romans 12:1 tell us, I beseech ye therefore brethren, by the mercies of God, that you present your bodies a living sacrifice, holy, and acceptable unto God, which is your reasonable service.

How am I going to satisfy the Lord? By trusting in Him. No matter how dark it gets, remember this—there are fringe benefits when you trust in the Lord. Hebrews 11:6 says without faith it's impossible to please Him for he that comes to God must believe. In other words you've got to trust Him. So whatever you must deal with now or in the future, keep trusting in the Lord. If you're out of work, trust in God. If the doctor says you won't live, trust in God. If your family packs up and walks away, trust in God, since the God I serve will hear. Hold to Psalm 86:7 In the day of my trouble I will call upon thee: for thou wilt answer me.

If

1 John 1:9

If we confess our sins, he is faithful and just to forgive us our sins, and to cleanse us from all unrighteousness.

Underline those little words *that if.* That means it might happen and it might not happen. If is the central word in the word life. If you drop the L off the front of the word life and E off the back, sandwiched right in the middle is the word **if**. That's why the old folk used to say, "I'll see you next Sunday if it's the Lord's will." The devil used that word when Jesus was in the wilderness. He said, "If you are the Son of God, command these stones to turn into bread." He said it again when Jesus was hanging on Calvary's cross. "If you be the Christ, save yourself and others and come down from the cross."

Indeed that word if is scattered all over the Bible. 2 Chronicles 7:14, If my people, which are called by my name, shall humble themselves, and pray, and seek my face, and turn from their wicked ways; then will I hear from heaven, and will forgive their sin, and will heal their land. Matthew 16:24, Then said Jesus unto his disciples, If any man will come after me, let him deny himself, and take up his cross, and follow me. John 12:32, And I, if I be lifted up from the earth, will draw all men unto me. John 15:7, If you abide in me, and my words abide in you, ye shall ask what ye will, and it shall be done unto you. Romans 10:9, That if thou shalt confess with thy mouth the Lord Jesus, and shalt believe in thine heart that God hath raised him from the dead, thou shalt be saved. 2 Corinthians 5:1, For we know that if our earthly house of this tabernacle were dissolved, we have a building of God, an house not made with hands, eternal in the heavens. 2 Corinthians 5:17, Therefore if any man be in Christ, he is a new creature: old things are passed away; behold, all things are become new. Galatians 6:3, If a man think himself to be something when he is nothing, he deceiveth himself. A powerful little word.

December

For Goodness' Sake

Psalm 25:7

Remember not the sins of my youth, nor my transgressions: according to thy mercy remember thou me for thy goodness' sake, O Lord.

Most of us are in accord in that we have had numerous opportunities in life to accomplish great goals and those occasions passed right on by. When cable TV first came on the scene, I had an opportunity to buy stock. I didn't think it was going to do that much, so I didn't want to tie my little money up in Cable TV; three stations were enough for me. At the time, I had no idea that it would expand so far. I missed that moment of golden opportunity.

Many of you ladies once knew a young man who was interested in you and even asked for your hand in marriage. However, because he wasn't groomed the right way with a winning smile or wearing the right clothes, you rejected him. Then Mr. Slick came by and you chose to go with him. And now Mr. Broad Shoulders and Mr. Physique that you ran off with has his shoulders drooping and his teeth no longer in his mouth. And you ran into that person that asked for your hand that you thought wasn't going to be nothing and he's residing in corporate America. You didn't want to tell him, but you told yourself you missed out.

Many go through school doing just enough just to pass. Some of you got fast too young. You got mannish too young. You had other things that would keep your attention rather than the classroom. You got wet behind the ears too soon and you learned too much too fast. You didn't think you would need the knowledge and you missed chances to move up the ladder of success. Some of you had babies too soon. Momma couldn't tell you nothing; you just had to go out there. Now you are weighted down. It takes almost as much as you make to keep your children going. So you missed opportunities. We can pray the psalm, According to your mercy, remember me O Lord for your goodness' sake.

When Opportunity Knocks

Matthew 19:20
The young man saith unto him, All these things have I kept from my youth up: what lack I yet?

Here is a text where a man had a great opportunity, but he missed it. The three synoptic writers, Matthew, Mark and Luke, discussed this young man. One writer says he was young. The other writer says he was rich. The other writer says he was a ruler. And by looking at all three accounts, we discover that he was a young rich ruler. When you look at his resume he had a lot to offer, because most of the time people don't have all three at the same time.

But when you are young there are several things you ought to do. First, you ought to train your mind while it's young and alert. You can think better and comprehend more while you're young. Secondly, straighten your life out. Don't waste and throw away your life while you're young. You can do some things while you're young that will damage you for the rest of your life. You don't want to get a bad record because when you reach a certain age, opportunities will come require a good record. You might miss some things that you could accomplish if hadn't messed up your record while you were young.

Thirdly, don't let others snatch youth from you. Don't let other fellows who are going nowhere stop you from going. Instead of hanging around with crack, be introduced to Jesus, the rock. He's all you need. If you want to get high, don't get high on substances and stuff; get high on Jesus. Jesus made me higher than I've ever been before. And when you have a hangover on drugs and alcohol, it makes you worse, but when you have a hangover on Jesus it makes you better. It puts joy in your heart, pep in your step and a glow in your eyes. The Jesus hangover will have you loving folk, but that other hangover will have you hating folk. You can eliminate some stuff and be ready for opportunity if you handle life better while you're young.

He Came Running

Mark 10:17

And when he was gone forth into the way, there came one running, and kneeled to him, and asked him, Good Master, what shall I do that I may inherit eternal life?

God had and still does have some rich folk. Abraham was a rich man with many possessions and descendants. Job was a rich man with a large family. Solomon was a very wealthy man. He was the richest on the block. There's nothing wrong with being rich, but the issue is how you handle your wealth. Some folk let money control them. When you learn how to control it, then money is a good servant. However, money is a very poor master.

The man who came running to Jesus was both young and rich. The Bible says it is easier for a camel to go through the eye of needle than for a rich man to enter into the kingdom of Heaven. In order for a camel to go through the city gate, the master had to first unload the camel. Then he had the camel bow down and crawl under the gate. Both poor and rich must do the same. Philippians 2:10 says at the name of Jesus every knee shall bow. Not only should you bow, but also you must unload. Hebrews 12:1 says to lay aside every weight and sin which so easily besets us and to run with patience the race that is set before us.

Not only does the text tell us about the man, but it also tells us about the master. Two young men met – the young rich ruler and young Jesus. This young man appears to have everything going for him that any youth should want to have. Yet he came running to Jesus. He was eager to get to the Lord. When you can find a young person running to Jesus, that's good isn't it? It's good to see young people at the house of the Lord, wanting to see Jesus and be taught how to read the Bible, how to pray, and how to act in church. It's good to find young people who want to see the Lord. The young ruler wanted to see Jesus so badly that he ran. Bow and take your load to Jesus!

The Appropriate Approach

Mark 10:17

And when he was gone forth into the way, there came one running, and kneeled to him, and asked him, Good Master, what shall I do that I may inherit eternal life?

nd kneeled to him. Not only did he run to see Jesus, but he also knew how to act when he got to Him; he fell on his knees. He didn't walk up and say, "Hey, doc. What's going on man?" He knew how to bow. You don't find many now even in church who know how to act. People will come to church and have no respect for the house of God. They walk in with a hat on their head and just sit up there. They might walk in with a cold drink and chips and all kind of junk right in the house of God. But it's good to find a young person that knows how to act. He bowed.

He also knew the right person to go to with his question. You see some things you can ask your school teacher. Some things you can ask folk on the job. Some things you can ask your parents, but there are some questions that nobody can answer for you except the Lord. He said, "Good master," which meant he also knew how to reverence the Lord. He said goodness. He didn't just say master. He said good master before asking his question.

By His response, at first it appeared that Jesus was angry with the young ruler. Jesus said, "Why do you call me good." Isn't that something? The man is wanting eternal life and Jesus puts him through a series of questions. But if the man was calling him good thinking that Jesus was just another man, Jesus was saying you are out of order, because if you're not looking at me as being God, I'm not good. Some of our Muslim brothers say he's a good man, but that He's not the Son of God. That isn't good enough. If you are just looking at me as being a man, I'm just a man. If you look at me as being God, I am good. Isaiah went on to call Him wonderful, counselor, mighty God, everlasting father, and prince of peace. He is our Good Master.

Already Done

Mark 10:17
...Good Master, what shall I do that I may inherit eternal life?

Don't miss this. What can I do to inherit eternal life? This messes up a lot of folk because folk come to church wanting to know, "What can I do to be saved? I want to know what can I do to get eternal life." We think salvation is received by what we are doing. You see, if you do something to get saved then you can stop doing it and be unsaved. No, you don't spell it D-O. You spell it D-O-N-E. It was done on Calvary's cross. Salvation is a gift. John 10:28 I gave unto them eternal life. If it's a gift you didn't earn it. If you earned it, it's not a gift. And since I didn't do anything to get saved, I can't do anything to stay saved. I'm staying saved by the power of God. He paid the price.

But the man kept pressing Jesus. He said, "You've got to let me do something to be saved. The Lord said, "What's written in the law?" Jesus said, "Thou shalt not commit adultery. Thou shalt not steal. Thou shalt not defraud. Thou shalt honor thy mother and thy father." Jesus quoted the last five commandments, which deal with man's relationship to man The first five deal with man's relationship to God. Jesus said, "How are you faring with your fellow man?" Hear the young man's answer, "All these have I kept from my youth up." You've got to give the him credit for being a pretty good young man.

Then Jesus looked at him and said, "One thing thou lacketh." What is your one thing that stands between you and God – something in your life that's kind of got you wrapped up and you can't give God your best. Jesus said, "Sell all you have and give it to the poor." Your God is your gold. You need to do a little switching from your gold to your God. And the Bible said that man walked away with a hung down head. I don't know what happened to that man but he left Jesus that day without eternal life.

Hardship

Psalm 57:1
Be merciful unto me, O God, be merciful unto me: for my soul trusteth in thee: yea, in the shadow of thy wings will I make my refuge, until these calamities be overpast.

David continually had serious problems with King Saul. If you're going to have problems with a person, you don't want it to be the king. Whatever the king says or does, that is law. But for some mysterious reasons, Saul had problems with David. Although David was a fine fellow, he was not the greatest character. He didn't know that God was preparing him for the same position of the man that was chasing him. That's why it's important to be careful when you're up because the person you look down on now, someday you might have to look up at. It is amazing how quickly God can switch things around.

David was a fugitive running from a king. He had to get help from others just to stay alive. And if you're going to get anywhere you need some help. Honest to goodness you need some help just to survive in life. I look at the many people that reached down to help me in polite and sincere ways. I've had others to be ugly and low down. But both helped me because I accept encouragement and correction. In addition, I also get help from folk that try to mash me down. Your enemies are the ones that really help you by taking you to your prayer closet. They will help you have a closer relationship with God.

God needed to take David through some things to learn some lessons. David needed to experience some situations, have some headaches and heartaches, let downs, set backs, and some back sets. It is bothersome when people that have never gone through things try to tell others how to hang on. Those who never had to say good bye to mom and dad tell you that you can make it. I like to know you've had some trials before you give too much advice. God allows us to go through some things so we can have a testimony.

Where Enemies Belong

Psalm 57:1
Be merciful unto me, O God, be merciful unto me: for my soul trusteth in thee.

David is in a cave standing against the wall along with all of his men, his servants, and his army. They are all standing there holding their breath because they know the king is in the neighborhood. And the king who is David's enemy is so sure that David is caught that he lies down and takes a nap. God says to David, "It's time to escape." David walks out by King Saul who is sound asleep. The soldiers are asleep. The soldiers of David say, "It's time to take Saul's life." Instead, David reaches down with his sword and cuts off a tiny bit of the coat of Saul and carries a piece of the material with him. His enemy is down and instead of destroying his enemy, he takes off a piece of his coat.

When you love the Lord, you can be sure of your security. Then David left and hid under a rock. Saul woke up discovering that David was no longer in the cave. When Saul came out looking for him, David said, Saul, look at the tip end of your garment. There is a piece cut off. I could have taken your life last night, but instead I spared your life. Even when you have your enemies at bay, don't try to destroy them. The Bible says to pray for your enemies. Do good to them that hate you and bless them that curse you. When you treat an enemy like an enemy treats you, you're just like the enemy. But you've got to be bigger and better than your enemy.

So David is still on the run. He's out of the cave, but he penned this Psalm. Be merciful unto me O God for my soul trusts in thee. David didn't have any confidence in Saul because he was still after him. His trust was in God. Don't have your trust in a government that's wishy washy. If you're going to have trust in somebody or something, let it be in the Lord, a true and a living God. Then put your enemies in God's hands.

Hide Me

Psalm 57:1

...Yea, in the shadow of thy wings will I make my refuge, until these calamities be overpast

In the shadow of thy wings will I make my refugee. David is asking the Lord to hide him. You can think of a mother hen that spreads her wings when trouble shows up and the little chickens come and find refugee under the wing of the mother hen. If a hawk comes down to try to devour the little chicken, it might get the mother, but it will miss the babies. It is said that once a field burned and a mother hen was found dead. But when they raised her up all of her little chicks were still living and were saved by hiding under the wings of the mother. David said, "I have found refugee under the wings of God." Have you found refugee under his wings? When you hide in God, your enemies will have to come through God to get to you.

David could look back to other times that the Lord did great things for him. When he was just a boy, he walked out before a giant Philistine who had been fighting all of his life. The odds where against David because everyone else was afraid, but he took his sling shot and five smooth stones and headed toward the giant. The Holy Ghost got in that rock and hit the giant's forehead. David knew God had rescued him. He said you did it for me.

If you are facing something now and you don't know how you're going to make it, just look back over the other times that God brought you through. You see if you are dealing with something, this is probably not the first time you've beat it. If you think about it, God brought you through something last year and the year before last. Ten years ago, you were in something and God brought you out. If you look back at your past record, you know nobody but God brought you to where you are. And just your past footsteps ought to give you enough encouragement to go on. So David said I need you to hide me.

Hear Me And Help Me

Psalm 57:2-3

I will cry unto God most high; unto God that performeth all things for me. He shall send from heaven, and save from the reproach of him that would swallow me up. Selah. God shall send forth his mercy and his truth.

David said, "I need you to hear me." There are some things that can happen in your life to keep God from hearing you. If you abide in sin, He will not hear you. If you want to talk to Him, you need to get it together. Don't go to Him any kind of way because He is not just an any kind of God. You must come to Him recognizing that you are nobody and that He is somebody. 2 Chronicles 7:14 says If my people which are called by my name will humble themselves Before you pray, you've got to first humble yourself and then pray.

Don't come to Him complaining about other folk. Don't approach Him talking about how good you are and how bad other folk are. You've got to come with mercy on your lips. Pray to God, "I know I've sinned and come short. I know I have not done the things you told me to do. I'm not pleading for justice, I'm pleading for mercy."

Help me. Save me from the reproach that will swallow me up. Maybe you are the kind of person who has every thing in order. You've got your stocks and bonds where they ought to be. Your health is in good shape. You don't need another good friend. However, I need his help. I need to start the year off by saying Lord, "If you don't help me, I can't stand the storms." I need Him walking by my side. I need him to be in me and around me. I need Him in my lonely hours to dry away my tears. In my sick hours, I need His help to heal me. In my broke hours, I need Him to finance me. In my dark hours, I need his help to give me light. When I'm wrong, I need his help to put me back on the right track. When I'm confused, I need his help to regulate my mind. I need the help of the Lord.

Lions On Every Side

Psalm 57:4

My soul is among lions: and I lie even among them that are set on fire, even the sons of men, whose teeth are spears and arrows, and their tongue a sharp sword.

My soul is among lions. My soul is hanging out with lions. In other words, everywhere I look I've got enemies. I have to step over enemies and go around enemies. My enemies look just like lions. What's so bad about a lion? Well the strongest part of a lion is his jaws. He is bad with his mouth. Also a lion is sneaky. He favors where he is. He can lay down on the ground and you can walk right up on him, because he looks just like the grass. You can't be sure he's on the ground. Before you know anything, he's right up on you. It's not so bad if you've just got one or maybe two in a lifetime, but David said, "I am surrounded. Every where I look, there is a lion."

Many of us do not know how blessed we really are. If you were born in a Christian family, thank God for that because you've been safeguarded from a lot of stuff. You grew up praying. You grew up coming to church school. You grew up reading the word of God teaching you how to avoid your enemies. But can you imagine being born in a Jehovah witness home? They will come to your door with a lie and many will believe. We have the truth and won't tell anyone, but they will spread a lie all over town. If the son or daughter gets sick, they can't give them their own blood. They try so hard to get you to follow them and yet they say only 144, 000 are going to heaven and the last count I heard they had over three million. What's the need of adding some more to the ship when it's already over loaded.

If you came up in a family that didn't know the Lord, you grew up among lions. If you send your children off to school where God's word can't be mentioned, you are putting them right in the midst of lions whose teeth are like swords and tongues are like arrows. Shelter us O Lord.

Fixed On The Father

Psalm 57:7, 9

My heart is fixed, O God, my heart is fixed: I will sing and give praise. I will praise thee, O Lord, among the people: I will sing unto thee among the nations.

My heart is fixed. You see you can't be wavering. You can't be unsure about who you are. You can't be in doubt about your salvation. No matter what anyone says, make sure your heart is fixed and your mind is made up. It is necessary for you to be on your way up.

I will praise thee. It is so important to remember to praise the Lord. David said that even while you've got enemies all around you and while there are lions on your trail, he said let me tell you how you can make. Just start praising the Lord. It doesn't matter how heavy your burdens are, just praise the Lord. It doesn't even make any difference how many enemies you have.

Maybe you've tried to talk to God and God didn't answer your prayer. David tells us to just start praising him. Somebody put out a song the other day that says when praises go up then blessings start coming down. Can you see the need of praising the Lord? You say, "But preacher, you don't know what I'm dealing with." Just praise him anyway. "Preacher, it's been rough on me." Just praise him anyway. "But preacher I've been in storm." But I can tell you the storm doesn't last forever. I'm so glad the God I serve will bring you through. Won't he do it? He will.

Many of you know what I'm talking about? You have been through some rough times, but God brought you through. You don't mind telling somebody, "Neighbor, whatever you are dealing with, if you make sure that your heart is fixed and your mind is made up, then you're on your way up. You can begin praising the Lord while you are still in the middle of the situation. Don't fix yourself on the lions, but fix yourself on the one who sends from heaven and delivers you from the lions.

Get Off Your High Horse

1 Peter 5:6

Humble yourselves therefore under the mighty hand of God, that he may exalt you in due time.

This text speaks of the day or season of time that you as a believer must suffer through in order for God to perfect, establish, strengthen, and settle you. Satan uses his best techniques during this period of time. It is also a time when burdens seems to be at their worst. People are on edge. We wet pillows with midnight tears. It seems as if money gets short and bills get longer. Phony friends seem to be plenteous. It is a time when everything seems to go wrong. You begin having conversations in your bedroom and in your car when no one is there except you. You search bookshelves to find the right book to read. You rent movies trying to find a solution to your problem. You may find yourself doing stuff that's not becoming to you.

There is something going on in the inside that you can't seem to explain. The people that you discuss it with know when you start talking they don't understand. There are others you want to tell, but you don't want them to know that you've sunk that low. So you start asking yourself, "How do I handle this kind of dilemma and keep going on?

There is an answer. There's a word that's tucked away in this book called Peter that will help us have a brighter future. You may want your problems to stay under cover. You don't want anybody else to know that you're going through what you're going through. But one thing you will have to do is start being honest with yourself. And then secondly, you'll need to be honest with God, because the only way God can help you is by you admitting your pride. Most of us try to handle our own dilemma. But if you could handle it, you wouldn't be in the shape you're in. We need the help and the assistance of others and especially the God that woke us up. The first instruction is for us to be humble. Simply put, you need to come off of your high horse.

Small In Your Own Sight

1 Peter 5:6
Humble yourselves therefore under the mighty hand of God, that he may exalt you in due time.

Humble yourself. So often we're so quick and glad to brag about our income on our job and where we live and what we drive. Then we are ashamed to admit that we have a real problem. But you can have all of the fixtures and the things of the world and still be miserable under the skin. This is because we spend our time trying to find out how to be happy when we ought to try to know joy. When you humble yourself, you admit that you have discovered that you can not handle this situation by yourself. You can't take enough pills to bring you back down. You can't drink enough. You can't be on enough drugs because once you come down off the high, you will still have the same problem. Humble yourself before the Almighty. Think of yourself in a lowly fashion admitting your neediness.

The mighty hand of God. Now I know that God is busy and we have to admit that he is a busy God because He keeps the earth moving on its axis and He keeps the solar system working together. He keeps all the planets from running and bumping into each other. He is a busy God. Every morning the sun rises and it sets in the evening. Out of six billion folk on planet earth, He visits every one every morning. He wipes the tears from all of our eyes and He answers every prayer. He visits every funeral. Every time a brother or sister gets ready to die, He walks beside them in the valley of the shadow of death.

He's a busy God, but in spite of his busyness, he still says to us, "Come unto me all you that labor and are heavy laden and I will give you rest. But don't come to me with a proud look; don't come to me lifted up in pride. Come to me in humility and with an apologetic heart. Come to me with patient submission and ask me to help you with your situation." This is something you cannot handle yourself.

In Due Time

1 Peter 5:5

Likewise, ye younger, submit yourselves unto the elder. Yea, all of you be subject one to another, and be clothed with humility: for God resisteth the proud, and giveth grace to the humble.

God resists the proud. When you come to God all proud, God steps back. When you come to God with your little ideas saying, "I can handle this by myself," then God steps back and lets you handle it. But when you surrender yourself to Him and say, "Lord I'm yours and you belong to me. Even if I could handle it, things would work better if you handle it. I am coming to you with a humble spirit asking you to take care of this matter yourself." Then God will exalt you in due time. You see God has a time set to lift you. We may think our time is the same time that our sister's time is. But God doesn't lift all of us at the same time. God has a season to bless you.

When you're doing well, it's difficult to get yourself to church. You've got to decide which car you are going to drive. You must decide what you want to eat. It takes two hours to figure out which suit you will wear. Then you have to choose which car to drive. After you get to church, you have to determine from which checkbook you will write out the check. It's hard to rush to the Lord when you have everything. Sometimes God has to take some stuff from you before you'll show up at His door.

When we didn't have anything, we showed up for worship. Rain or snow didn't stop us from coming to the Lord. When we're weary, wounded, and sad we come to Him. We are to cast our cares upon Him. The word cast means to commit. Take what I have out of my hand and place it in his hands. You see my hands are limited. My hands won't hold that much. His hands are much larger than mine. The stuff that would run me crazy God handles with ease. We need to know he will bless us, but in due time.

Stay On The Alert!

1 Peter 5:8

Be sober, be vigilant; because your adversary the devil, as a roaring lion, walketh about, seeking whom he may devour.

You do have an enemy. You need to be sober while God is bringing you out. In other words, you need to be awake. Be vigilant and be alert. Be ready to move at His command. The devil majors in trying to frighten you. He is as a roaring lion. Can you imagine walking up on a lion some where in the woods in a midnight hour and he walks up behind you and roars. I mean everything about you will shake. I don't care how bad you are. Somebody said they went out one day and had a gun and they were going to take care of somebody and somebody slipped up behind them. They ran all the way to the house before they remembered that they had a gun. The devil comes up on you suddenly like that to make you forget your defense. He does all he can to upset you and make you scared. He wants to make you forget who you are and whose you are.

He walks about as a roaring lion seeking whom he can devour. Oh he may be close to you. He may be trying to get you down. He comes to you sometimes in a midnight hour with all kinds of crazy thoughts. He whispers stuff in your mind. And he plants seeds in your life to make you think you're less than what you are or maybe make you think you're more than what you are. He will have you looking under eyed at somebody else. He uses all kinds of devices.

He wants to weaken your faith. The devil is not after your looks or your money. If he can weaken you in the faith, then you'll start backing off the Lord. You will stop reading your Bible and praying. You'll start replacing prayer meeting with some other junk. He's trying to get you to turn from the faith. But you've got to resist, resist, resist. Put up a fight. When you are submitted to the Lord, you can resist the devil because you got power. Keep on alert!

Afflictions Are Accomplishments

1 Peter 5:9
Whom resist stedfast in the faith, knowing that the same afflictions are accomplished in your brethren that are in the world.

Once you go through some things, you gain a real knowledge that you would not get if you had not gone through. You see every trial you go through is a lesson that God is teaching you. Some things you can learn in a seminary, some things you can learn at a university, and some things you can learn out of a book, but some things you've got to learn through experience.

My momma did the best she could in teaching me how to pray when I was just a boy. I learned my bedtime prayer. You could shake me anywhere and I could pray that prayer. But when I really learned how to pray was when I had to raise my own family. Sometimes I had more bills than money. I had a son that was suffering from a sickness. And sitting at the hospital night and day praying over my boy that God would deliver him and heal his body, that's when I learned what prayer was.

In order to really learn some truths, you've got to experience some stuff. It's good to read all you can, but if you haven't been there, you don't know the full meaning. That's why some folk don't know the goodness of God yet because they have not experienced anything except for a few little pains. But when you've really had to go through something in life and God has kept you with a sane mind and kept you walking up right, you can turn around and tell somebody, "The Lord was by my side." He is a caring God.

So resist the devil. Recognize who he is. He doesn't show up in red suits. He puts a lot of truth in with his lies or else you wouldn't believe them. We must also respect him. Don't play with him. Don't be making no little eggs calling them deviled eggs or devil's food cake. He is a devil. And whatever he can do to destroy you, he will do it.

The Squeeze Of Suffering

1 Peter 5:10

But the God of all grace, who hath called us unto his eternal glory by Christ Jesus, after that ye have suffered a while, make you perfect, stablish, strengthen, settle you.

But the God of all grace. The word grace has to do with the favor of God. Peter is saying that you are in his favor. That is great news. Being in Gods favor has lots of fringe benefits. He is the God of all grace meaning there must be measures of grace. You see one person who is suffering with sickness and there's another person who has a mental problem. The person going through sickness has got sick grace for healing. And the person with the mind confused has got regulating grace. In other words, he says whatever you're going through I've got grace to sustain your every need.

Who has called us unto his eternal glory. God has a higher calling on your life. Even though you are still sitting here on the runway, He has already given you clearance for another destination. This is not my eternal home. This is just my temporary dwelling place. I'm on the runway and there is a clearance from the tower that it's take off time already. He has called us unto his eternal glory. In other words, he's moving me up from trash and from filth. From condemnation to commendation. From misery to mercy. From darkness to light. From death to life. He says, "I have already called you to a higher calling."

When you have suffered a while. Now what good is suffering? Suffering actually brings the best out of us, but it also brings the mess out of us. You see you looking pretty in your pretty clothes and big smiles. But all of us have got some stuff in us that we can't take to heaven. You've got to get rid of it before you catch the morning train. Suffering squeezes the stuff out of us that God doesn't like. You won't come to church all proud and haughty, but you will walk in and say "Hallelujah, his grace has brought me!"

God's Gold

1 Peter 5:10
But the God of all grace, who hath called us unto his eternal glory by Christ Jesus, after that ye have suffered a while, make you perfect, stablish, strengthen, settle you.

God doesn't make you suffer because He hates you. He is bringing the best out of you. A goldsmith puts his gold in a pot and then turns the fire on. The goldsmith will go occasionally and stand over the pot and look. If he can't see the reflection of his face, he backs up and turns up the fire. When he can finally see the reflection of his face, he knows the gold is pure. In the same way the Lord puts us in the pot and turns up the fire of circumstances and suffering in our lives until He can see His reflection in our lives. You may not know why you are going through what you're going through. Know you are just in the fire. God has something better for you, but He has to get you ready for what He wants you to have. You are God's gold.

Suffering produces results in our lives. It will make you perfect or fit. The word perfect means mature. If you haven't gone through anything, you have a lot of childish stuff in you. A child wants a lot of attention. A child will pout. A child is jealous of another child who sits on his momma's knee. And a child will cry if they drop their toy or if you turn off the television. They pout and cry and have tantrums if they don't get their way. When you are mature, you will know that God is working in you for your good.

Establish you. Suffering will make you firm. You can build a fence by digging holes and putting in posts, but it won't be firm. You need to put cement in the bottom of the hole first. When you try to do stuff on you own, you're not established because winds of adversity will show up. The first lie you hear will knock you out or throw up your hands in the first crisis. But when God establishes you he cements you down with his love and firms you with his grace. When the winds of adversity come, you don't move.

Suffering Spawns Strength

1 Peter 5:10

But the God of all grace, who hath called us unto his eternal glory by Christ Jesus, after that ye have suffered a while, make you perfect, stablish, strengthen, settle you.

He will strengthen you. This means that God will make you forceful. Forceful means that you can stand through storms. But you can also hold on when other stuff comes up on you. When stuff unexpected shows up in your life, you don't give way. When death invades your family, you can walk to the grave and say absent from the body is to be present with the Lord. When sickness shows up and the doctor says you won't make it you can say weeping may endure for a night but joy will come in the morning. You need to be able to stand when adversity is pushing against you. When lies keep coming. When back biters keep back biting. When sickness keeps showing up. When jobs keep closing down. When money keeps running out. Whatever comes up on me, I'm not in this thing all by myself.

Settle you. It makes you fixed. I don't care what happens, I'm not going to turn God down. I don't care how dark it gets, I'm fixed with the Lord. It doesn't make any difference if He doesn't answer any more prayers. I've decided that I'm going to hold on to God's unchanging hand. I have decided the road may be rough and the going may get tough; the hills may be hard to climb, but I started out a long time ago and there is no doubt in my mind. I've decided to make Jesus my choice and since I know and I am convinced that he cares for me, I can cast all my cares up on him. Lord I'm not worried.

If you are a little weak right now and the devil is after you, let Isaiah 40:31 take hold. They that wait upon the Lord shall renew their strength; they shall mount up with wings as an eagle; they shall run and not be weary, they shall walk and not faint. His strength is made perfect in your weakness. He will strengthen you through suffering.

Heaven And Earth Touch

Luke 9:28
And it came to pass about an eight days after these sayings, he took Peter and John and James, and went up into a mountain to pray.

Jesus selected Peter, John, and James to go with Him up into a mountain to pray. What an incredible scene there is on this mountain. Heaven and earth kiss each other. We have visitors from heaven that came down to share with travelers on earth. It's a great scene to experience. This passage is so important that all of the three gospel writers chose to bring it to focus. There are some things that Matthew discusses that Mark does not. There are some things that Mark will bring to focus about which Luke has nothing at all to say. But here is a passage that Matthew, Mark and Luke all three bring in to focus.

In Matthew's gospel you will find this passage in chapter 17:1-9. In Mark's gospel it is in Mark 9:1-13. And then in Luke's Gospel it is in chapter 9:28-36. All three accounts come together to present to us this beautiful picture of heaven and earth sharing with each other. This is actually out of this world. You will see in this text some things that you have been questioning yourself about in relation to people that have already gone off the scene. What an awesome passage this portion of Scripture is to believers and it is such a moving passage that it can and will stir those that don't know Christ.

Matthew and Mark say that this is the beginning of a situation that had ended. That may sound strange, but Matthew, Mark, and Luke discuss a statement made by Simon Peter eight days previously that allows us to move forward in the body of Christ. Jesus asked his disciples, "Whom do men say that I am?" What is in the rumor mill? Notice that Jesus asked the right folk. He asked people that He knew loved Him. When people love you, they want what's best for you. He knew they would tell Him the truth.

A Real Revelation

Luke 9:19

They answering said, John the Baptist; but some say, Elias; and others say, that one of the old prophets is risen again.

Whom do men say that I, the Son of Man, am? Peter said, "Well we keep getting a lot of rumors, but they're all good. Some call you Elijah because of your ability to pray." Elijah was a great prayer. You remember he prayed one day and heaven opened and it rained during the drought. He said, "Some call you John the Baptist because of your preaching ability." John was an excellent preacher. He could preach so well that folk would leave the comfort of the pews in the temple and go down to Jordan just to hear John shout, "Repent for the kingdom of heaven is at hand."

But some called him Jeremiah. Jeremiah was a weeper. Jesus cried over the city of Jerusalem. He was seen weeping at the grave of Lazarus. So some say, "You are Jeremiah." Then Jesus said, "That sounds good, but whom do you say that I am?" Peter was anxious to answer. "You're the Christ of the living God." Jesus wanted to set Peter straight so Peter knew he was not the one who came up with this. Jesus said, "Flesh and blood did not reveal this unto you, Peter, but you have been shown this by my heavenly Father. Now you are Petros, a rock. However, upon the rock of the truth I will build my church and the very gates of hell shall not prevail against it."

Peter was filled with the Holy Spirit at that time. He proclaimed the same unusual statement that we have to make when we accept Christ as our personal Savior. But only three verses down, Jesus had to turn around and rebuke Peter for being a tool of Satan. You can be really caught in the spirit this minute and be in a whole different mindset later. Lots of times you can be so caught up in the Spirit that you think nothing can ever distract you. The devil likes to catch you at those moments. Don't think that the devil will leave you alone after a Holy Spirit encounter.

Close Companions

Mark 9:2
And after six days Jesus taketh with him Peter, and James, and John, and leadeth them up into an high mountain apart by themselves: and he was transfigured before them.

Jesus took Peter, James and John. When you look at this, you may think that Jesus was a little prejudiced. It looks like He had picks in His crowd, because He didn't have only Peter, James and John. He had many others who had joined Him as disciples. Often Jesus carried the three with him and left the others waiting. When Jairus' daughter was at the point of death and Jesus got ready to raise her, He brought three in the house with Him. When He went in the garden to pray concerning the bitter cup he was about to drink, He left all but three disciples on the outside. Why did He seem to be partial to some folk?

Some people won't let you get close. They will throw up stop signs to keep you back. Peter, James and John made sure that Jesus knew they wanted to be close to Him. John kept so close to Jesus that he would lay his head on His breast. When soldiers tried to arrest Jesus, Peter said he was willing to die to save the life of Christ. Passionately, He took out his sword and cut off the man's ear. When Jesus went to Samaria and came upon a crowd that didn't have respect for Him, James and John were with Him. They made a recommendation that Jesus would let them call heaven and order fire from heaven to come and consume all His enemies. So Jesus said, "These fellows love me enough to sacrifice all they have for me." Not only did they love Him enough, but they were also willing to be with Him.

They wanted to be close to the Lord. Is your heart's desire to be close to the Lord? Do you sincerely want to be next to Him? If you truly want to be close to Him, He will most certainly let you. I heard Him one day talking about you all, John 6:37 All that the Father giveth me shall come to me; and him that cometh to me I will in no wise cast out.

Repel The Repressive

Luke 9:30
And, behold, there talked with him two men, which were Moses and Elias.

L uke said, "Jesus went to the mountain to pray." Why did He go to pray? Well He was just a few days from Calvary and when you're getting ready to go and give your life for your enemies, you need to make sure you're headed in the right direction. Even when you know you are traveling down the right road, you still need some encouragement.

Now there are some folk who wouldn't encourage you if their life depended on it. When a person is miserable and sad they want everybody to be miserable and sad. Every time they talk, they have a sad conversation. They are always talking negative stuff. However, when you're in a storm, somebody needs to tell you it won't last forever. So Jesus went to be encouraged.

While on the mount, two men showed up, Moses and Elijah, neither of whom had lived ordinary lives or died ordinary deaths. Moses had spent eighty years of his life in preparation to do forty years of difficult work that he didn't particularly want to do. Most of us spend forty days in preparation to do eighty years of work. In the end, he allowed the folk he was leading to get on his nerves and God did not allow Moses to lead them into the promised land.

Elijah was a champion. He decided to do something out of the extraordinary. He walked down to King Ahab's palace with bugs in his hair and mud gushing from his toes and said, "As the Lord God liveth there shall be no dew nor rain until I give you word." And for three years and six months there was no dew or rain. But in spite of all the stuff he had going for him, he let one woman run him out of town. After Jezebel heard how bad he was, she sent a note telling Elijah to leave town or die. Elijah ran to the valley and asked the Lord to kill him. Don't allow people to discourage you to the point where you miss what God has in store for you.

Exiting Earth

Luke 9:31
Who appeared in glory, and spake of his decease which he should accomplish at Jerusalem.

Moses shows up. God wouldn't let him get to Canaan with the Israelites, but God preserved him and brought him over anyway. God got Elijah and brought him back. Here is the good part, these men were recognized by Peter, James and John. There were no videos or photos, but when Peter saw Moses and Elijah, he knew who they were. You will also know those you love when you get to heaven.

What could they be talking about on this hill called Mount Herman? You see Moses represented the law and Elijah represented the prophecy. Jesus came to fulfill the law and the prophecy. The jobs of Moses and Elijah were only temporary, but the Lord's job was eternal. The Bible says they came to talk about His decease. The word decease in the Greek text actually means exodus. Jesus was getting ready to make an exodus from planet earth. And God the Father sent these two heavenly hosts to tell Jesus, "Just go on. We did the best we could with the law, but we know you have done a better job. We did the best we could with the prophecy, but we know you will do a much better job.

These two men were qualified to talk to Jesus about his decease or departure. Elijah didn't experience death; he was caught up by a whirlwind and he disappeared in the air. Moses died but nobody was ever able to find his grave. Both men left in an unusual way but a few thousand years later this dead Moses shows up on Mount Herman. Isn't that something? I don't know how you all feel about it, but this helped me out because I discovered in reading the text that just because you leave here, it doesn't mean it's over for you. Too many folk think it's all over when you or your loved ones die. No! It's just a transfer from one place to the other. Don't get upset with folk when they've moved over to a better place. They encouraged Jesus to keep on going!

An Image Of The Father

Luke 9:32
But Peter and they that were with him were heavy with sleep: and when they were awake, they saw his glory, and the two men that stood with him.

While they were on the mountain, Jesus was changed, transfigured, or transformed. Now Jesus already had divinity, but it was covered with humanity. John 1:1 says in the beginning was the Word. A word is actually a thought that's been formulated into speech. Jesus said, "If you really want to know how God looks, look at me. If you want to know how God loves, watch how I love. If you want to know the power that my Father has, watch me raise folk from the dead." The Bible tells us in Genesis that God will provide Himself. In other words, He was going to wrap Himself up in human flesh and present himself as a lamb. And part of that came out on Mt. Herman when He was transfigured. Luke tried to describe what happened that day. He said it was an experience that you have never witnessed before. There are no words in the vocabulary that can describe how Jesus looked. He was white and shining and glittering and glowing.

While all of this was going on, Peter woke up and saw Moses, Elijah, and Jesus. Peter said, "It's good to be here." I'm praying for the day when I can come to church and folk walk in and act like it's good to be here. We forget about yesterday's problems and the things we've got to face tomorrow. Anywhere Jesus is, that's a good place to be.

While Jesus was speaking, a cloud came down and a voice spoke, "This is my beloved son in whom I am well pleased." You see Moses and Elijah came just to encourage Jesus. And the Bible says that when the cloud disappeared there was nobody there but Jesus only. I wonder what happened to Moses and Elijah. If you've been leaning on somebody other than Jesus, one of these days they are going to disappear. Jesus alone was left with them.

No Skeletons In The Closet

Luke 1:6

And they were both righteous before God, walking in all the commandments and ordinances of the Lord blameless.

The scene opens with the parents of one of the legends of the New Testament. I was impressed when I read the resume of the parents of this fellow named John. You don't hear a lot about Zacharias or Elisabeth, but they were people well bedded in the Word of God. So often when you read the resume of certain people, you discover that they have a lot of baggage that's been hidden. But it is a breath of fresh air when you can finally find a couple that loves and serves the Lord. In most cases you'll find one out of two. And in some homes there is no righteousness around the house at all. So when you can find a husband and a wife that are both living for the Lord, what a joy it is! It will be a sweet flight to heaven having husband and wife walking hand in hand in fellowship with God.

The Bible tells us how blessed this family really was. It says they were both righteous. And the text distinctly says they were righteous before God. Many people are righteous before God. There are a lot of people that are righteous before you. A lot of people will be righteous on their jobs. If you would get the right blood hound on their trail, you will come up with headed skeletons. You will see halos over their heads.

God is certainly the person that we should try to please. It is not your fellow man, because you want to please all of them any way. But you must make sure that you have the right relationship with God. And God is calling for holiness. God is calling for righteous living. No person should get comfortable in an unrighteous situation. No person should be satisfied if you're not living righteously for the Lord, because it has a way of slow walking us down. Elizabeth and Zacharias will go down in history as being righteous people.

Lives Of Faithfulness

Luke 1:7

And they had no child, because that Elisabeth was barren, and they both were now well stricken in years.

Although Elisabeth and Zacharias were Jewish people walking in all the commandments of the Lord, they were not perfect. There are no perfect people who live on planet earth. Nevertheless they were faithful to God. No person could finger them openly. They were doing all that would be pleasing to God. And because of them being such faithful people, God had some things in store for them.

Despite their righteousness, there were problems in the house. Know that living a holy life does not exclude problems. You can live as holy as you possibly can, but the difficult dilemmas and circumstances will show up. I remember hearing a story of two boys that got in trouble. One boy was righteous and the other one was unrighteous. When the unrighteous boy was in trouble, somebody told him to hold on and his response was, "I have nobody to hold on to." But when you are living a righteous life and problems come, you do have a problem solver. I would rather have Jesus and nobody else than to have everybody else and no Jesus. He is there to hold on to.

The problem in the house was they had no child. In the society we live in, that does not appear to be a problem. But in that society, people believed that if there was no boy in the house, then that the home was cursed. In order for the house to be blessed, a boy child had to be born. Elisabeth not only lacked a boy child, but she did not have any children at all. She was barren. She could not bring forth a child. And they were both now well stricken in age.

God, however, had not forgotten their lifetime of faithfulness from their youth. He wanted to reward that faithfulness. It's good to take your life while you're young and use it productively and positively for the Lord. Serve God in your youth. He will not forget you!

Make A Place To Meet God

Luke 1:8
And it came to pass, that while he executed the priest's office before God in the order of his course.

While Zacharias exchanged the priest's office. There were so many priests on the scene that often a priest didn't get a chance to serve in the temple except but once in a life time. According to the custom of the priest's office, his lot was to burn incense when he went into the temple of the Lord. It was time now for this Zacharias to go into the temple and offer incense. In other words, while he was praying he would send up this incense and it would envelope itself to go into the nostrils of God. It was their way of offering prayer to God.

What a wonderful privilege we have now to be able to pray. We don't have to wait on the priest to give us the go ahead, but we can bow anywhere at anytime and talk to God whenever we get ready. There was a time that a person was required to go to the priest with his problems. Then the priest would go in to the Holy of Holies to offer up the prayer and wait on God to answer him and he would come back and tell you what God said. But at Calvary the veil was split from the top to bottom allowing us to go directly to the mercy seat ourselves and tell God what we need. You can go boldly to the throne of God. No one else has to do your praying for you. God hears and answers your prayer.

Notice Zacharias was on the right hand side of the altar. It is believed that God spent his time on the right hand side of the altar. An angel of the Lord appeared and stood on the right side of the altar of incense. God made many promises to Zacharias and Elisabeth that day.

Zacharias was going where God was. You ought to keep a spot in your house where you can visit the Lord. People have bars in their houses and all kinds of other stuff. If God is important, make some knee bowing room where you go on daily basis and bow down and talk to God there.

A Marvelous Message

Luke 1:13-14

.. angel said unto him, Fear not, Zacharias: for thy prayer is heard;
..hy wife Elisabeth shall bear thee a son, and thou shalt call his name John.
..nd thou shalt have joy and gladness; and many shall rejoice at his birth.

Thou shall have joy and gladness. That's enough right there to start shouting about. When this boy comes, a whole lot of people are going to rejoice. For he shall be great in the sight of God. Most of us when our children are born have to wonder how they're going to be. We hope our son or daughter turns out to be all right. But Zacharias was promised by God that his boy was going to be great.

The Lord went on to promise that their son would not have wine or strong drinks. He didn't have to worry about his son being an alcoholic or getting strung out on drugs. Then the angel said the boy would be filled with the Holy Ghost even from his mother's womb. Now most of us have to wait until we accept Christ as our Savior to receive the Holy Ghost. But John was filled with the Holy Spirit before he got here. Many of the children of Israel shall he turn to the Lord their God. Your boy is going to be a soul winner. And he is not going to be a jack leg preacher. He's going to make a difference in the community.

The angel goes on, "He shall go before him in the spirit and the power of Elijah." John would represent or be like one of the greatest prophets that ever walked. What a joy it is to hear of a child having all these things going for him! And Zacharias could say, "He's my boy." Also he will turn the hearts of the fathers to the children. He's going to be a man that will unite families.

He will make ready a people preparing for the Lord. John is coming in on fire to win others for Christ. He will prepare the ones that are slothful and sluggish for the coming of the Lord. Zacharias should have been shouting! Instead, he was doubting.

Doubt Or Directions

Luke 1:18
And Zacharias said unto the angel, Whereby shall I know this? for I am an old man, and my wife well stricken in years.

After hearing of all the wonderful promises from the angel of the Lord, Zacharias said unto the angel, "Whereby shall I know this?" This was a comment of unbelief. Now here's what Zacharias was doing. He was asking God to give him another sign. He was actually doubting what the angel had said to him. There is another person in the Bible who received almost the same statement, yet she didn't doubt. Mary said in Luke 1:34 "How shall this be seeing I know not a man?"

There is a difference between what Zacharias and Mary said. Look at what resulted after their statements were made. God told Zacharias that he would be dumb, unable to speak. He condemned Zacharias right after he made the statement because Zacharias was doubting what God had said. However, God answered Mary positively. The angel answered, "The Holy Ghost shall come upon you and the power of the highest shall overshadow you." Now God gives an explanation to Mary, but he condemns Zacharias. It is because Mary didn't doubt, she was just asking for directions.

There is thin margin between doubt and faith or between a doubter and a person asking for directions. Sometimes we act like we are asking for directions but we are in fact doubting God at the same time. When you doubt God, you are actually calling God a liar. 1 John 5:10 He that believeth on the Son of God hath the witness in himself: he that believeth not God hath made him a liar; because he believeth not the record that God gave of his Son. When you fail to believe God, you make God a liar. And God doesn't take it lightly when you call him a liar.

Absorb The Word

Luke 1:20

Behold, thou shalt be dumb and not able to speak, until the day that these things shall be performed, because thou believest not my words, which shall be fulfilled in their season.

How is it that Zacharias, a priest, doubted God? Here is a man that was in conversation with God daily. He was praying to God for a special blessing, yet when testing time came, he failed because he doubted God. God gets upset with you when you don't trust him. It's like a father talking to his son about dinnertime. The father tells the son they will have dinner in a while. Daddy can handle it. About ten minutes later, the son asks, "Daddy, when we gonna eat?" In ten more minutes, he says, "Daddy, are you sure we gonna eat anything? I didn't see you bring nothing in." The father said, "Son, you've never missed a meal. We'll have dinner in a while." But what if this boy decided to go next door and eat at the neighbor's house because he didn't think his daddy was going to feed him. It would insult the father.

That's the way God feels when He promises you something and instead of waiting on God, you ease down to the slot machines. You say, "It's taking God too long so let me get my own money." This upsets God because you are down playing what God can do. He is a jealous God. God doesn't want you relying on anything except Him to supply your need. He doesn't even want you to rely on yourself.

Basically, we are on the same order spiritually as we are physically. If you don't take care of your body by eating properly, exercising, and drinking water you will have problems. Spiritually, we must do the same. We must read the word daily. All of your spiritual vitamins are in the word. Read it and review it continually. Also, research the Word. If you don't go into the depths of it you'll think it's saying one thing when it's really saying something else. Get into it. And then, release the Word!